THE
CHALLENGE
OF
EUTHANASIA

An Annotated Bibliography on Euthanasia and Related Subjects

Don V. Bailey

UNIVERSITY
PRESS OF
AMERICA

Lanham • New York • London

Copyright © 1990 by
University Press of America®, Inc.
4720 Boston Way
Lanham, Maryland 20706

3 Henrietta Street
London WC2E 8LU England

All rights reserved
Printed in the United States of America
British Cataloging in Publication Information Available

Library of Congress Cataloging-in-Publication Data

Bailey, Don V., 1932–   .
The challenge of euthanasia : an annotated bibliography
on euthanasia and related subjects / by Don V. Bailey.
          p.   cm.
Includes bibliographical references.
  1. Euthanasia—Abstracts.   2. Death—Abstracts.   3. Euthanasia—
Bibliography.   4. Death—Bibliography.   I. Title.
R726.B25   1990   179'.7—dc20   89–70604 CIP

ISBN 0–8191–7711–3 (alk. paper)

 The paper used in this publication meets the minimum requirements of
American National Standard for Information Sciences—Permanence
of Paper for Printed Library Materials, ANSI Z39.48–1984.

To Donna

It does not take much strength to do things,
but it requires a great strength to decide on what to do.

- Elbert Hubbard

ACKNOWLEDGEMENTS

To my knowledge, no book has ever been written without some assistance. The help and support in bringing this work to completion is gratefully acknowledged.

I am deeply indebted to my daughter, Donna, for her excellent typing skills, her faithfulness, and patience throughout the whole process of preparing the manuscript. Where there was chaos--a mishmash of citations and index numbers--she gave it order and form. I shall never forget the countless painstaking hours she sacrificed for me, from the book's first inception to its present form. What seemed to be an endless and difficult task has finally been completed. My heart-felt thanks to her.

Doctors Richard A. Body, Paul Feinberg, and Timothy Warner of Trinity Evangelical Divinity School, Deerfield, Illinois, were extremely helpful with suggestions, corrections and advice during the course of writing the manuscript. From the initial proposal, each has played a significant role in its composition. I am truly thankful for all their help.

My gratitude to Dr. Harold O. J. Brown also of Trinity Evangelical Divinity School who read the manuscript and sent it to Dr. Joseph Stanton, M.D., President of the Value of Life Committee, Brighton, Massachusetts. Dr. Stanton spent many hours reviewing it and offered valuable suggestions which not only improved the work but also helped uncover mistakes that may have otherwise gone undetected. His advice and promptings to submit the manuscript for publication were most encouraging and rewarding. I remain in his debt.

I highly commend the staff and personnel of the Palatine Public Library, Palatine, Illinois, for the kind, courteous, and professional service extended to me. They spent many hours researching materials inside and outside the library. The computer system and inter-library department were of inestimable value. Literally hundreds of various pieces were obtained, which were vital for this compilation. Without their cooperation and expertise this bibliography would have been much more difficult and time-consuming. I am indeed grateful for their help.

Further, I would like to thank Terry Dean, and Mel Hendrick of The Institute of Governmental Studies, University of California at Berkley, for their assistance in obtaining a list of 235 citations from The University of California's on-line catalog, MELVYL, on euthanasia and related subjects.

I would be remiss if I failed to express thanks to the various writers and producers whose works (books, articles, book reviews, abstracts, video and audio cassettes) make up this bibliography.

In addition, my sincere thanks to Mercy Ciero, Kathleen Hutchinson, and Diane Yamnitz for their valuable assistance during various phases of the project. And for the final layout and preparation for printing, I extend my deep appreciation to Natalie Maher and the staff of Patterson, Gray and Associates, Arlington Heights, Illinois, whose unique computer and software resources made it possible to meet a very aggressive schedule.

Finally, my deep appreciation to Albert Kopin, without whose generosity the completion of this work would have been virtually impossible.

TABLE OF CONTENTS

FOREWORD

The great surgeon, Rudolph Matas, in his autobiography, "The Soul of a Surgeon", reflected:

> "The transition between life and death should be gentle in the winter of life. Death under these conditions is invested with a certain grandeur and poetry if it comes to a man when he has completed his mission . . . There is nothing to fear, nothing to dread."

So it often was when death occurred amid loved ones gathered about bedside at home, a scene poignantly immortalized in Sir Luke Fildes' famous painting of the sick room. Apart from sudden, unexpected death, in the later half of the 20th century, dying at home became an unusual event. More commonly today, death approaches in sterile hospital surroundings, often in an intensive care unit, amid a panoply of machines, tubes and beeping monitors. Regulation limiting visits by family members and at times, seemingly brusque, albeit efficient "health care team" have replaced personal family doctor and familiar bedside nurse of yesteryear.

In an ironic paradox, medicine, which in this century saw life expectancy increase from 45 years to a more biblical three score and 10 or 15, is imputed to threaten the singular event of dying with a cold depersonalization and the natural fear associated therewith.

Thus today, calls for "death with dignity" and "patient autonomy" all too often are framed in tension against ethic and aspiration of medicine.

What treatment is medically indicated? What treatment is ethically optimal? What are the ethical obligations of institution, physician, nurse to patient, to patient's family? Does the patient have obligations or is patient autonomy unfettered and absolute? Are aim and ideal of patient and health care system mutually exclusive or are they parallel and complementary?

Such questions and tensions occupy center stage as health care turns into the decade of the nineties. Hospital ethics committees and ombudsmen to guard patient's rights are now permanent parts of the medical landscape.

"The Challenge of Euthanasia: An Annotated Bibliography on Euthanasia and Related Subjects" is a careful compendium of references to significant papers in the field. It fills a vacuum and represents one careful scholar's odyssey through the medical-ethical literature seeking understanding and resolution of problems associated with medical care and dying.

Comprehensive and carefully annotated, it should serve well those concerned with technological encroachments on the process of dying, that genetically inbred inevitably of all who are human.

University Press of America renders a valuable service in making this unique resource available.

Joseph R. Stanton, M.D., FACP
Value of Life Committee

PREFACE

The development of this project arose out of a deficiency in bibliographical aids on the subject of euthanasia. Surveys and research among libraries, hospitals, and health-care professionals revealed my presupposition true--a lack desired to be satisfied. I believe this project has succeeded in its purpose--made up the deficit.

Bibliographical data were acquired from the United States and countries around the world. After approximately two years of research, there remained the seemingly never-ending task of arranging and rearranging the information, and formulating the project. Finally, the decision was made to introduce it in Chapter 1 and divide the following Chapters (2-8) into two parts.

Part One comprises Chapters 2 and 3. Chapter 2 presents euthanasia as a challenge to me as a Christian and as a health-care professional, together with my personal views and experiences on the subject. The evaluation and conclusion make up the contents of Chapter 3.

Part Two is composed of the bibliography *per se*--Chapters 4 through 8. Chapter 4 lists the limited number of annotated bibliographies existing when the project was undertaken. The aids in the bibliography are characteristic of the attitudes and opinions of proponents and opponents alike.

No matter which view one espouses, all must admit that euthanasia is a formidable challenge--a challenge presenting apparently insurmountable problems, therefore, I have chosen to organize Chapters 5 through 8 under the following head-ings: Chapter 5--Euthanasia: The Homicidal Challenge; Chapter 6--Euthanasia: The Religious Challenge; Chapter 7--Euthanasia: The Sociological Challenge; and Chapter 8--Euthanasia: The Technological Challenge.

Chapter 5 classifies feticide, genocide, infanticide, and suicide under the heading of homicide. Works cited in Chapter 6 are chosen from two major religions: Christianity and Judaism. Sociologically-oriented fields are classified in Chapter 7 under the headings: economical, ethical, familial, individual, legal, medical, moral, philosophical, psychological, and social. Entries in Chapter 8 are works which treat euthanasia relative to technology--drugs, genetics, machines, and transplants.

Hopefully, this bibliography will be found an effective and rewarding reference.

CHAPTER 1

THE PROJECT INTRODUCED

Personal Interest in the Project

My personal interest in euthanasia has been enhanced by three factors: direct participation in health care, experience and counseling.

Direct Participation in Health Care

Direct participation in the health care field over a period of thirty-six years has brought me in touch with various disappointments and frustrations faced by physicians, administrators, nurses, technicians, social workers, pastoral care personnel, and other professionals who must wrestle with decision-making processes relative to death and dying. It is one thing to read and hear of traumatic issues having to do with life and death situations, but it is quite another to be present and involved in the process without knowing exactly what course of action is appropriate. The following case history is presented as an example of many incidents in which I was a participant which demanded a definite decision.

On this particular day all necessary life-saving and support equipment in the hospital was at the disposal of a young female patient who was in the prime of life but at the point of death. The patient was brought to the hospital emergency room and resuscitated for approximately forty-five minutes. At one point it seemed apparent that she had expired. All signs of death were obvious. The emergency-room team had reached its ultimate in trying to revive her.

The attending physician was ready to pronounce her dead. Her young age, however, seemed to spur the members of the team to make one last desperate attempt to save her life. She was at death's door. One last effort jerked her away from the threshold--she lived! She was transferred to the Intensive Care Unit, intubated, and put on the MA-1 Respirator for the following six days. The MA-1 Respirator is the type of machine that sustained Karen Ann Quinlan for an indefinite period (Quinlan 1977, 295).

The following day I visited the Intensive Care Unit to find the patient in a deep coma. Frantic efforts were still being made to pull her through the crisis. With these efforts the patient's condition continued to improve. After further treatment her neurological status seemed better, and she began to make progress toward rehabilitation, gaining control of the movement of her head and extremities, although with marked spasticity. She also began to take significant amounts of oral nourishment. The general degree of neurological recovery expected was questionable and took several months to evaluate. Gradual progress was made with physical therapy. The patient was discharged and went home. Her prognosis was good, and she made continued progress walking and talking, with a greater degree of control over her extremities.

I followed her progress for months afterward and found that her quality of life had become very poor, so much so that she had begun to act remarkably like a patient with severe muscular dystrophy--less control over her extremities. She was visited by her teenage friends who stood aghast at the repulsive change that had come over their once healthy, vibrant, and vivacious friend. She must now face the world and her peers with a different appearance--a quality of life totally different from that which she had enjoyed for eighteen years. Should she have been resuscitated? Would she have been better off dead rather than have to endure the remainder of her life in a gnarled and twisted contortion confined to a wheel chair? These and other questions rise to challenge those who take an active part in health care services on a daily basis.

The Influence of Personal Experience

One of the most influential components affecting my interest in the subject of euthanasia is experience. Thirteen years of surgical experience as a surgical technician (assistant on all major and minor surgery), and practical knowledge together with twenty-five years service as a hospital chaplain have equipped me with some measure of knowledge and wisdom. I have gained much insight into the dynamics which have brought about a change in the thinking processes of those who must deal with problems of life-and-death situations.

I have been involved in situations when I actually hoped for someone to die. For instance, the car of a family of five was rammed by a semitractor trailer, causing both to explode in flames. The driver of the truck, the father, mother, and one child who were in the car were killed. Two teen-age daughters survived, but received fourth-degree burns (more or less charring and blackening) over ninety percent of their bodies. For a period of days the heart-breaking task of the surgical team, of which I was a member, was to debride (pronounced *dabreed*: to remove foreign material and contaminated or devitalized tissue, usually by sharp dissection, until surrounding healthy tissue is exposed) their charred bodies, remove skin from German Police dogs, and apply it to the burned areas in order to retain the body fluids of each of the girls.

During the course of the procedure, the members of the surgical team literally prayed that both girls die, due to the extent of the burns and the excruciating pain they had to endure. Psychologically they suffered horrendously, with weird hallucinations of being chased by wild dogs, which plagued them whenever they were fortunate enough to fall asleep. Connie Lawerman has an excellent discussion on similar experiences in her article, "Life After Transplant", in which she states:

> In the early days of transplantation the psychiatric literature described cases in which recipients had bizarre reactions to the 'foreign organ.' For example, a black man who received a kidney from a white donor fantasized that the kidney was attacking him. In another case, a white Ku Klux Klan member became active in the NAACP after receiving a kidney from a black cadaver. When he discovered

that his donor brother was a homosexual, another patient acted as if his masculinity was threatened. And a heart transplant patient was haunted by a hallucination in which the donor returned for the heart. (Lawerman 1987, Sec. 10:10, 11)

Finally, God in his tender mercy took the girls to Himself--a sweet relief not only for them, but also for those who had tended and nursed their wounds.

Fifteen years have elapsed since that dreadful experience. I still weep when it comes to mind. As a result, I have a deep empathy for those who must suffer and wrestle day in and day out with the complexities of life and death. I, along with others, must rely on the type of source material recorded in this work.

The Contribution of Counseling

Counseling is another factor which has increased my interest in the subject under discussion. Questions from immediate family members, relatives, physicians and other health care professionals seeking answers have left me utterly helpless in a number of cases. At the same time, they have motivated me to try to find a solution, or at least provide some degree of sound advice to assist, as one decision or another must be made.

The daughter of a woman who was approximately eighty-four years of age came to me for counseling. She would soon be faced with the difficult decision on whether to remove the respirator which had sustained her mother for four months. After much consultation with her mother's physician, she decided to turn off the machine which kept her mother alive. Although saddened, she felt comfortable with the decision. All signs indicated that apart from the apparatus her mother would expire immediately. In order to remain within the limits of the law, a court order would have to be procured to turn off the equipment. As procedures were being implemented, her mother died while still being supported by the respirator. All who were involved in the patient's care were relieved of the responsibility of "pulling the plug."

Decisions like the above, and others which entail life-support issues, leave one with deep humility, respect, and reverence for life. In doing this project, I have drawn upon the practical knowledge which results from such experience.

The above factors have led me to recognize and acknowledge a need for the work herein undertaken.

The Need for the Project

Introduction to the Need

Frustration! That horrible word which describes what takes place inside a person when something comes between one's aim and desire.

A feeling of utter helplessness came over a surgeon friend when he asked for a special instrument during an operation, only to discover that the nurse neglected to include it in the instrument setup. Had he not been proficient in his field (general surgery), both he and the patient would have been in extreme difficulty. With make-shift improvisation, he was able to accomplish his aim--removal of an aortic aneurysm (the bulging out and weakening of the walls of the aorta, the large blood vessel leading from the heart).

Hopefully, one may not be faced with a problem such as the above. However, everyone at one time or another undergoes a frustrating moment. One such moment presented itself to me when I was asked to serve on a Medical Ethics Committee. The instrument I needed at the time was a much desired reference work on the subject of euthanasia. To be sure, there were many books and articles on the topic but a compilation of references was nowhere to be found. The committee *had* to work with the few articles at its disposal in the hospital library. The frustration was overcome and some basic guidelines were put together for future problems anticipated.

Subsequently, after further research I was still unable to locate such a work. Therefore, the aim of this project is to meet the above need by addressing the following: (1) a deficiency in biographical aids, (2) lack of reference material for health care professionals, (3) a counseling tool for clergy, and (4) an educational device for lay people.

Deficiency in Bibliographical Aids

While there may be bibliographical works on bioethics and medical, legal, and Christian ethics, to my knowledge there are very few, if any, annotated bibliographies on euthanasia. I attended a recent seminar which was sponsored by American Medical International Presbyterian/Saint Luke's and the Center for Applied Biomedical Ethics at Rose Medical Center, Denver, Colorado. The seminar was captioned, "Ethics On the Frontlines of Medical Care: The Value of Many Voices." The conference explored how differences in culture, religion, social relationships, and economics can and do complicate health care decision-making and performance.

Disagreement on some issues was expected, but my greatest disappointment was that of not finding bibliographical material on the subject of euthanasia. Many books were on display for perusal and purchase, but no bibliographies.

Later, I conducted a survey among ten hospitals throughout the Chicago area to determine if there were any bibliographies on the subject. The medical librarian in each of the hospitals was unable to produce anything resembling an annotated bibliography, however, each thought compiling one would be of value.

Computers in public libraries were accessed only to reveal that three published and unpublished works existed.

Lack of Reference Material for Health Care Professionals

I was told by a medical librarian of a large hospital that if he wanted to research the subject of euthanasia and/or related subjects, he would consult Index Medicus (an index of health care periodicals) for the desired information. Yet, he had no compiled annotated bibliography whereby he could short-cut his investigation.

Another librarian said that there was a shortage of compiled bibliographical material for medical ethics committees. She further stated that since problems with death and dying are becoming more complex, such committees will both need and desire a handy tool as an advisory and guide for shaping policies and guidelines. Certainly, with a project such as this at their disposal, they can deal more effectively with the problems confronting them.

A Counseling Tool for Clergy

That the Church of Christ must become more involved with the issues of the day goes without saying. The issue of death has always been present with man. The Church has consistently ministered to those undergoing the dying process, and has been a great source of solace to those who must stand by and watch their loved ones suffer and die. But, due to great strides in medical technology which allow people to be kept alive (or their death prolonged), clergy find themselves in a counseling dilemma--should life-supporting devices be removed and/or should wonder drugs which tend to prolong eventual death be withheld?

For assistance in dealing with the perplexity, clergy consult colleagues, search bookstores and libraries. At this point, an annotated bibliography would be of great benefit. There would be, on hand, a quick source of reference materials to aid in counseling people who are faced with a dying predicament.

One pastor stated that an incident arose with a member of his congregation whose loved one was being sustained on a respirator. The member did not know whether to have the machine turned off or allow it to remain on, thus keeping the patient alive indefinitely. The pastor admitted that he was not equipped with sufficient updated material to counsel his congregant. He said he would welcome such a project.

An Educational Device for Lay People

I have discussed the issue of death and dying with individuals from many walks of life and have found that, for the most part, people are very confused. As individuals are faced more and more with complex decision-making regarding loved ones, friends and themselves, they will need a source from which information can be gleaned. What reference would be more appropriate for such situations than this project?

In the book Zero People, Jeff Lane Hensley states in the preface:

> We then must work to educate people in order to stop taking innocent life. To educate others, we must first be well-informed ourselves. And that is the purpose of The Zero People, to provide an up-to-date handbook for those who desire to educate themselves, so they can in turn educate and persuade others. (Hensley 1983, Preface viii)

The above book is a compilation or pro-life articles and, of course, presents one view. However, this work presents books and articles of different persuasions, thereby giving a greater potential for education of its readers.

With a listing of descriptive material that presents different facets of the problem, lay persons will have a clear view from which concrete decisions and opinions can be formulated.

Relevance of the Project to the Hospital Chaplaincy

The project involves two groups within the confines of the chaplain's ministry: (1) health care professionals and (2) family members.

Relevance to Health Care Professionals

The hospital chaplain frequently finds himself in a counseling situation whereby he is requested to counsel physicians and other health care professionals on the problems which arise in life-and-death circumstances. With an annotated catalogue of this sort, he will have material on hand that will give quick reference to suggestions, and sound advice. Generally, most health care professionals know where they stand on the issue, but they need support from colleagues and others in their field. They will be able to find much of that support in the references listed in this project.

As the chaplain is called upon to serve on different committees which must address the subject of euthanasia, he will have at his disposal help which will enhance his effectiveness. Both he and other health care personnel will find the project invaluable as they confront the issues involved.

The chaplain as a health-care professional is occasionally obligated to write articles for periodicals dealing with death and dying. A bibliography will be an asset to his library.

Relevance to Family Members

The project also aims to benefit family members and relatives. Through the chaplain, they will have access to helpful decision-making materials. A guide to literature on the subject, of which he would otherwise be ignorant, will improve his service to family members.

I am convinced that interest, need, and relevance have gone a long way toward providing sufficient ground work for this undertaking.

Methodology of the Project

The following set of procedures has been employed in conducting the project: (1) library research, (2) interviews with health care and legal professionals, (3) interviews with relatives, (4) public media research, (5) interviews with counselors, (6) personal experience, and (7) questionnaires.

Library Research

Library research has entailed a search for works written on the subject of euthanasia. Both public and private libraries (including medical, legal, and university) have been accessed and investigated for books and articles which are related to the project.

Public Media Research

Many films and video tapes have been produced on the subject which explore virtually every question on death and dying. They, together with audio materials, are included in the project.

Interviews with Health Care
and Legal Professionals

The purpose of these interviews was not only to extract from physicians, nurses, administrators, and others in the field, information pertaining to the need for the project, but also to seek advice as to the choice of authoritative materials and where much of it could be found.

Interviews with Relatives

Family members and those who have had first-hand experience in dealing with the many problems of decision-making have been consulted as to how such a project would have helped them had it been in existence during their grief experience. They have been asked for suggestions which are incorporated into the project that will speak to their need and the needs of others faced with the dilemma as to whether or not "the plug should be pulled."

Interviews with Counselors

Counselors referred to here include professionals such as clergy, psychiatrists, psychologists, and social workers. Suggestions and advice on title selections have been sought.

Incorporation of Personal Experience

Thirty-eight years experience in the health-care profession have been drawn upon to complete the project. This includes familiarity with the internal working of the profession; connections with physicians, attorneys, judges, university professors, and many others who have had to cope with the problem of euthanasia.

Evaluation Questionnaires

Pertinent questions were addressed to health care professionals, legal professionals, librarians (public and private), clergy, and university professors for information to evaluate and determine the value of the project. Eight sets of questionnaires comprising fourteen questions each were sent to the above professionals. Out of the eight, only one expressed little interest in the project, but seemed to favor it if needed.

The above procedures have been most helpful toward the development of a creative, beneficial, and rewarding project.

Definition and Limitations of the Project

The specifics of the project will define and set forth its limitations.

Definition of the Project

The following will bring the project into clear focus: (1) meaning of the title, and (2) aspects of the work involved.

Meaning of the Title

The topic, "The Challenge of Euthanasia: An Annotated Bibliography of Euthanasia and Related Subjects" is defined as: (1) the incorporation of books, magazine and journal articles, pamphlets, films, videocassette and audiocassette materials dealing with the problems that occur within the framework of the dying process, (2) the different tasks imposed upon man to answer a multitude of questions raised by the enigma, and (3) to categorize and classify outstanding books on the subject, with a description of each.

Aspects of the Work Involved

The project is viewed from six different aspects relative to the challenge of euthanasia: (1) the personal challenge, (2) the challenge to find existing annotated bibliographies, (3) the homicidal challenge, (4) the religious challenge, (5) the sociological challenge, and (6) the technological challenge.

The personal challenge. This aspect deals with a personal response to the challenge of euthanasia as a Christian and as a health-care professional.

The challenge to find existing annotated bibliographies. These are entered in a separate chapter.

The homicidal challenge. The titles listed in this section incorporate works on feticide, genocide, infanticide and suicide.

The religious challenge. Religious works are dealt with in this part of the project. These will deal specifically with Christian and Judaic literature.

The sociological challenge. Every society has had to face the death-and-dying situation. A compilation of material from ten sociologically-oriented fields is treated: economical, ethical, familial, individual, legal, medical, moral, philosophical, psychological, and social.

The technological challenge. Literature dealing with technological advances in drugs, genetics, machines, transplants, and other areas of medical science which speak to the problems of meeting the challenge of euthanasia are included.

The above is a "nutshell" order of the plan and it is believed that it sufficiently covers most of the outstanding works which have been produced to date.

Limitations of the Project

The project has two limitations: boundary and selectivity.

The Boundary of the Project.

The boundary confines itself to literature which specifically addresses the subject of euthanasia and related subject, such as abortion. For example, abortion is related only if it involves aborting a fetus because of deformity that would affect "quality of life" should it be allowed to live.

Selectivity of Entries

Cognizant of the fact that voluminous material exists on the subject, especially treatments in articles, some restriction has been placed on the pieces selected. It was necessary to set certain criteria for the selection of each work. All articles have been chosen on the basis of the qualifications and scholarship of the writers, together with professional quality of publication.

Self-interest alone, in the topic selected for this project, has been sufficient cause for its production. However, when one considers the need for such a work, its relevance to the ministry both inside and outside the confines of the health care and legal professions, its merits become even more appealing.

PART ONE. RESPONSIBILITY

INTRODUCTION

When a ministerial student was told that euthanasia was to be the subject of this project, he thought I said "*youth in Asia*" and remarked "Why don't you do something on youth in America instead?" Upon questioning him, I discovered to my astonishment, that he had never heard of the word *euthanasia* much less understood its meaning.

The term *euthanasia* was first coined by W. E. Lecky in 1869. Coinage of the word was meant to convey its present broader usage. In antiquity, however, the word meant an "easy" or "happy" death in contrast with the present way in which it is used. Webster's has "[Gr, easy death, fr. *eu* + *thanatos* death - more at thanatos]: the act or practice of killing individuals (as persons or domestic animals) that are hopelessly sick or injured for reasons of mercy." (Webster's New Collegiate Dictionary 1981, s.v. "euthanasia")

Since its simple use by the Greek classicists it has become more complex due to great strides in medical technology and pharmacology. Not only has euthanasia become extremely complicated but it has also become very unpleasant even to participate in the practice of its mildest form. However, "someone" as said in the military, "must do the dirty duty." Removing life-supporting devices from a patient is indeed a *dirty* task and to maintain one on the same apparatuses indefinitely with no hope of life at all apart from such machinery, seems little less than obscene.

The issue demands a response from those who hold either the pro or con view. Whether one believes that every effort should be made to keep a patient alive or that pain and suffering should be alleviated by prematurely terminating life, the challenge remains one of serious responsibility.

17

CHAPTER 2

EUTHANASIA:
THE PERSONAL CHALLENGE

In reacting to the challenge of euthanasia, one realizes that it becomes even greater and more intense when looking at it from two different positions. From one perspective one must endeavor to see the issue from God's side, and from another view the human side. Therefore, the purpose of this chapter is to present my response to euthanasia, both as a Christian and as a professional.

A Christian Response

If one is conscious of God's presence and will, there are certain values that must be taken into account. The importance of these determines the Christian's response toward euthanasia. They are: (1) sanctity of life, (2) right to life, (3) dignity of life, and (4) innocents of life.

Sanctity of Life

Every Christian should ask the following questions: "What views of *sanctity of life* do I as a Christian espouse? What view *should* I hold?" No matter what persuasion one has, the latter question is more important because *sanctity of life* may be understood in an altogether different sense from that which the Scriptures convey. When dealing with life, dying, and death, it is important that the Christian's view be brought into line with Scripture. The Bible is God's "rule of thumb" by which all life should be measured. It is imperative that one's opinion of the sanctity-of-life issue has a firm basis as it relates to the Creator. Sanctity as it relates to Him touches upon (1) the holiness of God and (2) the authority of God.

The Holiness of God

Sanctity connotes holiness. The thought of sanctity cannot be entertained apart from thinking of God and the attribute of holiness. It would be very difficult indeed to separate the word from Him. Muller shows the inseparable relationship between God and sanctity:

> Sanctitas: sanctity, holiness, inward or intrinsic righteousness; the *sanctitas dei*, or holiness of God, refers to the absolute goodness of God's being and willing [sic]. It is a *sanctitas positiva*, or positive holiness, both intrinsically, in the essential goodness and righteousness of God, and extrinsically, in the goodness and righteousness of God's will toward his creatures, specifically, in his will that all creatures be holy as he himself is holy. It is also a *sanctitas negativa*, or negative holiness, in the sense that goodness and righteousness of God remain inviolate and eternally separate from all that is sinful or tainted in the created order. (Muller 1985, 270)

To disconnect sanctity from God and His holiness would be tantamount to separating the sun from its brightness. Likewise it would also be an extremely difficult and impossible task to divorce man from sanctity, e.g., God is the *causa prima* (the first cause or uncaused cause which set in motion all causes and their effects), and *causa formalis* (the formal cause which is the essence of the thing and determines what the thing caused is to be; e.g., the essence of myself is humanity and the essence of God is deity.) God is the source of all life, and seeing that He is the Author of life one becomes extremely aware that the holiness of the Creator is kindred to the life of humanity. Delitzch comments on God's holiness relative to man by saying that man is ". . . a creaturely copy of the holiness and blessedness of the divine life. This concrete essence of the divine likeness was shattered by sin; and it is only through Christ, the brightness of the glory of God and the expression of His essence (Heb. 1:3), that our nature is transformed into the image of God again (Col. 3:10; Eph. 4:24)." (Keil and Delitzch 1975, 1:62)

While man is presently a fallen being, he nevertheless has a direct link to the holiness of God. If the Christian's fellowman is seen in the light of God's holiness, there remains no difficulty in adopting and holding to the view of *sanctity of life*. Man's life is very special and must be cared for as such. Sanctity of life--from the womb to the tomb--is the responsive chord that should be sounded in the heart of every Christian who is entrusted with care for the lives and deaths of others.

The Authority of God

Sanctity not only connotes holiness but it also implies authority. Since God is *self-moved* (autozoos), has life in Himself and is the Author of life, He is the antecedent authority of all life. The life of God (vita dei) permeates all living creatures and He has power to sanction whatever or whomever lives, moves, and has being, whether that life is microcosmic or macrocosmic. "'For in Him we live and move and have our being . . . we are his offspring'" (Acts 17:28). God's authority provides the basis for a sanctity-of-life view. For without His authoritative influence, how can one speak of *sanctity* of life? It is therefore reasonable to assume that life is valuable because the authority of God has sanctioned it. His authority looms over all life in the light of two basic acts: (1) God created life and (2) God commanded against taking life.

God created life

Apart from this act no life would have come into existence. Only God would have existed. He chose, however, to create. How He instilled the life principle into beings other than man is rather difficult to tell from Scripture, other than, "Let the water teem with living creatures" (Gen. 1:20), and "Let the land produce living creatures" (Gen. 1:24). But with man it was uniquely different: ". . . the Lord God formed the man from the dust of the ground and breathed into his nostrils the breath of life, and the man became a living being" (Gen. 2:7). Exactly *how* God *inbreathed* life into man is not revealed, but the breath was "the breath of life." The Hebrew is plural--breath of lives--and assures that the one single act of breathing was the totality of all lives propagated through Adam. That, one single, unique, and special act resulted in the present lives of all humanity; thus, every life is special and unique to God, as was Adam. He alone gave life to man, and He alone is the one who has the authority to take it away. "When you take away their breath, they die and return to dust" (Ps. 104:29).

God commanded against taking life

That God opposed the taking of one person's life by another became obvious after the very first killing occurred. Cain's act of murder was the first recorded in history (Gen. 4:1-15). While no recorded injunction had been given to him not to kill, the severity of the crime was judged by his being banished from his parents and the presence of God to the "land of wanderings." "Cain was under no restrictions other than the dictates of his own conscience. He could not have known that centuries later his assault on Abel would be classified as a crime involving moral turpitude. More than 1,500 years passed before the Lord denounced homicide for the first time and fixed a penalty." (Scott 1979, 5-6)

The divine penalty was life for life. "Whoever sheds the blood of man, by man shall his blood be shed" (Gen. 9:6). The forfeiture of one life for taking another is based upon the fact that ". . . in the image of God has God made man" (Gen. 1:26, 27; 9:6). Just what the image of God implies is not revealed. However, God was very emphatic as to why man was never to take the life of his fellowman: man is made in God's likeness. God reiterates the command to Moses at Sinai (Exod. 20:13). We are reminded by James the Lord's brother of the fact that man is made after God's likeness (Jas. 3:9). Chafer writes: "To sin against man either by murder or by slander is reprovable on the ground of the divine image being resident in man. A sacredness appertains to human life. Man must respect his fellow man, not on the ground of kinship, but on the ground of the exalted truth that human life belongs to God. To injure man is to injure one who bears the image of God" (Chafer 1947, 2:18).

From the foregoing, it is imperative that a correct view of the sanctity of life involves the holiness and authority of God, both of which should be taken into account, if the Christian is to have a balanced attitude toward caring for not only those of like faith, but also for mankind in general. With a balanced attitude follows the recognition that all humankind has a right to life.

Right to Life

The Christian attitude toward euthanasia should involve a fundamental twofold consideration: this arises out of a correct sanctity-of-life view that all men have (1) a prescriptive right to life and (2) a Christian medical-ethical right to life.

A Prescriptive Right

From the moment God breathed into man's nostrils the breath of life, man has had the right to life (Gen. 2:7). Abel's life was infringed upon and his right to life was denied him (Gen. 4:8). Since that time God has repeatedly warned against usurping the right of another to live. Only He has the right to deny a person's right to live. Cain's answer when God asked, "Where is your brother?", was, "I don't know, am I my brother's keeper?" (Gen. 4:9). The question asked of Cain implies that he was responsible for his brother's well-being and that every man is liable to God for the life of a fellow human being. "Brother's keeper" implies protective measures toward another in sickness or in health (Matt. 25:36). Every human being has a right to lay claim to "the right to life" because God prescribed it.

A Christian Medical-Ethical Right

An individual's right to life also extends to the area of medical ethics. In the case of terminal illness, the Christian should take care not to become impatient with the prolonged suffering of a loved one and resort to measures which would deny the person's right to life. Everyone should be allowed to live until death, and when death approaches, the right to die should not be denied. For example, at the time of this writing I had been involved in making two very important decisions: (1) to admit my mother to a nursing home due to diagnostic broncho-genic carcinoma and (2) to give specific orders for those in charge of her care to withhold all treatment beyond the basic comforts of life (food, water, oxygen, and pain medication).

Each of the above decisions was made only after thoroughly discussing the matter with her and other family members. Cognizant of the fact that her case was terminal, and knowing that death was impending, and due to excruciating pain throughout her body, she requested that she be allowed to die without extraordinary measures to keep her alive. Her physicians had opted for surgery knowing that her condition was inoperable. Had surgery been performed she probably would not have survived. Had she survived, her existence would have been more miserable than that prior to surgery. Up to the very point of her death she, the family, and the health care team were positive that the right decision had been made. She lived until she died. Her death was neither prolonged nor was her life shortened.

For those who might become incapable of making rational decisions regarding a life-and-death situation and who would not want extraordinary measures taken to keep them alive, it would be wise to compose some sort of statement in the form of a "living will." This statement would express one's wishes relative to an uncontrollable situation. While such a statement is not a legal document, it would be an important guideline for family members and health care personnel in making decisions relative to one's condition. Paul Ramsey has suggested something on the order of the following statement.

To my Family, my physician,
my clergyman, my lawyer -

If the time comes when I can no longer actively take part in decisions for my own future, I wish this statement to stand as the testament of my wishes. If there is no reasonable expectation of my recovery from physical or mental and spiritual disability, I, _____, request that I be allowed to die and not be kept alive by artificial means or heroic measures. I ask also that drugs be mercifully administered to me for terminal suffering even if in relieving pain they may hasten the moment of death. I value life and the dignity of life, so that I am not asking that my life be directly taken, but that my dying not be unreasonably prolonged nor the dignity of life be destroyed. This request is made after careful reflection while I am in good health and spirits. Although this document is not legally binding, you who care for me will, I hope, feel morally bound to take it into account. I recognize that it places a heavy burden of responsibility upon you, and it is with the intention of sharing this responsibility that this statement is made. (Lammers and Verhey 1987, 189)

I believe this: that the incident involving my mother is descriptive of the basic meaning of euthanasia (good or easy death); that any action which tends to go beyond simply allowing one to die is homicidal in nature; that Christians should never be a party to so-called "mercy killing."

Dignity of Life

Dignity is derived from the Latin *dignatas* which means "goodness or dignity; i.e., goodness in the sense of merit, as distinct from bonitas, or moral goodness" (Muller 1985, 92). Webster has "1: the quality or state of being worthy, honored, or esteemed 2: a: a high rank office, or position b: a legal title of nobility or honor 3: archaic: dignitary 4: formal reserve of manner or language syn see decorum" (Webster's 1981, s.v. "dignity"). Leon Kass states in his section Toward an Analytic Of Dignity that "dignity is not something which, like a navel or a nervous system is to be expected or to be found in every human being" (Lammers and Verhey 1987, 204).

I see in the above definitions, dignity as it relates to position and possessions, and agree with Kass' statement to a certain degree; however, when one speaks of "dignity of life," the thought of what a person *is* rather than what he *has* comes into play. Therefore, dignity has to do with position, possessions, and *personage*. Dignity is to be found in all human beings because they are alive! It is life that gives dignity.

Life refers to that form of existence this side of physical death. *Dignity* of life means that life from conception to its last breath is venerated, not that man merits veneration on his own, but that God made man what he is--a living, breathing person. As long as man has breath, he has dignity. The last breath is, of course, that point at which death ensues. When death comes there is no dignity. Literally hundreds of articles have been written on the subject "Death with Dignity." It is my belief that death with the kind of dignity being discussed is impossible. Where is dignity when one has been subjugated by humanity's worst enemy? What dignity is exhibited when a great commander falls in battle? After many such struggles, General Douglas MacArthur was heard to say just prior to his death: "I've looked that old scoundrel death in the face many times. This time I think he has me on the ropes." (Manchester 1978, 704). It is true that the great general was dignified in life, but quite the contrary in death. Death stripped him of position, rank, and the greatest of all possessions--life. What dignity is to be found in the various ways that death comes to man? None. However, until death has victory over the physical body, dignity remains--the dignity of life.

The Christian's view of the dying process should not be dying but rather living until dead, and as long as one lives death has no dominion. Therefore, care should be taken to treat the living person with the respect due him because the individual lives even while in the process of dying. For the Christian, it might be better to speak of "life with dignity until dead" instead of "death with dignity."

Life with dignity should not entail the prolongation of a vegetable-state-type of existence. As one writer puts it: "The prolongation of a 'vegetable' state of physical life is cruel, degrading, and senseless. I am completely opposed to unnatural, artificial means of prolonging physical life when all awareness and mental powers have ceased" (Johnson 1986, 215). But life with dignity does entail prolonged care which honors the dying yet living person with reverence, respect, and love during his or her last days of life upon the earth. This is the Christian's utmost responsibility relative to fellow human beings.

Innocents of Life

The term *innocents* of life has been chosen to represent two special groups of individuals: (1) the unborn and (2) the newly born (neonate). *Innocents* refers to the fact that neither the unborn nor the newly born infant has an ability to control events which might threaten or do harm to its person, whether the events be accidental or intended. Since these two groups are vulnerable in that self-protection is impossible, it is imperative that Christians have a deep sense of responsibility toward them. They are of inestimable value, not only in the sight of those who hold them dear, but also are looked upon in God's eyes as being very precious indeed. The Savior was conceived, existed as an unborn infant, came into the world as a neonate, and could not have related to humanity as He did without having passed through the stages of human development. One might say that He has experienced humanity in all its forms of development and, as Creator, knows everything there is to know about these helpless infants. In fact, He escaped being victim of Herod's cruel action during the infant stage (Matt. 2:16-18).

The Unborn Infant

The Psalmist is explicit in expressing self-value in the sight of the Creator while in the prenatal state of existence: "For you created my inmost being; you knit me together in my mother's womb . . . my frame was not hidden from you when I was made in the secret place. When I was woven together in the depths of the earth, your eyes saw my unformed body. All the days ordained for me were written in your book before one of them came to be" (Ps. 139:13, 15, 16).

The great patriarch Job said: "Your hands shaped me and made me. . . . Remember that you molded me like clay. . . . Did you not pour me out like milk and curdle me like cheese, clothe me with skin and flesh and knit me together with bones and sinews? You gave me life and showed me kindness, and in your providence watched over my spirit" (Job 10:8-12). Both the Psalmist and Job agree on prenatal life and its worth. From conception to birth (the fetus and all its stages of growth), the Bible describes life in the womb. While many see this life as precious and worthy of protection and care, regardless of its physical and mental condition, others find invalid excuses for denying its right to a full term. According to them, euthanasia by abortion is preferable to allowing a child to be born and live a life of deformity and possibly severe pain.

Some advocate that unborn infants who are expected to have handicaps be aborted. Malcolm Muggeridge illustrates such a tragedy as an argument against the pro-abortionists:

> I wanted to tell you about a little playlet that some friends of mine devised. . . . The scene is a doctor's consulting room in Vienna round about 1770. A peasant woman comes in and tells the doctor that she is in her second month of pregnancy; that her husband is an alcoholic and has a syphilitic infection; that one of her children is mentally incapacitated and that there is a family history of deafness. The doctor listens, and finally agrees that there is a case for her to have her present pregnancy terminated. And so he has to fill in a form. Filling in the form he asks her name, but he can't quite hear when she tells him, so he says: 'Please spell it out.' And she spells out: 'B-E-E-T-H-O-V-E-N.' And then the sixth symphony strikes up. (Muggeridgte 1977, 5-10)

The above scene should strike a responsive chord in the hearts and minds of all Christians to take a strong stand against euthanasia enthusiasts who use quality of life as criteria for aborticide and infanticide. The writer believes, as do many others, that if prenatal life is allowed to be destroyed, such action will inevitably be another step toward unwarranted killing of the newborn.

Newborn Infants

The neonatal stage of life is a crucial period for survival. For those babies who are endangered at birth it has become necessary to set up neonatal intensive care units for the express purpose of assuring quality care and to guarantee a fair chance for life after birth. "A neonatal intensive care unit brings together sophisticated equipment and specially trained personnel to provide the optimal environment for assisting the endangered infant through a critical stage in the transition to extra-uterine life." (Jensen and Garland 1976, 1-2)

Obviously the health care profession, for the most part, recognizes the worth of these precious lives and does everything possible within its realm to care for and nurture them during this critical stage of their existence. Jensen presents a list of the various conditions in the newborn which require intensive care:

those born of diabetic or drug-addicted mothers;
infants whose mothers suffered blood poisoning
associated with pregnancy;
those born of Rh-negative mothers with rising
quantities of Rh antibodies in their blood;
infants born by Caesarean section because of a
variety of complications;
infants born after prolonged labor, especially
if the fetus has been in distress;
certain low birth-weight infants whether born
preterm or at term, post-term infants (more than
42 weeks gestation);
infants distressed at delivery (e.g. respiratory
distress);
multiple birth infants with potential problems;
infants with generalized infection (sepsis) or
exhibiting post delivery distress (e.g., cardiac,
respiratory, gastrointestinal);
jaundiced infants;
and those with congenital defects requiring immediate
treatment, such as heart malfunction or gastrointestinal blockage. (Jensen and Garland 1976, 2)

The authors go on to say that the various problems stated above "afflict many newborn infants, killing 12 of every 1,000 live born babies and producing permanent handicaps in at least as many more" (Jensen and Garland 1976, 3). Many of the conditions are improved or alleviated with proper care and treatment. However, many are not, and serious ethical questions arise, such as: (1) should the life of an infant who has severe brain damage be saved?, (2) should the life of an infant whose life would not be economically productive be saved?, (3) would it be wiser to let nature take its course and allow an infant to die?, (4) should parents be saddled with a mentally retarded child, (5) is it right to do everything possible to keep an infant alive?, and (6) would the active support of a life be a greater misfortune than death? The number of questions concerning the endangered lives of newborns does not end here but goes on ad infinitum. The questions seem to out number the patients.

If one is committed to saving all life, there will be very little danger of falling into the trap of uncontrolled practices of euthanasia. It is always better to err on the side of protecting and sustaining the lives of these little ones. Christians should commit themselves to saving the lives of all newborns if at all possible. Otherwise one begins to toboggan the hill from a higher ethical standard toward no moral ethics at all when it comes to caring for defective newborns. Joseph Fletcher, the ethicist, argues in favor of abortion after prenatal diagnosis based on detection of ". . . a variety of inborn errors of metabolism, chromosomal abnormalities and variants and polygenic conditions (e.g., spina bifida and anencephaly)." (Fletcher 1975, 292:75-77) Not only would he allow for the abortion of defective or poor quality fetuses, but he would also disregard restrictions against euthanasia for all defective infants (Fletcher 1975, 292:75). He views defective fetuses as "subhuman life."

Paul Ramsey takes the opposite view and equates genetically indicated abortion with infanticide. He rejects arguments for abortion that are based upon a positive prenatal diagnosis of a severe fetal disease and the socio-economic harm that will be done to the family, because he holds that the same arguments might be used under similar circumstances to justify infanticide. Infanticide is his term for deliberately bringing about the death of a newborn infant (Fletcher 1975, 292:75).

My sister, Jerry Rosborough, gave birth to two genetically defective children (undetermined encephalopathy). The older of the two was nine years of age when she died, and the younger died at age seven. Both children existed all their lives in a vegetable state, were blind, and unable to communicate. Eventually, both had to be placed in a children's hospital until death, because of severe respiratory problems. Doctors had advised the children's mother to "withhold antibiotics" and allow the children to die at an earlier age. She asked them if they had children and they replied, "Yes." She asked, "Would you withhold antibiotics from your children if they were in the same condition?" They replied, "No."

During visits to my sister's home, I observed, not only, the love and care that she and her husband, Jim, had for their two daughters, but also the way in which Carmen and Tanya responded to those affections. Obviously, God had a purpose for their existence. Their mother, at the date of this writing said, "I would give birth to the same identical children with all their defects if I had to do it over again. They were my daughters and I loved them no less than if they had been perfect in every way. As far as I'm concerned, they were perfect in my eyes and in God's. I miss them with all my heart and I know that I will see them in heaven with all their defects removed."

In 1973, the Supreme Court removed restrictions preventing the murder of fetuses, which led to the results of the Baby Doe incident in Bloomington, Indiana. Baby Doe was the neonate who was allowed to starve to death because of Down's Syndrome (a genetic defect resulting in degrees of retardation and possibly serious physical defects). It was the parents' decision to allow their baby to die. The court upheld their decision.

On April 22, 1982, George Will, a nationally syndicated columnist, wrote in the Washington Post:

> When a commentator has a direct personal interest in an issue, it behooves him to say so. Some of my best

friends are Down's Syndrome citizens. (Citizens is what Down's Syndrome children are if they avoid being homicide victims in hospitals.)

Jonathan Will, 10, a fourth-grader and Orioles fan (and the best wiffle-ball hitter in southern Maryland), has Down's Syndrome. He does not suffer from (as newspapers are want to say) Down's Syndrome. He suffers from nothing, except anxiety about the Orioles lousy start.

He is doing nicely, thank you. But he is bound to have quite enough problems dealing with society - receiving rights, let alone empathy. He can do without people like Infant Doe's parents, and courts like Indiana's asserting by their actions the principle that people like him are less than fully human. On the evidence, Down's Syndrome citizens have little to learn about being human from the people responsible for the death of Infant Doe. (Will 1984, 22)

Mr. Will has experienced what it means to have a child with Down's Syndrome and knows the difficulties involved in rearing a child who is so afflicted. But he also knows the feeling of fulfillment and satisfaction experienced when involved in the loving and caring aspect of a Down's Syndrome child.

On the one hand, some would rule that the Down's Syndrome child is defective, less than human, and because of that should be terminated. On the other hand, George Will would say that his son Jonathan is more human than they. So would say my sister.

I have strong feelings on this issue and stand shoulder to shoulder with the George Wills, Paul Ramseys, and Jerry and Jim Rosboroughs against those who are bent on the destruction of defective unborn and newborn infants. If the Psalmist and Job were alive today, they too, would position themselves against aborticide and infanticide.

A Professional Response

Euthanasia is defined as "mercy killing" of a patient whose quality of life is less than desired by either the patient or his peers, and, as a result of a hopeless pain-racking disease, is put out of his or her misery. The practice of euthanasia takes on four forms: (1) voluntary, passive euthanasia, (2) voluntary, active euthanasia, (3) involuntary, passive euthanasia, and (4) involuntary, active euthanasia.

Voluntary, Passive Euthanasia

This form of euthanasia is termed "palliative care" by the medical profession. The word *palliative* is from the Latin palliatus which means "to reduce the violence of." Palliative care eases the violent nature of disease and death by keeping the patient as comfortable as possible without resorting to extraordinary measures of life-sustaining equipment. The patient is resigned to inevitable death (indeed, has refused all treatment other than supportive care), and is well aware of what is taking place at all times. Pain-killing medication is never given to the point whereby the patient becomes irrational or is unaware of what is taking place (as discussed earlier regarding my mother under Christian medical-ethical right). For this patient, the health care team has ceased to attempt a cure. Only caring matters. When a physician can do nothing toward further healing of the patient, his license ceases. He is no different from a lay person. All who are involved with the patient; the physician, family, friends, nurses, social workers, and all others are obligated to provide supportive care, including psychological and emotional care until death.

Occasionally there is a fine line between allowing the patient to die (at his or her former request) and intervention on the part of physicians, which may involve them in legal difficulties. Two physicians were charged with murder for removing mechanical devices from a comatose patient, but the charges were later dismissed. Their case demonstrates the importance of respecting a patient's wish to be allowed to die

rather than revert to mechanical means of prolongation of death:

> Clarence Herbert was a 55-year-old security guard who had an intestinal obstructon that required an ileostomy. In May 1981 he had surgery to close the ileostomy. In the recovery room he had cardio-pulmonary arrest and never regained consciousness. Three days after the arrest, he remained comatose, with no motor function and with impaired brain stem function. The physicians judged that the patient's condition was hopeless. His wife and eight children wanted 'all machines taken off that sustains life.' The wishes of the family were consistent with Mr. Herbert's previous statements that he did not want to be kept alive by machines. After the ventilator was discontinued, he continued to breathe but remained comatose. Five days after the arrest, the family asked that intravenous fluids be discontinued. The patient died eleven days after the arrest. (Lo 1984, 101:248)

The court ruled that discontinuing intravenous fluids was not murder, and that according to the reasoning of The Presidential Commission for The Study of Ethical Problems in Medicine and Biomedical and Behavioral Research, competent persons may refuse life-sustaining treatment and families of incompetent patients may act as surrogate decision makers who should try to follow the patient's wishes. Conversation between the patient and his wife was sufficient, even though a "living will" had not been completed. "If the patient's wishes are unclear or unknown, the surrogates are to be guided by the patient's best interest. In irreversible illness, the surrogate may consider the patient's quality of life as well as the duration of life and, in particular, the likelihood of return to 'cognitive and sapient function'." (Lo 1984, 101:248)

As is seen, voluntary, passive euthanasia takes into account the patient's desires and best interest. I hold to this form of euthanasia for it is basically what the word means to convey--easy death. When an individual is terminal and/or has been diagnosed as hopeless (irreversible comatose state), and every effort has been made to bring about a cure and the patient or patient's family wants the natural course of events to transpire, it behooves all who are involved to step aside and allow that person to die without heroics.

Voluntary, Active Euthanasia

Voluntary, active euthanasia involves taking an active part in the death of a patient. While most would tend to steer clear of becoming a party to this action, there are many who lean toward a more active role in facilitating the patient's death. Patients are helped along in a number of ways: injections, pulling the plug, gunshot wounds, and assist suicide. The following case is an example of assist suicide:*

"What I wish more than anything in this world is that I could take some kind of pill . . . and end this" (Rollin 1985, 105). Ida Rollin was a seventy-six-year-old terminally-ill patient and mother of Betty Rollin, who obtained upon request enough medication to assist in her mother's suicide. Under the guise of not being able to sleep well, Ida telephoned her doctor and asked for a prescription for Nembutal. Prior to this, Betty had contacted a physician in Amsterdam, Holland by phone, who gave her information as to exactly what medication would be most appropriate toward an easy and speedy death for her mother. She was told that about twenty capsules of Nembutal would be enough to get the result she wanted. Ed, Betty's husband, picked them up at the drug store and gave them to Ida. After a few days more of planning and finally a decision on the day and time, the following incident took place after the three of them watched the clock for a while:

"Is it time now?" she asks . . . My mother looks at me, . . . bends forward to look at the clock, and answers the question herself, "Yes," she says, as if the end of the evening has come and the party is over, "It's time."

She sits up and takes the bottle of Nembutal in her hand. She opens the bottle and carefully taps its

---

contents onto an indented place on the blanket. She puts the bottle down . . . she turns back toward the table and grasps the bottle of soda water in her left hand and the opener in her right. She tries to open the bottle and fails . . . and after another try she does . . . she leans over in the direction of her knees and looks down at a small pile of shiny red capsules lying like candies on the yellow blanket. She picks up three or four of them in her fingers, places them on her tongue, lifts the glassful of soda water and, with a short swig, swallows them, then three more. Then three more. Soon she falls into a rhythm - pick them up, toss them on the tongue . . . she has stopped. The dent in the blanket where the capsules once were is empty. There are no more capsules. (Rollin 1985, 233-235)

The capsules did not take effect immediately. Words of love were exchanged and then Ida Rollin said, "Oh yes, I'm starting to feel it now. Oh, good. Remember, I am the most happy woman. And this is my wish. I want you to remember ..." (Rollin 1985, 233-235)

She fell asleep. Her daughter was finally able to vent her long suppressed emotions and broke out in sobs. "I sob heavily, but not for long. Because when I look up and see how still she is, I know that she has found the door she was looking for and that it has closed, gently, behind her." (Rollin 1985, 236)

One could hardly say that Betty Rollin murdered her mother when, after all, her mother, due to long days and hours of severe pain and suffering, desired to die and indeed wanted to commit suicide. But should she have become a party to her mother's desires? This question can only be answered in the light of another--Reader, what if your mother or father made the same request? What would you do, refuse or fulfill the request?

Involuntary, Passive Euthanasia

Unlike involuntary, active euthanasia, this form is a "do-nothing-approach." For example, the patient neither expresses a willingness to die nor is able to decide on the important issues of life and death, but is allowed to die. Responsible parties make no attempt to intervene by speeding up the dying process and exert no effort to prolong life by extraordinary measures. Nature is allowed to take its course, however, general nursing care is granted and efforts are made to keep the patient as comfortable as possible, including pain relief. Hydration and nutrition are given as dictated by the patient's thirst and hunger. This form of euthanasia is an indirect termination of life. Food (nasogastric feeding), antibiotics, and life sustaining equipment are considered for removal on occasion. The following case is illustrative of involuntary, passive euthanasia:

In a 1980 case from Delaware, In re Severns, the court authorized the patient's husband, following his appointment as her guardian and a court hearing, to refuse consent to surgical reinsertion of a tracheal feeding [sic] tube if it became necessary to sustain his comatose wife, to refuse placing his wife on a respirator, to refuse the administration of antibiotics if necessary to combat infection, and to authorize writing a 'no-code' order. The patient had been in a coma for a year following upper-brain death due to an automobile accident, but required none of these treatments at the time. Her condition was being maintained with a nasogastric tube. Its removal was neither requested nor authorized. The decision was prompted after a higher court in Delaware had concluded that a guardian could be authorized to withdraw life sustaining treatment, but only after a court hearing inquiring into all the facts and circumstances of the patient's condition and the presentation of clear and convincing evidence that the decision was appropriate under the circumstances. Evidence in the case showed all family members agreed the treatment proposed to be withheld was futile. Also, the patient's wish not to live as a 'vegetable' or by the use of 'extra-ordinary' medical means was manifest before her incapacity arose. (Meyers 1985, 145:127)

While from its very beginning the above case is an example of involuntary, passive euthanasia, it, nevertheless, eventually merged into a more active form and is plausible for five reasons: (1) the patient had been in a comatose state for one year, (2) there was evidence of brain death, (3) she was in a "vegetable state", (4) her condition was being maintained by a nasogastric tube, and (5) each of the family members was in agreement on the action taken.

Involuntary, Active Euthanasia

The Journal of the American Medical Association presented an article under the title "It's Over Debbie," describing what transpired between a gynecological resident and a terminal patient whom he felt had suffered enough and, therefore, someone (in this case, *he*) should take the responsibility of actively engaging in her demise. Involuntary, active euthanasia is just *that*--a second party makes decisions about whether or not decisions should be made to terminate a patient's life. The patient was a twenty-year-old woman, named Debbie, who was dying of ovarian cancer. She had been receiving an alcohol drip for sedation, nasal oxygen, and IV fluids. She had rapid inspirations, had not eaten or slept in two days, and had not responded to chemotherapy. She was being treated only with supportive care. The resident's appraisal of the patient's condition was not good. The doctor writes: "It was a gallows scene, a cruel mockery of her youth and unfulfilled potential. Her only words to me were, 'Let's get it over with'." The doctor did indeed proceed to *get it over with* according to his own description:

I retreated with my thoughts to the nurses' station. . . . I asked the nurse to draw 20mg of morphine sulfate into a syringe. Enough I thought to do the job. I took the syringe into the room and told the two women I was going to give Debbie something that would let her rest and to say goodbye. Debbie looked at the syringe, then laid her head on the pillow with her eyes open, watching what was left of the world. I injected the morphine intravenously and watched to see if my calculations on its effects would be correct. Within seconds her breathing slowed to a normal rate, her eyes closed, and her features softened as she seemed restful at last . . . I waited for the inevitable next effect of depressing the respiratory drive. With clock-like certainty, within four minutes the breathing rate slowed even more, then became irregular, then ceased . . . it's over Debbie. (It's Over Debbie 1988, 259:272)

At the date of this writing, no one knows for sure--other than the doctor who submitted the article-- whether or not this incident took place. An investigation is underway and if it did indeed transpire, a court order will procure the name of the doctor from the publisher, which may result in prosecution. In this case he set himself above the patient, other physicians, the patient's family, and other health care professionals. According to the article, he never at any time consulted anyone as to what his intentions were. One may argue for voluntary, active euthanasia in support of the doctor, but only on the basis of the patient's words "Let's get it over with." He stated that those were her *only* words to him. Voluntary, active euthanasia? Hardly. The overt actions of this doctor are what those who oppose involuntary, active euthanasia want to prevent.

In conclusion, euthanasia is insidious, from its mildest form to deliberate murder. Each form has its proponents and opponents alike. Whatever view, it behooves one to be extremely cautious in the practice thereof, for "Unless we recognize where we are going, . . . it will be only a matter of time before the Western ethic, with its respect for the value and equality of human life, ceases to be a living reality and is consigned to the archaic curiosities of history." (Hensley 1983, 171-17)

CHAPTER 3

EVALUATION AND CONCLUSION

Evaluation of the Project

The purpose of the project has been to provide an annotated bibliography on euthanasia and related subjects. I believe the goal has been reached. While it is difficult to evaluate a work such as this because of the fact that only I have been involved, there are, however, two criteria which give basis to fair judgment of the project: confirmation and education.

The Criterion of Confirmation

Question: Has the undertaking proved my premise? Answer: I believe it has in that it not only confirms my presupposition (a deficiency in bibliographical aids), but that it also confirms the necessity for doing this project.

The Presupposition Confirmed

While researching material for the project, I found that virtually no annotated bibliographies had been compiled. Some bibliographies exist, but only three which treat the subject specifically: Euthanasia - An Annotated Bibliography, The Euthanasia Controversy (1812-1974) A Bibliography with Select Annotations, and Abortion and Euthanasia: An Annotated Bibliography. These are cited in Chapter IV, along with others on the subjects of abortion, suicide, death and dying, and ethics, which contain citations on euthanasia. I had assumed beforehand that few works, if any, on the subject were in existence. I was correct in my presupposition.

41

The Need Confirmed

I knew there was need for such a bibliography, and out of this need the project was born, as stated in Chapter I. Not only has my presupposition been confirmed, but the need for the project has been substantiated by the fact that so few bibliographies on the subject were found. Others may exist than those mentioned above, but if so, this writer has failed to locate them through Index Medicus, the University of California, Institute of Governmental Studies computer search system, and the Palatine Public Library research program CLSI computer catalogue database.

In answer to the questionnaire I sent to professionals, a doctor responded: "It would be very valuable for the work of our ethics committee (of which I am a member). In my experience, most health care professionals have read very little about euthanasia; the availability of such a bibliography would help in solving that problem."

The Criterion of Education

A second criterion for evaluating the project is that of education. Since I alone have been involved, I can speak only insofar as to how *I* have been affected from an educational point of view. That an educational process was in operation during the course of the project will be shown by the following components of education: (1) information, (2) understanding, and (3) edification.

The Information Component

I have received information from many areas of the world, and have touched on most of the socio-related fields, thus giving me a greater insight into the different views of individuals in the areas of religion, education and health care.

The Understanding Component

My understanding of euthanasia has increased considerably through pursuing books and articles written from different viewpoints. I am more cognizant and considerate of why and how others feel about the subject.

The Edification Component

The edifying effect of having done the project has gone a long way toward building on prior knowledge of euthanasia and strengthening my Judeo-Christian belief. I am more knowledgeable of the degrees of different arguments on the subject.

Conclusion

This project set out to present the challenge of euthanasia as it is reflected in the literature of those who have opposing views by bringing together a compilation of citations which describe briefly how each writer or groups of writers approach the challenge. It lists all outstanding up-to-date works on the subject relative to homicide: feticide, genocide, infanticide, and suicide; religion: Christianity and Judaism; sociology: economical, ethical, familial, individual, legal, medical, moral, philosophical, psychological, and social; and technology: drugs, genetics, machines, and transplants.

It is hoped that this work will have, not only, benefited the writer, but that it will have also contributed to those who may use it as a research tool toward answering many perplexing questions, brought on by one of the most difficult challenges facing mankind--the challenge of euthanasia.

PART TWO. BIBLIOGRAPHY

INTRODUCTION

Items listed in the following chapters have been selected from works which cover virtually every area of euthanasia. Chapter IV lists annotated bibliographies which have been located while doing this project. Chapter V classifies feticide, genocide, infanticide, and suicide under the heading of homicide. Works cited in Chapter VI are chosen from two major religions: Christianity and Judaism. Sociologically-oriented fields are classified in Chapter VII under the headings of: economical, ethical, familial, individual, legal, medical, moral, philosophical, psychological, and social. Entries in Chapter VIII are works which treat euthanasia relative to technology: drugs, genetics, machines, and transplants. Duplication of entries has been chosen rather than cross-referencing because the former is found to be more convenient and of greater ease to the investigator. An addendum has been added pertinent to the widely-publicized Linares case, which transpired in 1989, after the manuscript for this book was written. Author and title indexes are provided for quick search of works throughout the bibliography and are indexed according to citation number.

CHAPTER 4

EUTHANASIA:
GENERAL ANNOTATED BIBLIOGRAPHIES

1) Clouser, Danner K., and Arthur Zucker. Abortion and Euthanasia: An Annotated Bibliography. Philadelphia: Society for Health and Human Values, 1974.

> A scholarly and precise bibliography on abortion and euthanasia. Much of it consists of periodical annotations, although there are citations from books. Many pro and con articles are cited which present both sides of an argument. The authors say: "cross-referencing is meant to be helpful but not exhaustive." The work is a good tool for those who want to do fast research, especially in medical periodicals.

2) Euthanasia-An Annotated Bibliography. New York: Euthanasia Educational Fund, 250 W. 57th St. (10019), 1970.

3) Fulton, Robert, ed. Death, Grief and Bereavement: A Bibliography 1845-1975. New York: Arno, 1976.

> Over 4,000 entries mainly composed of journal articles, with a subject index. Good for research work.

4) Martinson, Ida Marie. The Dying Child. The Family and The Health Professionals: An Annotated Bibliography. St. Paul, Minn.: 2303 Doswell St. (55108), 1976.

> Management and care of the dying child. Some eighty items are listed. A helpful work although limited.

49

5) MediaGuide on Death and Dying. New York: Biomedical Communications, 1978.

A descriptive bibliography of some two hundred films, tapes and slide programs. Good to have on hand.

6) Euthanasia and the Right to Die. Bethesda, MD. National Library of Medicine, 1977.

Order from: Literature Search Program
MEDLARS Management Section
National Library of Medicine
8600 Rockville Pike
Bethesda, Maryland 20014

7) Nevins, Madeline M., ed. Annotated Bibliography of Bioethics: Selected 1976 Titles. Rockville, Md.: Information Planning Associates, 1977.

Twelve hundred citations of annotated references from journal literature of bioethics for 1976. Categories covered are: general works, mental health, death and dying, medical research, professional/ patient relationship, genetics/fertilization and pregnancy, population control, medical technology, and health care. Those interested in bioethics will find this a useful resource guide.

8) Prentice, Ann E. Suicide: A Selective Bibliography. Metuchen, N.J.: Scarecrow, 1974.

A bibliography which compiles over two thousand two hundred citations. The citations are grouped under headings such as books, theses and dissertations, articles in books, articles from the popular press, articles from religious journals, articles from legal journals, suicide and state legislation, articles from medical and other scientific journals, literary works (criticisms, novels, short stories, plays, poetry), and films, tapes and recordings. The book is indexed by author and subject, and gives one ready help in the area of suicide. It is highly recommended for speedy research work.

9) Simpson, Michael A. Dying, Death, and Grief: A Critically Annotated Bibliography and Source Book of Thanatology and Terminal Care. New York and London: Plenum, 1979.

An overly *critical* bibliography denouncing many works with witticism and sarcasm, but at the same time is efficient and to be commended for good annotation--apart from its sarcastic remarks, of course. It covers "death" literature thoroughly and is well arranged. Content-wise it is loaded. Categories used in classification: annotated list of books; supplementary list of books; subject index; author index; journals; films; audio-visual materials; teaching materials, kits, etc.; European literature (French, Scandinavian, German, and Dutch); key journal references; films and audio-visual media available in Great Britain; and stop press additions. Highly recommended for research material.

10) Sollitto, Sharmon, and Robert Veatch, eds. A Selected and Partially Annotated Bibliography of Society, Ethics and the Life Sciences. New York: The Hastings Center 1979-80.

11) Triche, Charles W., and Diane S. Triche. The Euthanasia Controversy (1812-1974) A Bibliography with Select Annotations. New York: Whiston, 1975.

This work is for the most part well done and does not annotate every entry (makes no claim to do so), but at the same time is comprehensive and well structured. It is divided into three sections: (1) books and essays, (2) subject index to periodical literature, and (3) author index. Each citation is numbered for quick reference. Probably should be rated as the best on the subject of euthanasia. Anyone wanting to research newspaper articles on euthanasia--there are many--will find references at their fingertips. It is highly recommended.

12) Vernick, Joel L. Selected Bibliography on Death and Dying. (Prepared by Information Office, National Institute of Child Health and Human Development, Bethesda, Md.) U.S. National Institute of Health: for sale by the Supt. of Documents, U.S. Printing Office, Washington, D.C., 1969.

CHAPTER 5

EUTHANASIA:
THE HOMICIDAL CHALLENGE

Feticide

13) Devine, Philip E. The Ethics of Homicide. Ithaca: Cornell University Press, 1978.

A professor of philosophy offers some compelling insights into homocide. A thoughtful examination of all forms of killing. He includes abortion, capital punishment, euthanasia, suicide, war and murder. Particularly interesting is Part II which discusses infanticide and our institutions; infanticide and rights; and other views on infanticide. Part III discusses fetuses and "human vegetables"; abortion and the fetus, and the comatose. Part IV presents the justifications for homicide which are, according to Devine: euthanasia (chiefly involuntary), consensual homicide, voluntary euthanasia, and suicide. His arguments are both provocative and controversial.

14) Englehardt, H. Tristram, Jr. "The Endings and Beginnings of Persons: Death, Abortion, and Infanticide." Chap. in The Foundations of Bioethics. New York: Oxford University Press, 1986.

A scholarly discussion of the status of the fetus. The worth of the fetus is determined by the attitude of the mother toward it, however, some responsibility is allotted to the father. Englehardt briefly traces the history of infanticide and evaluates the conditions under which an infant should or should not be disposed of.

15) Humphries, S. V. "The Problems of Theraputic Abortion and Infanticide." The Central American Journal of Medicine 24 (April 1978): 77-79.

According to Humphries, even though a fetus is a human species,it is not a person, but only a potential one if allowed to develop fully. He lists moral objections and side effects to abortion. "If," as he says in the above article, "we accept the justification of abortion, it is difficult to defend the practice of going to great lengths to preserve the lives of newborn babies with gross defects."

16) Lamm, R.D., and S. Davison. "Abortion and Euthanasia." Rocky Mountain Medical Journal 68 (February 1971): 40-42.

Discusses the conflict of abortion with the 1967 Colorado abortion statute and attempts to show that abortion of an unquickened or non-viable fetus is not recognized as the taking of a "life."

17) Persaud, T., ed. Problems of Birth Defects. Baltimore: University Park Press, 1977.

From Hippocrates to Thalidomide and beyond. A compilation of fifty-seven papers on historical aspects, epidemiology, mechanisms, genetics, causes, prenatal diagnosis, management, and social aspects of birth defects. Good for basic reference and descriptions of various physical problems of unborn and newborn infants.

18) Ramsey, Paul. The Ethics of Fetal Research. New Haven and London: Yale University Press, 1975.

The ethics of fetal research distinguishes between fetal research and fetal politics. First, Ramsey outlines various types of fetal research and acknowledges their potential benefits. He then presents a description of the development of proposed American guidelines up to the National Research Act, passed by Congress in 1974, with a comparison to England's "Peel Report." Moral and ethical problems involved in fetal research are considered, along with how medical policy is formulated in America. This book is an excellent guideline for those who want to know *how* to think about fetal research.

19) Scully, Thomas, and Celia Scully. Playing God: The New World of Medical Choices. New York: Simon and Schuster, 1987.

A collaboration by husband and wife, with whom the reader feels an affinity because of their compassion and care for patients and families alike. Their concern is revealed through the subject content of Playing God. One learns how to make choices relative to health care while reading this work: choices in choosing the right physician for one's self and family; building the right relationship with one's physician; patients' rights and how to exercise them; "living will" and the power of attorney; transplantation of human organs; different ways of making babies; dilemmas on treatment and nontreatment; who should be the spokesperson for a child who has a disabling, life-threatening, or terminal illness; making life-and-death decisions for another adult; how to get action when you have been wronged through malpractice and billing fraud. A very important feature of the book is the appendices, which are "packed" with information on bills of rights in most areas of health care. The Scullys state, "The whole purpose of this book is to help you understand the issues and their ethical underpinnings, how to protect yourself, and where to go for help." Having researched many "how to" books, I find this one to be at the top of the list, and recommend it very highly to be read and digested by all who are interested in the subject of euthanasia, in order to help make the right decisions in the area of health care. It is well indexed, and would be a handy tool for discussion groups.

Genocide

20) Alexander, L. "Medical Science Under Dictatorship." New England Journal of Medicine 241 (July 1949): 39-47.

An analysis of Nazi medicine and its evils. An expression of wonder as to how doctors and others could condone such practice--a practice which is nothing short of cold-blooded murder. Alexander believes that the Nazi view of life and its disrespect for life, no matter what the "quality," is a logical and dangerous step toward euthanasia.

21) Barrington, M. R. "Apologia for Suicide." In Euthanasia and the Right to Die, ed. A. B. Downing. New York: Humanities, 1970.

A convincing argument for the right to suicide. Barrington condones the practice and belittles the belief that suicide is sinful. When at the extreme of a life situation due to poor "quality," she advocates suicide and voluntary euthanasia. A well planned life is one that does not leave out "planned" suicide. For those who hold to her views, this article should be supportive.

22) Betowski, E. P. "Prolongation of Life in Terminal Illness." CA 10 (January/February 1960): 25-27.

An argument that the difference between ordinary and extraordinary means will not in and of itself solve the problem of euthanasia.

23) Blakely, P. L. "Mercy Killing Turns Back the Clock." America (November 4 1939).

An emotional argument that "mercy killing" will indeed turn back the clock because continual advances in medicine will not be likely or necessary if euthanasia becomes a practice, and that a society which fails to care for its citizens will not have required characteristics for maintaining an enduring one. It will be an irresponsible one, to say the least.

24) Chesterton, G. K. "Euthanasia and Murder." American Review 8 (February 1937): 487-490.

Chesterton says that laws are meant to prevent one from doing the things that he or she would enjoy doing. We are all capable of committing criminal acts and, therefore, should create laws that would prohibit our acting foolishly, otherwise, our foolishness will run rampant.

25) Clouser, K. D. "'The Sanctity of Life': An Analysis of a Concept." Annals of Internal Medicine 78 (1973): 119-125.

Clouser shows that the phrase "sanctity of life" is muddled and inconclusive. He thinks it should be expressed in a moral rule, such as "do not take human life." He explains and analyzes the rule.

26) Cohen, Bernice H., Abraham M. Lilenfeld, and P. C. Huang, eds. Genetic Issues in Public Health and Medicine. Springfield, Ill.: Charles C. Thomas, 1978.

Brings into focus genetic knowledge and its concomitant problems in the social, political, legal, and moral-ethical areas. Space is given to the discussion of genetic material and the environment, prenatal diagnosis of genetic disorders, population screening and surveillance, investigations and programs in special population segments, genetic counselling and intervention, and present capabilities and future possibilities. Anyone interested in genetics and where society is headed in this area would find the book of interest. Includes bibliographical references and index.

27) Collin, V. J. "Limits of Medical Responsibility in Prolonging Life." Journal of The American Medical Association 206 (October 1968): 389-392.

That medicine is obligated to enhance life as much as possible is reason enough for Collin's opinion not to maintain mere biological life, if that life is poor quality and beyond recovery. To discontinue treatment or therapy is not morally wrong if biological existence is all that is to be hoped for, Collin maintains. The author leaves the responsibility to the physician and his expertise in determining the condition and state of the patient who is to be denied therapy or life-sustaining treatment. Collin contends that the doctor need only be concerned with the patient. The family's best interests will follow.

28) Comfort, A. "A Vote for Humanity." Medical Opinion and Review 7 (February 1971): 28-29.

The possibility of a better life for the aged has been made by geriatrics, however, according to Comfort, even though he feels that being old and chronically ill is not good reason for euthanasia, there are, nevertheless, occasions where treatment should be withheld. The doctor's "good judgement" seems to be his criteria.

29) Cunningham, M. F. "To Live and to Die Humanly." Religious Humanism (Summer 1969).

Cunningham leans toward active euthanasia and suggests that the physician has a right to administer euthanasia when the mind of a person does not function (fails to function). It is his thesis that the physician is morally bound to participate in the death of those who have a sub-human existence.

30) "Doctor at the Bar." Newsweek 35 (January 16 1950): 20.

> Dr. Herman Sander is accused of administering a fatal injection of air (40cc) into the vein of his cancer patient, Abbie Borroto. At the request of Mr. Borroto, Dr. Sander complied with four injections--10cc each injection.

31) Duff, R. "Intentionally Killing the Innocent." Analysis 34 (October 1973): 1619.

> An argument against Geddes, "On the Intrinsic Wrongness of Killing Innocent People," Analysis 33 (1972): 93-97. Geddes' claim is that if one can describe what he did without reference to a death caused by said agent, the death was without intention. Duff counters with an illustration of cannibalism, and does so effectively.

32) "Euthanasia.", editorial. Lancet 2 (August 1961): 351.

> In opposition to "The Case for Voluntary Euthanasia" which was published by the Euthanasia Society, the editors charge that doctors are too free and active in practicing euthanasia, especially as having to do with terminal cancer patients who want to die because of extreme pain. Pain is no excuse for ending a life of the terminally ill when pain among patients with locomotive diseases is greater. If pain is to be the criteria, where will it all end?

33) "Euthanasia Rejected by French Academy of Moral and Political Sciences." Today's Health 28 (April 1950): 65.

> The French Academy denounces any form of euthanasia and cites accounts of the Nazi atrocities during World War II. What better argument could be propounded than academy's vivid presentation of the death chambers?

34) Filbey, E. E., and K. E. Reid. "Some Overtones of Euthanasia." Hospital Topics 43 (September 1965): 55-58.

The different forms of euthanasia are discussed, along with two questions raised: 1) can anyone be justified in deciding when to kill? and 2) would all the necessary legal machinery further depersonalize the hospital room? Machinery has its place in reducing patients to a non-human status.

35) Fletcher, Joseph. "The Patient's Right to Die." In Euthanasia and the Right to Die. A. B. Downing, ed. New York: Humanities, 1970.

Fletcher distinguishes none whatsoever between allowing to die and killing. He defends mercy killing and suggests that a law protecting those who practice voluntary active euthanasia be passed, thus putting the burden of proof on those who are opposed to prove that the killing was other than benevolent acts.

36) Glatt, M. M., Anthony J. Pelosi, and Christian Sawter. "From Nazi Holocaust to Nuclear Holocaust." Lancet 8507 (September 1986): 632.

Letters to the editor which give a lucid account of genocide as allowed and practiced by physicians under Hitler's regime. This discussion centers on a paper written by Dr. Hanauske-Abel in the August issue, 1986.

37) Human Life Review 2 (Spring 1976): 27-70. Articles on the right to die and euthanasia.

M. J. Sobran, Jr. discusses the right to die and suicide and concludes that these concepts devalue life. C. Everett Koop focuses on the dilemmas in euthanasia and abortion. Virgil Blum and Charles Sykes compare the euthanasia movement to Hitler's genetics policy in Germany.

38) "It's Over Debbie." Journal of The American Medical
Association 259 (January 1988): 272.

An unknown physician shares in detail the
steps he took to kill a terminally ill patient. A
good example of active euthanasia, although one
may argue in defense of voluntary euthanasia based
on the statement "Lets get it over with." Read the
article and decide for yourself.

39) Johnson, Eric W. Older and Wiser. New York: Walker,
1987.

A moving account of how the elderly feel
about growing older, eventually meeting with man's
last experience--Death. They express their feelings
about dying with dignity, the right to die, the
senselessness of prolonging a painful death, the right
of choosing *how* to die and living wills. Much of
the book is composed of questions and answers. It
is very easy to read and would probably lend itself
to discussion groups.

40) Kane, Robert L., and Rosalie A. Kane. Long-Term
Care in Six Countries: Implications for the United
States. Washington, D.C.: U.S. Government Printing
Office, n.d.

A comparative analysis of the extent and
mechanisms for delivery of long-term care to the
aged in England, Scotland, Sweden, Norway, The
Netherlands, and Israel. Concluding section discusses common themes and problems, rising costs, and
implications for the United States. Everyone in
health care delivery for the elderly *and* other
professionals should be aware of the information
compiled in this report.

41) Kluge, Eike-Henner. The Practice of Death. New
Haven: Yale University Press, 1975.

A philosophical discussion of decision-making

on the subjects of euthanasia, suicide, abortion, infanticide, and senicide. Straightforward.

42) Langer, William L. "Infanticide: A Historical Survey." History of Childhood Quarterly 1 (1974): 353-365.

Dr. Langer presents an overview of the history of infanticide. He discusses the practices of the people of antiquity and their attitudes toward newborn infants. Infanticide was committed in many cases because of over-population and food supply. He states that among non-Christian peoples (with the exception of the Jews) infanticide has from time immemorial been accepted procedure for disposing of sickly infants. Langer concludes that even though infanticide is not practiced during the present day, as it has been in the past, it is nevertheless still with us.

43) Levisohn, A. A. "Voluntary Mercy Deaths." Journal of Forensic Medicine 8 (April/June 1961): 57-79.

This article is pro euthanasia. Court cases are cited throughout. Legal language about murder is analyzed. Levisohn states that relative to euthanasia there are laws which deal with other areas in technology, but none for medicine. He feels that laws should be made to deal specifically with doctors who want to practice euthanasia--laws to help them in their decision making. The author believes that the anti-euthanasia view is religious in nature and, therefore, should not be written into law.

44) Lifton, Robert Jay. The Nazi Doctors: Medical Killing and the Psychology of Genocide. New York: Basic Books, 1986.

The subject of the book is the monstrous scheme of the Nazi doctors to rid the world of Jews (polluting Jewish genes). Lifton traces step-by-step procedures as to how extermination was possible by involved medical personnel without which the process could not have taken place. After reading the book, one realizes the danger of being led down the same path as the Nazi doctors, and that euthanasia, if practiced to extremes, could well be the first step toward genocide.

45) London, Jack. "The Law of Life." In Best Short Stories of Jack London. Garden City, NY.: Doubleday, 1953.

A perfect example of euthanasia as practiced among the Indians. Old Koskoosh is left behind by his tribe to die in the snow, during which time he thinks about life and death. Although he tells them all is well, he is resentful that they left him to die all alone.

46) Mansson, Helge H. "Justifying the Final Solution." Omega 3 (May 1972): 79-87.

A reaction of university students to the suggestion that "unfit" persons should be put to death, as a final solution to alleviate suffering and over-population, was fifty percent in agreement.

47) Medical Science in the Fight Against Genocide. New York: Campaigne, 1983.

A publication of selected transcripts from 1982-83 conferences of the Club of Life, with supplementary articles. Touches on different aspects of genocide and its results.

48) Mother Teresa Speaks at The National Right to Life Convention '85. Washington, D.C.: 30 min., color, $25., Video VHS. National Right to Life Educational Trust Fund, 419 7th St., N.W., Suite 402 (20004).

Mother Teresa, strongly but lovingly, urges all to protect and value human life at every stage of development. One will find that she is a heavyweight contender for life, no matter what the quality.

49) Reverence For Life--Father John Powell. Allen, Tex.: 90 min. (30 min. each part), color, $94.50 with study guide, Video VHS or Beta. Argus Communications, P.O. Box 7000, One DLM PARK (75002).

Expose on the historical and present day attempt to destroy our reverence for life. Powell describes the legal and medical efforts to replace it with the pragmatic "Quality of Life" ethic. He projects the consequences if we fail to stand up now and be counted for life. Part I: Reenactment of the Nazi Nightmare; Part II: Contemporary American Scene; Part III: Challenge to Conviction: The Call to Action.

50) Scully, Thomas, and Celia Scully. Playing God: The New World of Medical Choices. New York: Simon and Schuster, 1987.

A collaboration by husband and wife, with whom the reader feels an affinity because of their compassion and care shown for patients and families alike. Their concern is revealed through the subject content of Playing God. One learns how to make choices relative to health care while reading this work: choices in choosing the right physician for one's self and family; building the right relationship with one's physician; patients' rights and how to exercise them; "living will" and the power of attorney; transplantation of human organs; different ways of making babies; dilemmas on treatment and non-treatment; who should be the spokesperson for a child who has a disabling, life-threatening, or terminal illness; making life-and-death decisions for another adult; how to get action when you have been wronged through malpractice and billing fraud. A very important feature of the book is the appendices, which are "packed" with information on bills of rights in most areas of health care. The Scullys state, "The whole purpose of this book is to help you understand the issues and their ethical underpinnings, how to protect yourself, and where to go for help." Having researched many "how to" books, I find this one to be at the top of the list, and recommend it very highly, to be read and digested by all who are interested in the subject of euthanasia, in order to help make the right decisions in the area of health care. It is well indexed, and would be a handy tool for discussion groups.

51) The Slippery Slope. Toronto, Canada: 31 min., color, 16mm. Sale $475; Rental $50. Peter Gerresten Productions, 118 Castlefield Ave. (M4R 1G4).

This film is a critical examination of the issues surrounding the "Baby Doe" incident and the impact on human life. It deals with infanticide and euthanasia. It also deals with issues surrounding care of children with handicaps, care for older dying patients, "living wills," and merch killing.

52) "Three Score Years and Twelve." Christianity Today 17 (February 16 1973): 36.

This article is in opposition to a plan by a group in Chautauqua County, New York who proposes that suicide be allowed at age 72. The group advocates mandatory death at 144 years of age.

53) U. S. Senate. Death With Dignity: An Inquiry Into Related Public Issues. Washington, D.C.: U.S. Government Printing Office, 1972.

This document includes hearings before the Special Committee on Aging, and testimony of Rep. Walter Sackett, endorsing a recommendation to allow ninety percent of one thousand five hundred severely retarded children in Florida state hospitals to die.

Infanticide

54) Baylor Law Review 27 (Winter 1975). Symposium Issue on Euthanasia.

The symposium dealt with the following: "Euthanasia: Why No Legislation"; "The Physician's Dilemma: A Doctor's View: What the Law Should Be"; "Death? When Does it Occur?"; "Medical Death"; "Bill of Rights for the Dying Patient"; "Medical Technology as It Exists Today"; "The Family Deals with Death"; "The Living Will, Coping with the historical Event of Death"; "The Physician's Criminal Liability for the Practice of Euthanasia"; "Euthanasia: The Three-In-One Issue"; "Euthanasia vs. The Right to Live"; "Euthanasia, Medical Treatment and the Mongoloid Child: Death as a Treatment of Choice"; and "Death With Dignity: The Physician's Civil Liability." Practically every area of euthanasia was discussed. The subject of infanticide is suggested under the discussion "Euthanasia, Medical Treatment and The Mongoloid Child: Death as a Treatment of Choice."

55) Campbell, M., and R. Duff. "Moral and Ethical Dilemmas in the Special Care Nursery." New England Journal of Medicine 289 (October 1973): 890-894.

Moral and ethical issues surrounding decisions to allow certain babies to die are presented by Campbell and Duff. They believe it is perfectly alright to allow infants to die who have poor "quality of life" (withhold treatment). A review of records in a special-care nursery found that over a 2 1/2 year period, 14 percent of the deaths were the result of withholding treatment from abnormal infants. The family is taken into consideration as being the ultimate decision makers in allowing the infant to die. Special guidelines are suggested in order that the decision to withhold treatment should not be abused.

56) Carr, Charles A., and Donna Carr, eds. <u>Hospice Approaches to Pediatric Care</u>. New York: Springer, 1985.

Examples are presented which demonstrate how hospice care can become part of the pediatric scene. Individuals who are concerned for care of children with chronic illness, brain damage, and other areas which deal with dying children, can benefit greatly from this book.

57) Cohen, Douglas. "To Live or Let Die?" <u>Australian and New England Journal of Surgery</u> 56 (March 1986): 429-432.

This article examines the history of infanticide and some motivating reasons for infanticide. Personhood is discussed relative to abortion and infanticide. Selective non-treatment such as no surgery, nutrition, fluids, and drugs is mentioned along with legal liability.

58) Colen, B. D. "A Time to Die." <u>Washington Post</u> (March 10-12, 1974).

A series of three newspaper articles dealing with actual cases on decisions to die. Doctors and relatives of dying patients were interviewed. The march 10 issue deals with traumatic victims. Neonates (newborns) are dealt with in the March 11 edition. The copy of March 12 deals with patients who are terminally ill.

59) "Premies and Politics." Chap. in <u>Hard Choices</u>. New York: G.P. Putnam's Sons, 1986.

An excellent treatment of infanticide. The author reviews early accounts of killing defective newborns and brings the reader up to date on the latest cases having to do with treating or not treating the defective infant. Discussion of parental responsibility regarding deformed children recalls such cases as "Baby Doe", Roe vs. Wade, and Baby Andrew.

60) Damme, Catherine. "Infanticide: The Worth of an Infant Under Law." Medical History 22 (1978): 1-24.

An examination of medieval values and customs relating to the neonate and the low status in which the infant was held by society. The position has been institutionalized in English laws, which the American jurisprudential system has inherited, evidenced in Roe vs. Wade. Highly recommended for the study of infanticide.

61) David. 55 min., 16mm, color. Sale $700; Rental $75.00. Filmakers Library, 133 East 58th St., New York.

A portrait of a Down's Syndrome youth. potential of the human mind, and spirit of the mentally disabled. All who oppose the view that Down's Syndrome children are less than human should see this film.

62) Death In The Nursery. Boston: WNEV TV Documentary. 60 min., color.

Carlton Sherwood, a Pulitzer Prize and Peabody Award recipient, investigates and reports on infanticide in the U. S. For more information contact National Right to Life's Public Relations Department, 419 Seventh St., N.W., Suite 500, Washington, D.C. 20004.

63) Devine, Philip E. The Ethics of Homicide. Ithaca: Cornell University Press, 1978.

A professor of philosophy offers insights into homicide by examining all forms of killing. He includes abortion, capital punishment, euthanasia, suicide, war, and murder. Particularly interesting is Part II, which discusses infanticide and our institutions; infanticide and rights; and other views on infanticide. Part III discusses fetuses and "human vegetables"; abortion and the fetus, and the comatose. Part IV presents the justifications for homicide which are, according to Devine: euthanasia (chiefly involuntary), consensual homicide, voluntary euthanasia, and suicide. His arguments are both provocative and controversial.

64) Englehardt, H. Tristram, Jr. "Euthanasia and Children: The Injury of Continued Existence." Journal of Pediatrics 83 (July 1973): 170-171.

A presentation of legal cases which have bearing on the "quality of life" rated below normal. According to the author, a person's "quality of life", if below normal could be used negatively to deny his or her right to live. In this case, vulnerable children are at risk. Englehardt believes that the moral rights would bring great pressure to bear on physicians involved.

65) _____. "The Endings and Beginnings of Persons Death, Abortion, and Infanticide." Chap. in The Foundations of Bioethics. New York: Oxford University Press, 1986.

A scholarly discussion of the status of the fetus. The worth of the fetus is determined by the attitude of the mother toward it, however, some responsibility is allotted to the father. Englehardt briefly traces the history of infanticide and evaluates the conditions under which an infant should or should not be disposed of.

66) _____. The Foundations of Bioethics. New York: Oxford University Press, 1986.

A bold and provocative book which raises questions having to do with contemporary issues such as abortion, infanticide, and euthanasia.

67) Englehardt, H. Tristram, Jr., and Stuart F. Spicker, eds. Philosophy and Medicine. Vol. 18, Medical Ethics in Antiquity: Philosophical Perspectives on Abortion and Euthanasia, by Paul Carrick. Boston: D. Reidel, 1985.

An exploration of the origins and development of medical ethics as practiced by the ancient Greek and Roman physicians, together with their views on abortion and euthanasia. Infanticide and suicide are also examined. The Hippocratic oath is examined relative to abortion, infanticide, euthanasia, and suicide. The book is in three parts. Part One explores the social setting of Greek medicine. Part Two specifically deals with the beginning of Greek medical ethics, and Part Three examines a variety of divergent Greco-Roman ethical views and opinions on abortion and euthanasia. An excellent work. Scholarly done, well indexed, and should be in the libraries of those who are interested in historical aspects of euthanasia and related subjects.

68) Erdahl, Lowell D. "Mercy Killing and Its Pro-Life Alternatives." Chap. in Pro-Life/Pro-Peace. Minneapolis: Augsburg, 1986.

This chapter presents a pro-life-view defense against "mercy killing" as such, although Erdahl seems willing to consider passive euthanasia necessary, depending upon the condition of the patient. Concerning deformed infants, he strongly feels the need to preserve their lives if corrective surgery will give them a meaningful life. Appendix I contains questions and suggestions for reflection and discussion (session 6 on "mercy killing and its pro-life alternatives" lists 12 thought provoking questions on the subject).

69) Etzoioni, Amitai. "Moral and Social Implications of Genetic Manipulation." When Is It Moral to Modify Man?, ed. Claude A. Frazier, 267-269. Springfield, Ill.: Charles C. Thomas, 1973.

A brief discussion of how genetic control and manipulation can be a curse to man rather than a blessing. One danger mentioned is the fact that defective genes may be found in a floating fetus and lead to abortion (infanticide). This short article raises serious questions.

70) Evans, M. "Power to Kill: Homicide as Euthanasia." American Opinion 17 (January 1974): 39-41.

Reflections on the inconsistent attitudes of the public toward abortion and euthanasia. Some implications of the government's implementation of euthanasia.

71) Fletcher, Joseph. Humanhood: Essays in Biomedical Ethics. Buffalo, N.Y.: Prometheus Books, 1979.

A humanist's examination of subjects in the forefront of argumentations, among which are genetic engineering, fetal research, responsibilities to the unborn, abortion, infanticide, euthanasia, suicide, and human experimentation.

72) Freeman, J. "Is There a Right to Die--Quickly?" Journal of Pediatrics 80 (May 1972): 904-905.

According to Freeman, infants who have serious birth defects should be killed rather than have their lives prolonged indefinitely. Prolonga tion would result in much suffering not only for them, but also for their parents and those who serve their health care needs.

73) Gift of Life/Right to Die. 15 min., B&W. Rental, EMC No. 7320. Champaign, Ill.: Indiana University Audio-Visual Center and Visual Aids Service, Division of University Extension, University of Illinois (61822), 1968.

A short film discussing one person's death and another who becomes an organ recipient of the former. Other ethical issues are mentioned, such as euthanasia for infants who are malformed, and individuals who suffer from catastrophic disease.

74) Gillon, Raanan. "Ordinary and Extraordinary Means." British Medical Journal 292 (January 1986): 259-261.

A scholarly discussion on the Roman Catholic view of ordinary and extraordinary means. The importance of the patient's permission is tantamount relative to withholding or discontinuing treatment. Burdensomeness of treatment (risks, cost, and other difficulties) is also taken into consideration, along with burdens on others. Withholding of nutritional support for infants with an encephaly, severe brain damage, and total necrotising enterocolitus would be appropriate because of prolonged treatment for the remainder of the infant's life.

75) Gimbel, Barry. "Infanticide - Who Makes the Decision?" Wisconsin Medical Journal 73 (May 1974): 10-11.

Based on two court cases surrounding two deformed babies on which surgery was performed. According to Gimbel, the ultimate decision should be made by the parents of children whose quality of life is questioned.

76) Glover, Jonathan. Causing Death and Saving Lives. Harmondsworth: Penguin Books, 1977.

A lucid discussion presenting the arguments used in prohibiting or justifying the killing of others. It deals with: moral theory, autonomy and rights, ends and means; not striving to keep alive;

abortion, infanticide, suicide, voluntary and involuntary euthanasia, choices between people in allocating resources, assassination, and war. A skillful work and highly recommended for those interested in euthanasia and problems surrounding it.

77) Gregg, W. W. "Right to Kill." North American Review 237 (March 1934): 239-249.

Active and passive euthanasia are discussed, along with abortion, infanticide, and capital punishment. An analysis of legal and moral implications is offered.

78) Gustafson, James M. "Mongolism, Parental Desires, and the Right to Life." Perspectives in Biology and Medicine 16 (Summer 1973): 529-557.

The discussion centers around the decision not to perform life-saving surgery on a mongoloid newborn. Arguments used to support such a decision are presented, but Gustafson concludes that such a decision should not have been made.

79) Holder, Angela Roddey. Legal Issues in Pediatrics and Adolescent Medicine. New York: Wiley, 1977.

A handbook for the physician who is interested in combating those who are opposed to his rights as he operates within the confines of the medical profession. Holder identifies many legal issues confronting pediatricians, neonatologists, and others who treat minors. Among the problems she discusses are genetic counselling, genetic screening, fetal research, and the physician's liability to treat deformed newborns. Discussion of allowing the malformed infant to die is presented with the fact that it cannot be covered up, but must be openly addressed. Moral issues are also treated with which pediatricians are faced as they must come to terms with the question of whether to treat or not to treat severely deformed infants.

80) Horan, Dennis J., and David Mall, eds. Death, Dying and Euthanasia. Washington, D.C.: University Publications of America, 1977.

Controversial aspects of euthanasia are discussed, such as: involuntary euthanasia of the defective newborn; ethical, moral, and legal aspects of "mercy killing"; the feasibility of legalized euthanasia; and the right of the individual to reject treatment.

81) Horan and Dela Hoyde, eds. Infanticide and the Handicapped Newborn. Provo, Utah: Brigham Young University Press: 1981.

A scholarly work which evaluates the moral and medical issues raised by infanticide in America.

82) Human Life Review 2 (Spring 1976): 27-70.

M. J. Sobran, Jr. discusses the right to die and suicide and concludes that these concepts devalue life. C. Everett Koop focuses on the dilemmas in euthanasia and abortion. Virgil Blum and Charles Sykes compare the euthanasia movement to Hitler's genetics policy in Germany.

83) Humphries, S. V. "The Problems of Therapeutic Abortion and Infanticide." The Central American Journal of Medicine 24 (April 1978): 77-79.

Humphries' view is that a fetus, though a human species, is not a person but is a potential one if allowed to develop fully. He lists moral objections and side effects to abortion. "If," as he says in the above article, "we accept the justification of abortion, it is difficult to defend the practice of going to great lengths to preserve the lives of newborn babies with gross defects."

84) Kluge, Eike-Henner. The Practice of Death. New Haven: Yale University Press, 1975.

A philosophical discussion of decision making on the subjects of euthanasia, suicide, abortion, infanticide, and senicide. Straightforward.

85) Kohl, Marvin, ed. Infanticide and the Value of Life. Buffalo, N.Y.: Prometheus Books, 1978.

Examined are the religious, medical, legal, and ethical issues surrounding infanticide. Familiar personalities writing are: Joseph Fletcher, Arval A. Morris, Glanville Williams, Joseph Margolis, Richard Brandt, Peter Black, Immanuel Jababovits, and Leonard Weber. Indexed, with bibliography.

86) Lachs, John. "Humane Treatment and Treatment of Humans." New England Journal of Medicine 294 (April 1976): 838-840.

A presentation of a classic case having to do with the treatment and attitude of care toward hydrocephalic infants. Infants such as these are looked upon by the author as non-persons--not humans, but human shapes.

87) Langer, William L. "Infanticide: A Historical Survey." History of Childhood Quarterly 1 (1974): 353-365.

Dr. Langer presents an overview of the history of infanticide. He discusses the practices of the people of antiquity and their attitudes toward newborn infants. Infanticide was committed in many cases because of over-population and food supply. He states that among non-Christian peoples (with the exception of the Jews) infanticide has from time immemorial been accepted procedure for disposing of sickly infants. Langer concludes that even though infanticide is not practiced during the present day as it has been in the past, it is nevertheless still with us.

88) Lantos, John. "Baby Doe Five Years Later." New England Journal of Medicine 317 (August 1987): 444-447.

The author reviews the unfortunate case of Baby Doe who was allowed to die of starvation in an Indiana hospital, and the controversy which erupted between the Reagan administration and the Supreme Court decision legalizing abortion. For additional reference see "The Story of Baby Doe." New England Journal of Medicine 309 (1983): 644

89) "License to Live." Christianity Today 18 (July 1974): 22-23.

An editorial warning against the acceptance of legalized abortion in that it would result in forced sterilization, passive euthanasia, and eventually active euthanasia. An alarm for Christians to speak out in opposition.

90) Manney, James, and John C. Blattner. "Infanticide: Murder or Mercy?" Journal of Christian Nursing (Summer 1985): 10-14.

Manney and Blattner mention in brief how unwanted infants have been disposed of in the past which, if compared to present-day practices, show very little difference. The authors are opposed to infanticide in any form and present a strong defense against it by pointing out the dark side of human thinking in its attitude toward helpless infants who are malformed. According to the writers, it is imperative that a true definition of infanticide be understood, that the new ethic of "quality of life" be rejected, which opposes the old ethic of Judeo-Christian moral tradition, i.e., there is intrinsic worth and equal value of every human life regardless of its stage of development or condition.

91) <u>May's Miracle</u>. New York: 28 min., color, 16mm. $450. Filmakers Library, 133 E. 58th St.

In a modern world where defective babies are being rejected by some parents and doctors and left to die, the story of May Lemke and her adopted son, Leslie, stands as an effective witness against the practices of abortion and infanticide.

92) <u>Mother Teresa Speaks at The National Right to Life Convention '85</u>. Washington, D.C.: 30 min., color, $25., Video VHS, National Right to Life Educational Trust Fund, 419 7th St., N.W., Suite 402 (20004).

Mother Teresa urges all to protect and value human life at all stages of development.

93) Murray, Thomas, and Arthur L. Caplan, eds. <u>Which Babies Shall Live?: Humanistic Dimensions of the Care of Imperiled Newborns</u>. Clifton, N.Y.: Humana, 1985.

A collection of essays discussing seriously-ill newborns. This work draws on the insights of philosophers, a historian,, theologian, an anthropologist and others. The essays are in four groups: "The Child, Medicine and Science," "Caretakers: Images and Attitudes," "Religion, Suffering and Mortality," and "Images of the Abandoned." Truly, this book offers a new perspective in the cause of catastrophically ill newborns.

94) <u>Oklahoma Infanticide</u>. Washington, D.C.: 67 min., (Part I: 37 min.; Part II: 30 min.), color, $25. Video VHS, National Right to Life Educational Trust Fund, 419 7th St., N.W., Suite 402 (20004).

A Cable News Network Documentary. Part I: Carlton Sherwood investigates incidents of infanticide in the U.S., treatment vs. non-treatment of handicapped newborn babies, "Quality of Life" selection processes, includes excerpts from the film "Who Should Survive." Part II: "Debate . . . " Nat

Henthoff, columnist for The Village Voice vs. Dr. Anthony Shaw, pediatric surgeon and author of "Quality of Life" formula.

95) Persaud, T., ed. Problems of Birth Defects. Baltimore: University Park Press, 1977.

From Hippocrates to Thalidomide and beyond. A compilation of fifty-seven papers on historical aspects, epidemiology, mechanisms, genetics, causes, prenatal diagnosis, management, and social aspects of birth defects. Good for basic reference and description of various physical problems of unborn and newborn infants.

96) Potts, Malcolm, Peter Diggory, and John Peel. Abortion. New York: Cambridge University Press, 1977.

A scholarly thesis which is well documented. The hypothesis presented is that no society has been able to adjust or advance socio-economically without recourse to abortion. The authors are sympathetic to the illegal abortionists, one of whom was the inventor of the Karman Curette for vacuum aspiration. The authors' presentation supports their thesis that abortion precedes a society's effective use of contraception and is a necessary adjunct to contraception. Those who are anti-abortionist will not agree that abortion on a large or small scale is the answer to any society's socio-economic problems.

97) Reverence For Life--Father John Powell. Allen, Tex.: 90 min., (30 min. each part), color, $94.50 with study guide, Video VHS or Beta; Argus Communications, P.O. Box 7000, One DLM Park, Allen (75002).

An expose on the historical and present day attempt to destroy our reverence for life. Powell describes the legal and medical efforts to replace it with the pragmatic "Quality of Life" ethic. He projects the consequences if we fail to stand up now and be counted for life. Part I: Reenactment of the

Nazi Nightmare; Part II: Contemporary American Scene; Part III: Challenge to Conviction: The Call to Action.

98) Sempos, Christopher, and Richard Cooper. "Passive Euthanasia." Archives of Internal Medicine 143 (July 1983): 1492.

A letter written to oppose the thought that parents may be justified in allowing their children with profound mental retardation to be killed, which is incompatible with social experiences.

99) Scully, Thomas, and Celia Scully. Playing God: The New World of Medical Choices. New York: Simon and Schuster, 1987.

A collaboration by husband and wife, with whom the reader feels an affinity because of their compassion and care for patients alike. Their concern is revealed through the subject content of Playing God. One learns how to make choices relative to health care while reading this work: choices in choosing the right physician for one's self and family; building the right relationship with one's physician; patients' rights and how to exercise them; "living will" and the power of attorney; transplantation of human organs; different ways of making babies; dilemmas on treatment and non-treatment; who should be the spokesperson for a child who has a disabling, life-threatening, or terminal illness; making life-and-death decisions for another adult; how to get action when you have been wronged through malpractice and billing fraud. A very important feature of the book is the appendices, which are "packed" with information on bills of rights in most areas of health care. The Scullys state, "The whole purpose of this book is to help you understand the issues and their ethical underpinnings, how to protect yourself, and where to go for help." Having researched many "how to" books, I find this one to be at the top of the list, and recommend it very highly to be read and digested by all who are interested in the subject of euthanasia, in order to help make the right decisions in the area of health care. It is well indexed, and would be a handy tool for discussion groups.

100) Stehbens, William E. "Euthanasia." New Zealand Medical Journal 99 (March 1986): 190-193.

A debate of the inconsistency of society's view of death and euthanasia, especially voluntary euthanasia. Dr. Stehbens sees no difference between active and passive euthanasia. In the light of techniques which enable the patient to be kept alive indefinitely, he believes that doctors should be allowed to decide when it is useless to keep a patient alive without fear of being charged with unprofessional conduct. Regarding deformed infants, Stehbens believes that interference to prolong the lives of those incapable of ever experiencing a near normal existence is undesirable, if not cruel. He points out that involuntary, active euthanasia is unacceptable in a free society and that involuntary, passive euthanasia , which includes severe irremedial brain damage, grossly malformed infants, and irreversible coma patients, is a form of life that has caused untold misery and cost to family members. He agrees with others that arguments for moral mercy killing outweigh those that oppose it, and concludes that the moralists are beginning to concede that there will be an irreversible trend toward mercy killing.

101) Temkin, Owsei, William K. Frankena, and Sanford H. Kadish. Respect for Life in Medicine, Philosophy, and the Law. Baltimore: The Johns Hopkins University Press, 1976.

Respect for life is approached from different perspectives which shed light on the subject in different ways. Temkin discusses the history of medicine and how early medicine understood respect for life. The philosophical approach by William Frankena interprets respect for life and how moral philosophy should define it. Kadish presents how the law treats different cases of taking human life. Euthanasia, abortion, infanticide, and other means of taking life are interwoven throughout the book.

102) "The Prognosis for Babies with Meningomyelocele and High Lumbar Paraplegia at Birth." Lancet 8462 (November 1985): 996-997.

A comment by a working group on whether or not there continues to be an ethical justification for selective treatment of spina bifida babies. The group is convinced that in certain cases, active steps to shorten a baby's life should not be taken.

103) The Slippery Slope. Toronto, Canada: 31 min., color, 16mm. Sale $475; Rental $50. Peter Gerresten Productions, 118 Castlefield Ave. (M4R 1G4).

This film is a critical examination of the issues surrounding the "Baby Doe" incident and the impact on human life. It deals with infanticide and euthanasia. It also deals with issues surrounding care of children with handicaps, care for older dying patients, "living wills," and mercy killing.

104) U. S. Senate. Death With Dignity: An Inquiry Into Related Public Issues. Washington, D.C.: U. S. Government Printing Office, 1972.

This document includes hearings before the Special Committee on Aging and the testimony of Rep. Walter Sackett, endorsing a recommendation to allow ninety percent of one thousand five hundred severely retarded children in Florida state hospitals to die.

105) Venes, Joan, Joseph C. Maroon, Thomas Shannon, Barbara Geach, et al. "Severely Deformed Infants." New England Journal of Medicine 295 (July 1976): 115-116.

Six letters by physicians in answer to an article (New England Journal of Medicine 294: 838, April, 1976) by Dr. Lacks, who characterized hydrocephalic children as being "non-persons."

106) Weiss, Anne E. Bioethics: Dilemmas in Modern Medicine. Hillside, N.J.: Enslow, 1985.

Weiss makes difficult subjects comprehensible, such as right to life, organs for sale, the Baby Doe rule, experimenting on humans, who gets health care, genetic engineering, rights of patients, and the right to die. After reading this book, one will have a good understanding of what bioethics is all about.

107) Whitelaw, Andrew. "Death as Option in Neonatal Intensive Care." Lancet 8502 (August 1986): 328-331.

According to Whitelaw, many physicians believe there are circumstances in which infants should be allowed to die without having their lives prolonged. He mentions that seventy five infants were so seriously ill that withdrawal of treatment was considered. Criteria for withdrawal of treatment from a particular infant had to be based on certainty of total incapacity and a unanimous decision among the nursing staff caring for the child. Treatment was withdrawn from fifty one of the seventy five patients. The parents of forty seven infants accepted the decision and all the infants died. Parents of four chose continued intensive care, and two infants survived with disabilities. Treatment of twenty four cases was continued. Seventeen survived and seven died. Agreement was unanimous among staff and parents that treatment should be withdrawn and that treatment on purely legal grounds is not justifiable.

108) <u>Who Should Survive?</u> 26 min., color. Rental/Sale. Joseph
P. Kennedy Foundation. Media Center, University
Extension, University of California, Berkeley, Calif.
(94720), 1972.

Issues surround a mongoloid infant who is
allowed to die. Experts discuss the legal, scientific,
and ethical aspects of the case. For those who want
to explore these aspects of euthanasia.

109) <u>Who Speaks for the Baby?</u> New York, N.Y.: 20 min.,
color. 3/4" Video Cassette. 15 Columbus Circle
(10023).

Parents of a mongoloid baby are reluctant to
give consent for surgery to solve life-saving
problems for the infant. The pediatrician proceeds
to seek a court order to operate. Should he? Should
the child be allowed to live or die--a difficult
question which the content of the tape seeks to
answer. A National Continuing Medical Education
tape. Subscribers only.

<u>Suicide</u>

110) Allred, V. C. "Euthanasia - Legal Aspects." <u>Linacre</u>
<u>Quarterly</u> 14 (April 1947): 1-15.

Legal aspects of euthanasia are treated. Cases
explained are: mercy killings, suicide pacts, abortion, and duelling. The legal guild involved in each
case is explained. Legal definitions and statutes are
quoted. Discussions of natural and divine laws are
incorporated.

111) Barrington, M. R. "Apologia for Suicide." In <u>Euthanasia</u>
<u>and the Right to Die</u>, ed. A. B. Downing. New
York: Humanities, 1970.

A convincing argument for the right to suicide.
Barrington condones the practice and belittles the

belief that suicide is sinful. When at the extreme of a life situation due to poor "quality," she advocates suicide and voluntary euthanasia. A well planned life is one that does not leave out "planned" suicide. For those who hold to her views, this article should be supportive.

112) Battin, Pabst M. Ethical Issues in Suicide. Englewood Cliffs, N.J.: Prentice-Hall, 1982.

Margaret Battin is a philosopher who writes for an intelligent readership. The problems considered by her in this work are of widespread importance and are treated effectively as well as intelligently. In the introduction, the current view of suicide is discussed, which incorporates: the scientific view, the treatment of suicide, the legal dilemma, and the suicide taboo. Moving into the body of the book, arguments for and against the moral permissibility of suicide are presented. The arguments are arranged in two parts. Part I comprises traditional arguments concerning suicide, among which are: religious views of suicide, social arguments concerning suicide, and suicide and the value of life. Part II is contemporary in character and compiles up-to-date issues on suicide. Beginning with Chapter 4, the concept of rational suicide and its criteria is presented. Chapter 5 expounds paternalism and suicide, which deals with paternalistic intervention in suicide, and the facilitation thereof. Chapter 6 graphically sets forth the rights of suicide, together with suicide as being a right within itself, and the rights and roles of others who are involved. After reading the book, one will discover that the author has an automist view of suicide, which sees the act as ". . . potentially rational and dignity-promoting . . ." Yet she ". . . applauds the sincere efforts of suicide-prevention workers and researchers to prevent suicide which is irrationally or pathologically chosen, and welcomes those voices who remind us of the value of life." (See page 195 in work cited.) This work is truly philosophical in content.

113) Battin, Pabst M., and David J. Mayo. Suicide: The Philosophical Issues. New York: St. Martin's, 1980.

Contemporary essays by philosophers, psychiatrists, legal theorists, literary, and religious personalities, which bring together a body of material answering to the issues which are relative to suicide. Explored are such questions as: Does a person have a right to end his or her own life? Is suicide always an irrational choice? Is suicide evidence of insanity? Do other persons have a right to intervene into a suicidal attempt or assist someone in taking his or her life? Can suicide be meaningful, legal, or morally right? Debated are the following philosophical issues:

Did Socrates commit Suicide?
The Concept of Suicide
Suicide and Self-Sacrifice
Suicide: Some Theological Reflections
Suicide and Covenant
Apologia for Suicide
The Ethics of Not-Being: Individual Options for Suicide
The Rationality of Suicide
Irrational Suicide
On Choosing Death
Suicide and False Desires
Suicide as Instrument and Expression
The Art of Suicide
Manipulated Suicide
The Ethics of Suicide
Choosing the Time to Die
Suicide Prevention and the Value of Human Life
The Right to Suicide: A Psychiatrist's View
Suicide and the Inalienable Right to Life
A Constitutional Right to Suicide
Assisting Suicide: A Problem for the Criminal Law
Suicide: A Fundamental Human Right?
Suicide and Virtue

The reader will discover that the discussions in this work involve primarily conceptual and moral issues. Also spoken to are professionals in areas of psychiatry, counselling, nursing, general medicine, religious practice, and law. A book which calls forth respect for the intelligent scholarly gifts of its contributors.

114) Cavanagh, J. R. "Chaplain and the Dying Patient." Hospital Progress 52 (November 1971): 35-40.

The ethical and pastoral relationship of the chaplain and patient are discussed. Irreversible and reversible illness are defined, along with further discussion on dying, death, ordinary and extraordinary means of life prolongation. Murder and suicide are defined. Student nurses are surveyed and their reactions to the dying patient are recorded.

115) Clark, David B., Jr. "Voluntary Euthanasia and the Hemlock Society." American Journal of Psychiatry 143 (November 1986): 1503, 1504.

A defense of the Hemlock Society in response to an article "Is It Normal for Terminally Ill Patients to Desire Death?"

The article states that the Hemlock Society condones and assists in suicide by terminally ill patients.

116) "Deed of Friendship: Mary Happer Shot by Friend." Newsweek 65 (April 26 1965): 30.

After witnessing constant suffering of her friend, Mary Happer, Dorothy Butts shot her in an act of "mercy" and then committed suicide.

117) Desmond, Stewart. Socrates and the Soul of Man. Boston: Beacon, 1951.

The work incorporates a fresh translation of Plato's Phaedo, in which Plato describes the last hours of Socrates. The book documents the fact that man during Plato's and Socrates' period became aware that man is a personality (soul). It is more or less a memorial to Socrates. A very emotional account of the death of one of the "greats" of philosophical thinking.

118) Devine, Philip E. The Ethics of Homicide. Ithaca: Cornell University Press, 1978.

A professor of philosophy offers insights into homicide by examining all forms of killing. He includes abortion, capital punishment, euthanasia, suicide, war, and murder. Particularly interesting is Part II, which discusses infanticide and our institutions; infanticide and rights; and other views on infanticide. Part III discusses fetuses and "human vegetables"; abortion and the fetus, and the comatose. Part IV presents the justifications for homicide which are, according to Devine: euthanasia (chiefly involuntary), consensual homicide, voluntary euthanasia, and suicide. His arguments are both provocative and controversial.

119) Donne, John. Biathanatos. New York: Arno, 1976.

A lasting study of "self-homicide." An examination of suicide and death.

120) Englehardt, H. Tristram, Jr., and Stuart F. Spicker, eds. Philosophy and Medicine. Vol. 18, Medical Ethics in Antiquity: Philosophical Perspectives on Abortion and Euthanasia, by Paul Carrick. Boston: D. Reidel, 1985.

An exploration of the origins and development of medical ethics as practiced by the ancient Greek and Roman physicians together with their views on abortion and euthanasia. Infanticide and suicide are also examined. The Hippocratic oath is examined relative to abortion, infanticide, euthanasia, and suicide. The book is in three parts. Part One explores the social setting of Greek medicine. Part Two specifically deals with the beginning of Greek medical ethics, and Part Three examines a variety of divergent Greco-Roman ethical views and opinions on abortion and euthanasia. An excellent work. Scholarly done, well indexed, and should be in the libraries of those who are interested in historical aspects of euthanasia and related subjects.

121) Englehardt, H. Tristram, Jr. "Free and Informed Consent, Refusal of Treatment, and the Health Care Team: The Many Faces of Freedom." Chap. in The Foundations of Bioethics. New York: Oxford University Press, 1986.

In this chapter there is an excellent section on "suicide, euthanasia, and the choice of a style for dying," p. 301. The author shares his thoughts on the right to be left alone and the context of death; intending death, foreseeing death, and refusing treatment; advance directives, proxy covenant, and stopping treatment on the incompetent; suicide and assisted suicide; and euthanasia.

122) "Euthanasia: A Study in Comparative Criminal Law." University of Pennsylvania Law Review 103 (December 1954): 350-389.

Suicide and mercy killing are discussed, defined, and compared with criminal law.

123) "Euthanasia." Spectator 88 (February 1, 1902): 175-176.

A series of letters putting forth various views on euthanasia. Euthanasia and legislation, and euthanasia and suicide are discussed relative to the Christian ethic.

124) Fletcher, Joseph. Humanhood: Essays in Biomedical
Ethics. Buffalo, N.Y.: Prometheus Books, 1979.

Perplexities confronting modern man, such as
genetic engineering, transplantation, fetal research,
recombinant DNA, abortion, suicide, and euthanasia
are discussed by this well known ethicist. In the
early chapters he establishes standards of humanhood and chooses progress and rationalism over the
rights and loving concern of individuals. These
essays are well written.

125) Glover, Jonathan. Causing Death and Saving Lives.
Harmondsworth: Penguin Books, 1977.

A lucid discussion presenting the arguments
used in prohibiting or justifying the killing of
others. It deals with: moral theory, autonomy and
rights, ends and means; not striving to keep alive;
abortion, infanticide, suicide, voluntary and involuntary euthanasia, choices between people in
allocating resources, assassination, and war. A skillful work and highly recommended for those interested in euthanasia and problems surrounding it.

126) Hall, William T. "Legalized Suicide." Delaware State
Medical Journal 40 (February 1968): 50-51.

Dr. Hall's conclusion--after discussing the
process of dying with his family and patients--is that
they would approve of legalized suicide.

127) Haverwas, Stanley, and Richard Bondi. "Memory,
Community and the Reasons for Living: Theological
and Ethical Reflections on Suicide and Euthanasia."
Journal of the American Academy of Religion 44
(1976): 439-452.

The purpose of this essay is to try and see what
significance suicide and euthanasia have in the
Christian community, and how the memory and
narrative framework of that community provide
resources for determining an appropriate position on

suicide and euthanasia. An experimental model of how moral notions operate within the story, and convictions that sustain human communities is advanced. It is suggested that suicide and euthanasia are in disagreement with the Christian view and must, therefore, be repudiated.

128) Hendin, Herbert. Suicide in America. New York: W.W. Norton, 1982.

The last chapter, "The Right to Suicide," is an argument against the right to suicide. The reasons for suicide are discussed together with the tendency toward promoting suicide in England and America. The author concludes that our society is leaning more toward helping one another die rather than helping one another live.

129) Higgins, Colin. Harold and Maude. New York: Avon Books, 1975.

A humorous book about Harold and Maude, two people who enjoy attending funerals for pastime and amusement. Harold attempts suicide many times and Maude finally commits suicide in order to have some control over her own death--a form of euthanasia.

130) Holland R. F. "Suicide." In Moral Problems, ed. J. Rachels. New York: Harper and Row, 1971.

The author tries to find out what one may count as suicide and the factors that cause it. He differentiates between taking one's life for others and killing oneself for selfish reasons. He seems to think that religion is rather hard on suicide and blankets it as *all* wrong.

131) Hook, Sidney. "The Ethics of Suicide." In <u>Beneficent Euthanasia</u>, ed. Marvin Kohl, 57-69. Buffalo, N.Y.: Prometheus Books, 1975.

An attempt by the author through the method of moral and philosophical analysis to show that any system of thought which absolutely refuses to condone suicide as a rational possibility is irresponsibly optimistic or utterly immoral. He classifies the major arguments against suicide: (1) suicide is against society, (2) suicide is cowardly, (3) suicide is a violation of our duty to God, (4) suicide is unnatural, (5) suicide is an insult to human dignity, and (6) suicide is cruel in that it inflicts pain upon one's family and friends. Hook counters each argument. Whether or not he is successful is left to the reader for judgement.

132) Horan, Dennis J. <u>Death, Dying and Euthanasia</u>. Washington, D.C.: University Publications of America, Inc., 1977.

An impressive collection of works by authors from various fields: physicians, attorneys, ethicists, clergy, philosophers, and others who write with conviction on euthanasia. The works, most of which are reprints from periodicals, are classified under 7 headings: (1) Death: When Does It Occur and How Do We Define It?, (2) Death as a Treatment of Choice?: Involuntary Euthanasia of the Defective Newborn, (3) Euthanasia: Ethical, Religious, and Moral Aspects, (4) Euthanasia: The Legal Aspects of "Mercy Killing," (5) How Should Medicine and Society Treat the Dying?, (6) Legalized Euthanasia: Social Attitudes and Governmental Policies, and (7) Suicide and the Patient's Right to Reject Medical Treatment. The editors list the contributors in the back of the book. Good for research.

133) Human Life Review 2 (Spring 1976): 27-70 Articles on the right to die and euthanasia.

M. J. Sobran, Jr. discusses the right to die and suicide, and concludes that these concepts devalue life. C. Everett Koop focuses on the dilemmas in euthanasia and abortion. Virgil Blum and Charles Sykes compare the euthanasia movement to Hitler's genetics policy in Germany.

134) Humphrey, Derek. "Suicide and Euthanasia Special Types of Partner Relationships." Suicide and Life-Threatening Behavior 15 (Summer 1985): 65,66.

Humphrey initiates dialogue with Dr. H. Pohlmeier, who wrote the above article in which Pohlmeier, stated that euthanasia societies engage in assist suicide. Humphrey, who belongs to the Hemlock Society of Los Angeles, responded with "If we 'performed suicide' I would not be here to write this letter, would I?" Pohlmeier replies to Humphrey.

135) Humphrey, Derek, and Ann Wickett. "Helping Another to Die." Chap. in The Right to Die. New York: Harper and Row, 1986.

The husband-and-wife team join together in this chapter to write on assist suicide. In it they deal with two questions: "Do my religious and philosophical beliefs permit me to participate in this requested death?" and "Am I upholding the dying person's autonomy--his free choice in life's decisions--by helping?" Much support for the chapter is sought from such proponents of assist suicide as Joseph Fletcher and Margaret Pabst Battin. The Humphreys also present cases of individuals who have helped others to die. The reader will conclude that the Humphreys definitely condone the practice of active euthanasia.

136) _____. "Mercy Killing and the Law." Chap. in The Right to Die. New York: Harper and Row 1986.

The authors trace mercy killing issues as related to law, and present some interesting cases. They begin with Dr. Kraai, who injected three large doses of insulin into the chest cavity of a long time friend, Frederick C. Wagner, who was suffering from Alzheimer's Disease and gangrene. Other interesting and shocking cases are reviewed, with a brief look at "mercy killing" in the Swiss, German, and United Kingdom legal codes. Also, see "An upsurge in mercy killing and double suicide" in the same book.

137) Kluge, Eike-Henner. The Practice of Death. New Haven: Yale University Press, 1975.

A philosophical discussion of decision making on the subjects of euthanasia, suicide, abortion, infanticide, and senicide. Straightforward.

138) Langone, John. Death Is A Noun. Boston: Little, Brown, 1972.

An objective look at death, euthanasia, abortion, capital punishment, murder, suicide, and the afterlife.

139) "Mercy Killing." New Republic 127 (January 1950): 6.

A discussion of assist suicide, with reference to the case of Dr. Sander, who injected 40cc of air into his cancer patient.

140) Miller, Marvin. Suicide After Sixty: The Final Alternative. New York: Springer, 1979.

This is Volume 2 of a five volume series, the others being: Vol. 1: Between Life and Death, Vol. 3: Children's Conceptions of Death, Vol. 4: Death and the Creative Life, and Vol. 5: Hospice Care. Volume 2 documents reasons why many of the elderly commit suicide. Among the reasons cited are early retirement, fixed income, social isolation, declining health, and dependency. The book substantiates the fact that there are more suicides among the elderly than other age groups. The author focuses on multiple losses of the elderly, which lead them to decreased ability to cope with their situation. The book looks inside the relation between geriatric suicide and euthanasia, with a chapter on the physician and life-terminating events. Case histories are also provided. Dr. Miller is founder of the Suicide Information Center in San Diego, California, and brings much of his expertise to bear on the subject of this book.

141) Morgan, Ernest. A Manual of Death Education and Simple Burial. Burnsville, N.C.: Celo, 1977.

Apart from death in general, there are sections on coping with dying, grief, and ground rules for self-termination (suicide).

142) Murphy, George E. "The Physician's Responsibility for Suicide." Annals of Internal Medicine 82 (March 1975): 301-308.

A thought provoking article, treated in two parts. Part I, "An Error of Commission," shows studies of persons committing suicide, the majority of whom have been in contact with a physician within hours to a few months before death. Doctor Murphy concludes that the principal opportunity for suicide prevention begins in the physician's office. He believes that a study of persons committing suicide while under medical care may bring to view some areas of management errors, either in commission or omission. Murphy discloses: "Over half of those who died by overdose had received a prescription within a week or two before dying, or had an unlimited prescription for a . . . lethal amount of the hypnotic substance ingested." Further, he points out that individuals receiving smaller prescriptions supplemented them with "on hand" medications they already had in their possession. The study revealed that in over half of the cases, the physician supplied the lethal amount--an error of commission.

In Part II, "Errors of Omission," Murphy sadly discloses the fact that failure of physicians to detect depressive illnesses in forty nine patients out of sixty nine resulted in suicide. The depression was rarely treated due to ignorance. He states that "The failure to diagnose and to treat depressive illness and the failure to be informed about the risk factors in these cases represent missed opportunities for preventive intervention." This two-part article is invaluable for those interested in euthanasia patients who want to commit suicide and/or want assistance in the act.

143) Nevins, Madeline M., ed. A Bioethical Perspective on Death and Dying: Summaries of the Literature. Rockville, Md.: Information Planning Associates, 1977.

This work contains two hundred seventeen abstracts from the first twelve issues of the Bioethics Digest. Such issues explore the following: attitudes toward death, death education, definitions of death, euthanasia, care of the dying, bereavement, and suicide. The annotations are satisfactory.

144) Portwood, Doris. Common-Sense Suicide. New York: Dodd-Mead, 1978.

Portwood puts forward straight facts in defense of what she terms "rational" suicide. She calls for the legalization of suicide for those who are in a pitiable state of health. Those who are in favor of her argument would indeed feel comfortable while reading her book.

145) _____. "Common-Sense Suicide for the Elderly."
In Problems of Death: Opposing Viewpoints, ed.
David L. Bender, 128-130. St. Paul, Minn.: Green-
haven, 1981.

    A free lance writer argues that the aged should
hold the legal right to arrange their own death by
suicide.

146) Raanan, G. "Suicide and Voluntary Euthanasia: Historical Perspective." In Euthanasia and the Right to
Die, ed. A. B. Downing, New York: Humanities,
1970.

    A brief historical sketch of ideas surrounding
suicide and voluntary euthanasia, along with various reasons for and against suicide are stated.
Personalities, movements, and philosophies are
discussed.

147) Rosenberg, Jay F. Thinking Clearly About Death.
Englewood Cliffs, N.J.: Prentice-Hall, 1983.

    Interesting topics, such as: why life itself is not
a value, mercy killing and letting die, and rational
suicide are among others discussed in this volume.
The book as a whole constitutes those questions
about death to which philosophers have addressed
themselves through the centuries.

148) Rosner, Fred, and J. David Bleich, ed. Jewish Bioethics.
New York: Sanhedrin, 1979.

    In this volume, outstanding medical and rab-
binic experts bring together discussions which
deal with Jewish bioethics. On the subject of
euthanasia, there is a section," Death and Dying,"
which deals in depth with: The Jewish Attitude
Toward Euthanasia; The Quinlan Case: A Jewish
Perspective; Establishing Criteria of Death; The
Halakhic Definition of Death; Neurological Death
and Time of Death Statutes; and Suicide in Jewish
Law. The reader who is interested in Jewish views

on euthanasia will profit greatly from this edited work.

149) Steinbrook, Robert, and Bernard Lo. "The Case of Elizabeth Bouvia." Archives of Internal Medicine 146 (January 1986): 161-164.

An interesting case concerning assist suicide. The patient wanted to die and then changed her mind. Hospital attorneys said she wanted the hospital staff to assist in suicide. Her request was denied by the actions of the chief of psychiatry, who said he would "forcibly feed her." A discussion of a competent patient's right to determine medical care is presented.

150) The Literature of Death and Dying. New York: Arno, 1977.

The Literature of Death and Dying is a forty-volume collection on the subject of death, the content of which is extremely varied. It deals with the subject from the seventeenth century through the 1960s. Included are anthropological studies, religious essays, suicide, immortality, funerals, and history. Volumes can be ordered separately. More information can be obtained from the publisher.

151) "Thesis Abstracts." Calvin Theological Journal 20 (1985): 355.

"The Moral Revolution: Humanism vs. Christianity," by Clifford Earl Bajema, "presents the contrast between two ethical approaches to the issue of treatment termination decisions. The first, that of euthanasia, defends indirect or direct mercy killing and suicide . . . the second (endorsed) approach, that of benemortasia, works within the moral parameters of patient consent and imminence of death to determine when a person should be allowed to die and be provided only with palliative care, while life supports are withheld or even withdrawn." (Thesis Abstracts 1985)

152) Thomson, A. R. A Dictionary of Medical Ethics and Practice. Bristol: John Wright and Sons, 1977.

Among other things, the author gives accounts of bereavement, moment of death, brain death, suicide, and euthanasia. There is also a piece on "care of the dying." One will find the work moralistic and sincere.

153) "Three Score Years and Twelve." Christianity Today 17 (February 16, 1973): 36.

This article is in opposition to a plan by a group in Chautauqua County, New York who proposes that suicide be allowed at age 72. The group advocates mandatory death at 144 years of age.

154) Vincent,Merville O. "Suicide - A Christian Perspective: Suicide Prevention - Where There's Hope There is Life." In Is It Moral to Modify Man?, ed. Claude A. Frazier, 129-147. Springfield, Ill.: Charles C. Thomas, 1973.

A Christian psychiatrist looks at the question ". . . what role, if any, does Christianity have in alleviating the kind of suffering that results in self-destructive behavior? Does Christianity have anything to offer except . . . thou shalt not?'" Dr. Vincent appeals to Scripture and finds that while the Bible does not moralize on certain suicidal acts, it does not condone the practice. He lists and discusses the myths about suicide, and faith as being the factor of preventing suicide. He emphasizes that Christians should change society and provide hope for the hopeless. Anyone reading this article will find neither justification nor encouragement in committing suicide by euthanasia.

155) Wallace, Samuel E., and Albin Eser, eds. Suicide and Euthanasia. Knoxville: The University of Tennessee Press, 1981.

An edited work by a professor of sociology at the University of Tennessee, and a professor of criminal and comparative law at the University of Tubingen in West Germany. The essays address a wide variety of issues related to suicide and euthanasia: social suicide, suicide among cancer patients, defending suicide, the right to live and the right to die, voluntary euthanasia, "sanctity" and "quality" of life in a historical-comparative view, and legal structure of the "living will." Collectively, the essays apply a variety of perspectives on unexplored areas relating to the study of death. The book provides a very helpful bibliography citing works which directly relate suicide and euthanasia, and is highly recommended.

156) Waltzer, Herbert. "People Who Choose to Die." In Is It Moral to Modify Man?, ed. Claude A. Frazier, 102-110. Springfield, Ill.: Charles C. Thomas, 1973.

An excellent discussion on people who choose to die, specifically by suicide. Individuals who succeed, whether conscious or unconscious, are considered. The right to suicide by euthanasia practices is mentioned, but only briefly; however, what is written is thoughtful.

157) West, Jessamyn. The Woman Said Yes: Encounters With Life and Death. New York: Fawcett Book Group, 1977.

West gives an account of her own fight for life and supports her sister's desire for death rather than a drug-dominated existence. She also gives an account of assist suicide, whereby she helped her sister commit suicide rather than face a prolonged dying process resulting from cancer of the bowel.

CHAPTER 6

EUTHANASIA:
THE RELIGIOUS CHALLENGE

The Reply of Christianity

158) Adams, Tom R. "Is It Ever Right To Withhold Treatment Or 'Pull The Plug' On A Terminally Ill Patient?" Illinois Baptist 81 (June 1987): 4.

A discussion of a biblical perspective on euthanasia as a proper understanding of the sanctity of life.

159) Amulree, Lord, et. al. On Dying Well: An Anglican Contribution To The Debate on Euthanasia. London: Church Information Office, 1975.

Euthanasia from the Anglican point of view. Argues against voluntary euthanasia, and emphasizes care and compassion for the dying person. Focuses on good quality terminal care. Moral, legal, and theological aspects are considered. A commendable work, well done by a distinguished working party from the field of medicine and theology.

160) Barnes, W. E. "Science, Religion and Moral Judgement." Nature 166 (September 16, 1950): 455-457.

A bishop discusses euthanasia's role in solving many of the world's problems; its role in capital offenses, the eradication of abnormal genes, and over-population.

101

161) Bartlett, Robert H., Walter M. Whitehouse, Jr., and Jeremiah G. Turcotte, eds. Life Support Systems in Intensive Care. Chicago: Year Book Medical, 1984.

This volume is for practitioners in "intensive care." The contributors cover a wide range of professionals from departments of surgery, physiologists, internists, engineers, and physicians who are oriented in biomedical engineering and legal/ethical fields. There are four sections to the book. Section one deals with the monitoring of artificial organs. Sections two and three cover the basic pathophysiology of disease states and organ failure. Section four, "Ethics and Values," written by a physician and a professor of religion, discusses ethical considerations associated with the terminally ill. This section would probably be of the most interest to clergy personnel, however, the material presented would benefit anyone interested in health care.

162) Beauchamp,Tom L., and LeRoy Walters. Contemporary Issues in Bioethics. Encino and Belmont, Calif.: Dickenson, 1978.

A co-edition by a theologian and philosopher at the Kennedy Institute for Bioethics at Georgetown University. Sections included are on moral and conceptual foundations, patient-physician relationship, life and death, allocation of health resources, human experimentation, and behavioral and biomedical technology. Important judicial documents are included. The Hippocratic oath and the Quinlan case are examined. Policy statements, such as the Harvard Medical School Definition of Irreversible Coma and articles by professionals in other fields go together to compile the anthology. Each essay is well written, and taken together make a book that is recommended for teachers who desire to inform students of the issues confronting medical science. The book is a major effort to address perplexing problems.

163) Behnke, J. A., and S. Bok, eds. The Dilemmas of Euthanasia. Garden City, N.Y.: Anchor/Doubleday, 1975.

Four anthologies on philosophical, legal, theological, and medical articles, active and passive euthanasia, suicide, and care for the dying.

164) Blaker, C. W. "Thanatopsis." Christian Century 83 (December 7, 1966): 1503-1506.

An account of a patient who was kept alive by machines for eight years. A discussion of death, the definition of death, and the time when it is right for man to intervene into the situation. ". . .Man is justified in tampering with the transition between the two."

165) Brown, Harold O. J. "Euthanasia: Drawing New Distinctions." Journal of Christian Nursing (Fall 1986): 10-14.

An imperative for Christians to distinguish between varieties of euthanasia, and to recognize that there is very little difference between "passive" euthanasia and "active" euthanasia. Degrees, distinctions, and problems of euthanasia are discussed.

166) Bryant, D'Orsay D., III. "The Doctor and Death." Journal of The National Medical Association 78 (March 1986): 221-235.

A well-thought-through article. Emphasis is placed on the fact that doctors need to discuss death with their patients, and that communication is vital in order to help them during the process. Bryant also emphasizes that death comes to all, even Americans, who have a tendency to deny it more than other peoples around the world. He mentions that technological devices abound throughout the health care industry for the purpose of prolonging death, all by which man attempts to play God. God will remove man whenever He is ready to do so.

Importance is placed on "Christ's death, resurrection, and return. Hope for the Christian is anchored in these.

167) "Catholic Physicians Stress Respect for Life." Hospital Progress 51 (November 1970): 13-14.

According to these physicians, all human life must be respected, and physicians are not obligated to use every technique and means of technology to keep a patient alive who is incurably ill.

168) Cavanagh, J. R. "Chaplain and the Dying Patient." Hospital Progress 52 (November 1971): 35-40.

The ethical and pastoral relationship of the chaplain and patient are discussed. Irreversible and reversible illness are defined, along with further discussion on dying, death, ordinary, and extra-ordinary means of life prolongation. Murder and suicide are defined. Student nurses are surveyed and their reactions and attitudes to the dying patient are recorded.

169) Cooper, R. M. "Euthanasia and the Notion of Death With Dignity." Christianity Today 90 (February 21, 1973): 225-227.

The author stresses human dignity and pain. Pain is accepted as part of the human condition. According to Cooper, to deny pain as a human ingredient is worse than pain itself.

170) Curran, Charles and Michael de Bakey. Decisions: Life or Death. 30 min., B&W Rental/Sale. Association Films, and MacMillan Films.

The ethics of heart transplants and medical technology are discussed by a leading heart surgeon. A religious professional also takes part in the discussion.

171) Dayringer, Richard. "Death Ethics." American Protestant Hospital Association Bulletin 44 (1980): 1-9.

"Death Ethics" seeks to answer such questions as: 'When does death occur?'; 'How long should life be prolonged?'; and 'Should death ever be allowed to occur?' These questions are answered to some degree by a discussion of the definition of death, the prolonging of life, and a brief historical survey of euthanasia and its forms. A case history is presented to illustrate some of the concepts set forth in the article. It is a quick survey of the ethics of death.

172) "Euthanasia." Spectator 88 (February 1902): 175-176.

A series of letters putting forth various views on euthanasia. Euthanasia and legislation, and euthanasia and suicide are discussed relative to the Christian ethic.

173) Fletcher, John. "Abortion, Euthanasia, and Care of Defective Newborns." New England Journal of Medicine 292 (January 1975): 75-77.

John Fletcher sets forth two opposing views: that of Paul Ramsey and Joseph Fletcher. Ramsey equates genetically indicated abortion with infanticide, whereas, Joseph Fletcher not only equates the morality of abortion with selective euthanasia but also approves. To paraphrase the abstract, the author points out that though the two arguments are radically different, they are similar. Yet there are different moral features between the two--the post natal existence has an opportunity for treatment, and parental support. Because of the different moral features, decision for abortion after prenatal diagnosis does not necessarily commit the parents to euthanasia in the management of a seriously damaged or deformed infant. John Fletcher would argue that if we hold to the Judeo-Christian view, we ought to care for the defective newborn as though our relationships with God depended on the outcome, and the basis of our dignity depended on the same.

174) Gariepy, G. "Euthanasia and Death." Catholic Hospital, Canada 2 (March-April 1974): 131-133.

An examination of euthanasia and death relative to the position of the Catholic Church, the family, and health care professionals.

175) Gilder, S. S. B. "Christians and Euthanasia." Canadian Medical Association Journal 108 (January 20, 1973): 141.

Information on Christian viewpoints of euthanasia taken from two documents; a report of the General Synod of the Dutch Reformed Church, and Duncan Vere's English work.

176) Gillon, Raanan. "Ordinary and Extraordinary Means." British Medical Journal 292 (January 1986): 259-261.

A scholarly discussion on the Roman Catholic view of ordinary and extraordinary means. The importance of the patient's permission is tantamount relative to withholding or discontinuing treatment. Burdensomeness of treatment (risks, cost, and other difficulties) is also taken into consideration, along with burdens on others. Withholding of nutritional support for infants with an encephaly, severe brain damage, and total necrotising enterocolitus would be appropriate because of prolonged treatment for the remainder of the infant's life.

177) Graham, Billy. Facing Death and the Life Hereafter. Waco, Tex.: Word Books, 1987.

Graham covers a number of the aspects of death in this book. It should be read in its entirety. In his excellent chapter, "How Long is Borrowed Time?", Mr. Graham shares his thoughts on the fact that all have a right to die, and should not be forced to live a life when it only prolongs death.

Passive and active euthanasia are defined and discussed, along with illustrations from case histories. Graham is careful to include the importance of doing God's will. Scripture application is highlighted throughout. An excellent book on preparation for the great event.

178) Haverwas, Stanley, and Richard Bondi. "Memory, Community and the Reasons for Living: Theological and Ethical Reflections on Suicide and Euthanasia." Journal of the American Academy of Religion 44 (1976): 439-452.

The purpose of this essay is to try and see what significance suicide and euthanasia have in the Christian community, and how the memory and narrative framework of that community provide resources for determining an appropriate position on suicide and euthanasia. An experimental model of how moral notions operate within the story, and how the convictions that sustain human communities is advanced. It is suggested that suicide and euthanasia are in disagreement with the Christian view and must, therefore, be repudiated.

179) Hilhorse, Henri W. A. "Religion and Euthanasia in the Netherlands: Exploring a Diffuse Relationship." Social Compass 30 (1983): 491-502.

In this work, the author's intention is to discuss euthanasia and its relationship to religion in The Netherlands. He shows that for the most part religion and euthanasia are opposites, and that religion is not in favor of pro-euthanasia attitudes. As to institutions, the non-religious institutions, such as humanist organizations and euthanasia societies, are more in favor of euthanasia based on individual right of self-determination. Concerning individuals who are religious, there seems to be favoritism for euthanasia over and above the stand of religious institutions, however, religious individuals are less in favor of euthanasia than are non-religious individuals. Within the medical profession, doctors, nurses, and other health care professionals act within the framework of their religious belief, and are for the most part opposed to euthanasia. Only a small percentage think and act in favor of euthanasia. The author's purpose is realized in this article in that he does indeed give revealing insight into the practice of euthanasia throughout The Netherlands.

180) Hofling, C. K. "Life-Death Decisions May Undermine M.D.'s Mental Health." Frontiers in Hospital Psychiatry 5 (March 1968): 3

Hofling is emphatic in believing that decision making with regard to euthanasia should be a team effort composed of a group effort. The expertise of the physician, clergyman, family, and friends should be brought to bear on the decision.

181) Holifield, Brooks E. Health and Medicine in the Methodist Tradition: Journey Toward Wholeness. New York: Crossroad, 1986.

An exploration of health and medicine in the Methodist tradition. It covers such themes as well-being, sexuality, passages, morality, dignity, madness, healing, caring, suffering, and dying.

182) Holst, Lawrence E., ed. Hospital Ministry: The Role of the Chaplain Today. New York: Crossroad, 1985.

An appealing work on the spiritual dimension of health care. The book seeks to present the role of the chaplain as someone who goes beyond the physical pain, and enters the suffering world of the patient's soul pain, his relationship to God, and theology.

183) Humphrey, Derek, and Ann Wickett. "Religion and Euthanasia." Chap. in The Right to Die. New York: Harper and Row, 1986.

This chapter briefly describes the views of Roman Catholics, Jews, Lutherans, and others relative to euthanasia. There is also a list of religions and their tenets which specifies whether or not each is opposed, accepts, or leaves it to individual decision on passive and active forms of practice.

184) Hurley, Mark J. "The Value of Human Life: Challenge to a Brave New World." Hospital Progress 58 (February 1977): 70-73.

There are two basic questions addressed in this article on the value of life in the U.S.: 1) what premium is placed on human life in this country?; and 2) whose whose concept of values and whose perception of human life will assume ascendancy? Since there is so much difference in cultural practices, attitudes, and and religious beliefs of the various peoples living in the United States, is there a danger of the standards and practices of one group being forced upon another? The author writes on how the value of human life has eroded in America. He traces the history of abuses of life, and points out that some philosophers advocate infanticide, while others still value life, and are undertaking heroic means to protect, preserve, and enhance it. The writer believes that there is a danger of one view being accepted to the detriment of others, however, he states that there is a line beyond which tolerance should not go, and appeals to the fact that history affirms the basic concepts of life, dignity, human value, and worth. Old Testament times are given as examples of what true human liberty means. Our two hundred year old Declaration of Independence is an example of how different peoples of different cultures come together under one covenant to form one society in which true freedom and liberty can be pursued with respect to each citizen's views and concepts.

185) Jackson, Douglas M. Human Life and Human Worth. Christian Medical Fellowship, 1970.

What a Christian surgeon thinks of life, death, and the value of human life. A good appraisal.

186) Jackson, E. "Is Euthanasia Christian?" Christian Century 67 (March 8 1950): 300-301.

This article is divided into three parts: medical, theological, and legal. Each of these aspects are discussed relative to Christianity.

187) Jones, W. H. S. "From The Oath According To Hippocrates In So Far As A Christian May Swear It." In Ethics in Medicine: Historical Perspectives and Contemporary Concerns, ed. Stanley Joel Reiser, Arthur J. Dyck, and William J. Curran. Cambridge, Mass.: MIT, 1977.

The Hippocratic Oath is edited to fit the beliefs of Christians. Jones notes the different changes made by early Christians. This may be a good quote for Christians who need support for combating strong views in favor of euthanasia.

188) Jungel, Eberhard. Death: The Riddle and The Mystery. Philadelphia: Westminster, 1975.

A translation by a European Christian theologian. Examines Old and New Testament attitudes toward death, and demonstrates how theology can deal with medical and sociological problems surrounding death. A very efficient work.

189) Kapusta, Morton Allan, and Solomon Frank. "The Book of Job and the Modern View of Depression." Annals of Internal Medicine 86 (May 1977): 667-672.

A recommended study of the book of Job and depression. The authors present the book as being an instrument to provide professionals of the day with a realistic approach to the problems of life. Its disclosure of depression is the same as the modern view of depression. There are clues throughout the book that distinguish between normal grief and deep depression. Kapusta and Frank are convinced that Job not only gives a good description and meaning of depression, but that it also provides solutions for dealing with modern depression. Chapter 30 of Job provides answers that are vital for results of depression. The authors say, ". . .part of the wisdom of the Book of Job is a timeless medical masterpiece that provides an unexcelled standard of clinical observation and medical intervention." While this study is not specifically on the subject of euthanasia, it provides insight into the depression that occurs as a result of grief on the part of those who deal with the problems of euthanasia. It is highly recommended for all who experience depression, regardless of the cause.

190) Karo, Nancy, and Alvera Mickelsen. Adventure in Dying. Chicago: Moody Press, 1976

A paperback with an academic view of death and its actuality. A story of Karo's husband's experience with malignant cancer until his death. The story of a young Baptist minister who continues to preach up to the very end.

191) Kelly, G. "The Duty of Using Artificial Means of Preserving Life." Theological Studies 11 (1950): 203.

A review of Catholic literature on the difference between ordinary and extraordinary means. Kelly makes the distinction between preserving life when there is *no* hope and preserving life when there *is* hope of recovery. According to Catholic teaching, treatment may be withheld from the hopeless as long as sacraments have been given.

192) Koop, C. Everett <u>The Right To Live: The Right To Die</u>. Wheaton, Ill.: Tyndale House, 1976.

A famous pediatric surgeon gives his views on abortion and mercy killing. He examines current attitudes and trends from different perspectives: medical, personal, social and theological. He discusses the Supreme Court ruling and the Quinlan case. As the Surgeon General of the U.S., what Dr. Koop has to say in this book is highly significant and important.

193) Kreeft, Peter J. <u>Love Is Stronger Than Death</u>. New York: Harper and Row, 1979.

Both Christian and philosophical in answering the questions; what is death, and why do we die?

194) <u>Learning To Live With The Dying</u>. New York, N.Y.: 39 min. Color. Videocassette. Rental. 15 Columbus Circle (10023).

A National Continuing Medical Education tape sharing management of the terminally ill patients with patients and family. A discussion involving medical students, physicians, and a minister. For use by NCME subscribers only.

195) "License to Live." <u>Christianity Today</u> 18 (July 1974): 22-23.

An editorial warning against the acceptance of legalized abortion in that it would result in forced sterilization, passive euthanasia, and eventually active euthanasia. An alarm for Christians to speak out in opposition.

196) Mack, Arien, ed. <u>Death in the American Experience</u>. New York: Schocken Books, 1973.

A paperback book reprinted from the Fall issue of Social Research. A compilation of essays including: "Being and Becoming Dead," by Eric Cassell;

"The Sacral Power of Death in Contemporary Experience," by William May; "Death in the Judaic and Christian Tradition," by Roy Eckhardt; and Johannes Fabian writes on "How Others Die-Reflections on the Anthropology of Death."

197) McCormick, Richard A. Health and Medicine in the Catholic Tradition: Tradition in Transition. New York: Crossroads, 1985.

An exploration of health and medicine in the Catholic tradition, and its changes. Themes covered are well-being, sexuality, passages, morality, dignity, madness, healing, caring, suffering, and dying.

198) "M.D.'s, Clergy Discuss Prolonging Life." American Medical Association News 9 (May 9 1966): 1.

Bishop Fulton J. Sheen, Paul S. Rhoads, Reverend Granger E. Westberg, and Botthard Booth engage in a discussion of prolonging a patient's life by extraordinary means. Artificial devices such as the artificial kidney and artificial heart are discussed.

199) Maguire, Daniel C. "A Catholic View of Mercy Killing." In Beneficent Euthanasia, ed. Marvin Kohl, 34-43. Buffalo, N.Y.: Prometheus Books, 1975.

Maguire's position is that in a medical context, it may be moral and should be legal to speed up the death process by active euthanasia through overdose of drugs, etc., and that the use of extraordinary means is optional. He attempts to justify his position by showing that it is relatively in line with historical Catholic ethical theory.

200) Manney, James, and John C. Blattner. "Infanticide: Murder or Mercy?" Journal of Christian Nursing (Summer 1985): 10-14.

Manney and Blattner mention in brief how unwanted infants have been disposed of in the past which, if compared to present-day practices, show very little difference. The authors are opposed to infanticide in any form and present a strong defense against it by pointing out the dark side of human thinking in its attitude toward helpless infants who are malformed. According to the writers, it is imperative that a true definition of infanticide be understood, that the new ethic of "quality of life" be rejected, which opposes the old ethic of Judeo-Christian moral tradition, i.e., there is intrinsic worth and equal value of every human life regardless of its stage of development or condition.

201) Manning, K. M., "A Catholic Viewpoint." The Australian Family Physician 15 (April 1986): 493, 496, 497.

The points expressed in this article are not the official position of the Catholic church, but the views of Monsignor Manning. He discusses in brief the following: abortion, artificial insemination, in vitro fertilization, embryo experimentation, euthanasia, suicide, sterilization, malformed newborns, organ donation, homografts, blood transfusion, contraception, sexual habits and perversions, lesbianism and homosexuality, masturbation, circumcision, premarital sex (fornication), and adultery. On euthanasia, he holds to the Catholic moral position that one may not directly cause his or her own death, or the death of another by deliberately performing an act toward taking that life, or deliberate omission of treatment due an individual.

202) Marty, Martin E. Health and Medicine in the Lutheran Tradition: Being Well. New York: Crossroads, 1983.

An exploration of health and medicine in the Lutheran tradition. It covers such themes as well-being, sexuality, passages, morality, dignity, madness, healing, caring, suffering, and dying.

203) Miller, William A. When Going to Pieces Holds You Together. Minneapolis: Augsburg, 1976.

Miller is a hospital chaplain who deals with the attitudes of people experiencing grief. A superb work for those who are in the caring professions.

204) Moberg, David C., ed. Spiritual Well-Being: Sociological Perspectives. Lanham, Md.: University Press of America, 1979.

A Judeo-Christian orientation on the religious beliefs of the aged. Death, preparation for death, and the right to die are presented with hope for immortality.

205) Morgan, John L., John Henley, and Doris McCaughey. "The Anglican and Uniting Church Viewpoints." Australian Family Physician 15 (March 1986): 264, 265.

The article is part of a series on the relationship between medical and religious ethics. According to the authors, Anglicanism places high premium on the conscience of the individual.There are few strictly defined medical areas of morality for which specific Anglican teachings are available. They are, however, sensitive to some issues, one of which seems to be euthanasia. As to mercy killing or active euthanasia, the Anglican Church is opposed to the deliberate ending of a person's life, but does not advocate keeping people alive at all costs. As to malformed infants, the Church leaves pertinent decisions to medical expertise. The Uniting Church decides within the laws of the state on life and death issues, but has serious reservations about any form of direct euthanasia.

206) Murray, Thomas, and Arthur L. Caplan, eds. Which Babies Shall Live?: Humanistic Dimensions of the Care of Imperiled Newborns. Clifton, N.Y.: Humana, 1985.

A collection of essays discussing seriously-ill newborns. This work draws on the insights of philosophers, a historical, theologian, an anthropologist, and others. The essays are in four groups: "The Child, Medicine and Science"; "Caretakers: Images and Attitudes"; "Religion, Suffering and Mortality" and "Images of the Abandoned." this book offers a new perspective in the case of catastrophically ill newborns.

207) Nelson, Leonard J., ed. The Death Decision. Ann Arbor, Michigan: Servant Books, 1984.

A collection of essays from the Fourth Annual Christianity and Law Seminar presented November 11-13, 1982 at the City of Faith Continuing Education Center in Tulsa, Oklahoma, sponsored by the O. W. Coburn School of Law of Oral Roberts University. The contributors are composed of such men as Harold O. J. Brown, John Eidsmore, Leonard J. Nelson III, John T. Noonan, Walter Probert, Charles E. Rice, Peter J. Riga, and George Huntston Williams. The above experts address the legal and ethical issues emerging on the frontier of today's new biology, including: abortion, euthanasia, treatment of newborns, genetic screening, bioengineering, and reproductive techniques. "Who decides when it's time for someone to die?" is what the book is all about. A book which presents the Christian stand on important issues.

208) Nelson, Robert. "Live and Let Live...and Die When You Must." Journal of The Perkins School of Theology 39 (January 1986): 1-9.

An encouragement not only for Christians to "live and let live" by encouraging and assisting others, but to promote caring for one's fellow man, no matter what one's religion, culture, or ethnic group may be. This, of course, is based on the fact that Jesus Himself is the source of all life.

209) Oates, Wayne E. Pastoral Care and Counselling In Grief and Separation. Vol. 9, Philadelphia: Fortress, 1976.

A professor of psychiatry and pioneer in the field of pastoral care deals with grief and separation and presents a helpful bibliography in this small work.

210) Oden, Thomas C. Should Treatment Be Terminated? Moral Guidelines for Christian Families and Pastors. New York: Harper and Row, 1976.

Arguments which favor and oppose ending treatment of the terminally ill are addressed, along with problems having to do with truth-telling, organ donation, home care, and legal limits. Disagreements between families and physicians are discussed, with other issues such as "living wills" and refusal of medical treatment.

211) O'Rourke, Kevin D. "Christian Affirmation of Life." Hospital Progress 55 (July 1974): 65-67.

For the Christian who is interested in signing a "living will." An expression of the Christian's faith relative to death as being the last act upon entrance to everlasting life.

212) Pope Pius XII. "The Prolongation of Life," The Pope Speaks 4 (Spring 1958): 393-398.

An address of Pope Pius XII to an International Congress of Anesthesiologists, wherein he discusses the problems of anesthesiology, the practice of resuscitation, administering of the sacraments, the fact of death, a doctor's rights and duties, extreme unction, and "when is one dead?" A Catholic insight into the problem of euthanasia.

213) Provonsha, J. W. "The Prolongation of Life." Bulletin of The American Protestant Hospital Association 35 (Spring 1971): 14-16.

"Shall I do anything to hasten death?" and "How long should a patient be kept alive?" Unless one brings love (agape) into solving such difficult questions, the Christian is at a loss for an answer. Love should be applied to specific situations. Provonsha stresses the "greatest of these"--love.

214) Rahner, Karl. On The Theology Of Death. New York: Seabury, 1967.

Explains the Catholic theological viewpoint of the different aspects of death. A clear look at how death is viewed within the Catholic church.

215) Ramsey, Paul. The Patient As Person. New Haven, Conn.: Yale University Press, 1970.

A comprehensive moral analysis of euthanasia, the use of ordinary and extraordinary means for preserving life, and moral responsibilities toward the dying.

216) _____. Ethics at the Edge of Life: Medical and Legal Interactions. New Haven, Conn.: Yale University Press, 1978.

A serious study of the medical, legal and moral issues which come together in a depressing society. Ramsey, one of the more conservative theologians and ethicists of the present, addresses moral issues at the "first of life." These issues involve the Supreme Court decision regarding a Missouri statute which regulates abortion. The last six chapters which address the "last of life" discuss "dying well enough," the care of infants, and the Quinlan case, followed by a study of treatment withdrawn from a mentally incompetent man. Throughout Ramsey's study, discouragement and distress is obvious due to the fact that he sees very little hope in society's attempt to better the situation, i.e., take a stand against the low respect and regard for life. Those who share Ramsey's views will be encouraged to know that there are still those who stand in the gap for human dignity and the right to life.

217) "Right to Die - Opinion of Physicians, ChurchMen and Press." Literary Digest 120 (November 23 1935): 17.

Can an individual who is racked with pain, who is incurable, choose to die mercifully? The issue is discussed from various viewpoints.

218) Rosner, Fred. "The Jewish Attitude Toward Euthanasia." New York State Journal of Medicine 67 (September 1967): 2499-2506.

Rosner gives a detailed account of Protestant, Catholic, and Jewish views of euthanasia, with emphasis on the Jewish. According to the Bible and Talmud, he can find no justification for active euthanasia, although there is, he believes, justification and support for passive euthanasia.

219) Schmitt, Abraham. Dialogue with Death. Waco: Word Books, 1976.

Schmitt means by "dialoguing with death" the importance of one's perceptions and grappling with all the implications involved. He addresses the theological, biblical, and ethical principles relative to death and dying. The book is informative for "setting up" seminars on the subject.

220) Smith, David H. Heath and Medicine in the Anglican Tradition: Conscience, Community, and Compromise. New York: Crossroads, 1986.

A study of health and medicine in the Anglican tradition, covering the following themes: wellbeing, sexuality, passages, morality, dignity, madness, healing, caring, suffering, and dying.

222) Spilka, Bernard, John D. Spangler, and M. Priscilla Ray. "The Role of Theology in Pastoral Care for the Dying." Theology Today 38 (April 1981): 16-29.

This article is based on the hypothesis that a more conservative theological view toward the terminally ill is more satisfying and offers a greater measure of accomplishment than does the liberal theological view. The method of proving this hypothesis was to take a sampling of one hundred twenty seven clergy; seventy United Methodists, eighteen Presbyterians, twenty Lutherans (LCA and ALC) and nineteen Conservative Baptists. Questionnaires were sent to each and completed by the respondents. Fifteen clergy were selected from each group and interviewed. Their goals, feelings, and desires were explored in depth relative to their death-work. Helpfulness of theology, effectiveness in death-work, goals in working with the dying, theological conservatism, perspectives on death, informing the patient, and attitudes toward euthanasia were explored, which proved the hypothesis to be true.

223) Taylor, Jeremy. The Rule and Exercises of Holy Dying: In Which Are Described the Means and Instruments of Preparing Ourselves and Others Respectfully for a Blessed Death. New York: Arno, 1976.

Written by the chaplain to King Charles I of England, in which he stresses death education and preparation for death. Taylor also proposes suggestions for helping the dying. A historically significant book.

224) The Patient's Right to Die. Videotape Library, 60 min. B&W, Videocassette. Walter Reed Army Medical Center, Washington, D.C., 20307.

Discusses moral and ethical dilemmas on preservation of life, and active and passive euthanasia. Theological in approach.

225) The Right to Life. 27 min. Audiocassette. Sale. Thomas More Associates, 180 N. Wabash, Chicago, Ill. 60601.

Abortion and euthanasia seen from a religious viewpoint.

226) "Thesis Abstracts." Calvin Theological Journal 20 (1985): 355.

"The Moral Revolution: Humanism vs. Christianity", by Clifford Earl Bajema, "presents the contrast between two ethical approaches to the issue of treatment termination decisions. The first, that of euthanasia, defends indirect or direct mercy killing and suicide. . . . the second (endorsed) approach, that of benemortasia, works within the moral parameters of patient consent and imminence of death to determine when a person should be allowed to die and be provided only with palliative care, while life supports are withheld or even withdrawn." (Thesis Abstracts 1985)

227) Vaux, Kenneth. Biomedical Ethics: Morality for the New Medicine. New York: Harper and Row, 1974.

Dr. Vaux is a Presbyterian minister and professor of ethics and brings a wealth of material out of his experience. He shares many insights on ethical problems. The book is a help for physicians and others who need assistance in making decisions in the sensitive area of health care. He points out that disciplines which were at one time helpful are not outdated because they are pre-technological and, therefore, new disciplines need to be formulated. The first part of the book is a summary of historical roots of medical ethics. It discusses Judaism, Islam, Catholicism, Protestantism, and Marxism, and ends with some insight into the Nuremburg trials. The second half of the book centers on ethical concerns in biomedicine; genetic manipulation, organ transplantation, controlling man, and immortalizing man, which deals with death. Theological terms are used which should be appealing to the clergy, as well as the theologians.

228) _____. Health and Medicine in the Reformed Tradition: Promise, Providence, and Care. New York: Crossroads, 1984.

The author covers health and medicine in the Reformed tradition. Among the themes covered are: well-being, sexuality, passages, morality, dignity, madness, healing, caring, suffering and dying.

229) Vere, Duncan W. Voluntary Euthanasia: Is There an Alternative? London: Christian Medical Fellowship, 1970.

The Christian response to euthanasia. Defines death and the difficulties of those who are incapable of deciding. A short work of sixty one pages.

230) Vincent, Merville O. "Suicide - A Christian perspective: Suicide Prevention - Where There's Hope There is Life." In Is It Moral to Modify Man?, ed. Claude A. Frazier, 129147. Springfield, Illinois: Charles C. Thomas, 1973.

A Christian psychiatrist looks at the question ". . .what role, if any, does Christianity have in alleviating the kind of suffering that results in self-destructive behavior? Does Christianity have anything to offer except. . .thou shalt not?'" Dr. Vincent appeals to Scripture and finds that while the Bible does not moralize on certain suicidal acts, it does not condone the practice. He lists and discusses the myths about suicide and faith as being the factor of preventing suicide. He emphasizes that Christians should change society and provide hope for the hopeless. Anyone reading this article will find neither justification nor encouragement in committing suicide by euthanasia.

231) Wilson, Jerry B. Death By Decision: The Medical, Moral, and Legal Dilemmas of Euthanasia. Philadelphia: The Western Press, 1975.

An attempt to shed light on the euthanasia debate. A well organized study of the subject which traces ancient practices of euthanasia to the present day. The author examines the medical, moral, and legal aspects of the subject, and presents pros and cons on its different forms. He has a tendency to support limited practices of euthanasia. The book is easy to read, and has an extensive bibliography.

232) "Who Should Decide? The Case of Karen Quinlan." Christianity and Crisis 35 (January 1976): 322-331.

Robert Veatch,the distinguished ethicist, along with others, comments on the Quinlan case and its disposition. For the most part, they are opposed to the decision. They are reluctant in allowing the medical profession to decide such issues.

The Reply Of Judaism

233) Beauchamp, Tom L., and LeRoy Walters. Contemporary Issues in Bioethics. Encino and Belmont, Calif.: Dickenson, 1978.

A co-edition by a theologian and philosopher at the Kennedy Institute for Bioethics at Georgetown University. Sections included are on moral and conceptual foundations, patient-physician relationship, life and death, allocation of health resources, human experimentation, and behavioral and biomedical technology. Important judicial documents are included. The Hippocratic oath and the Quinlan case are examined. Policy statements, such as the Harvard Medical School Definition of Irreversible Coma and articles by professionals in other fields go together to compile the anthology. Each essay is well written, and taken together make a book that is recommended for teachers who desire to inform students of the issues confronting medical science. The book is a major effort to address perplexing problems.

234) Bryant, D'Orsay D., III. "The Doctor and Death." Journal of The National Medical Association 78 (March 1986): 221-235.

A well-thought-through article. Emphasis is placed on the fact that doctors need to discuss death with their patients, and that communication is vital in order to help them during the process. Bryant also emphasizes that death comes to all, even Americans, who have a tendency to deny it more than other peoples around the world. He mentions that technological devices abound throughout the health care industry for the purpose of prolonging death, all by which man attempts to play God. God will remove man according to His own good time. Importance is placed on Christ's death, resurrection, and return. Hope for the Christian is anchored in these.

235) Encyclopedia Judaica, 1971 ed. s. v. "Euthanasia."

Presents the Hebrew meaning of euthanasia along with the Jewish view of life and death. Very strong on the value of human life and worth of the individual. Anyone doing a paper and/or article on the subject should incorporate this information. Excellent!

236) Feldman, David M. Health and Medicine in the Jewish Tradition: L'Hayyim - To Life. New York: Crossroad, 1986.

This book is among others which grew out of Project X: Health/Medicine and Faith Traditions. This particular one explores health and medicine in the Jewish tradition involving ten themes: well-being, sexuality, passages, morality, dignity, madness, healing, caring, suffering, and dying.

237) Fletcher, John. "Abortion, Euthanasia, and Care of Defective Newborns." New England Journal of Medicine 292 (January 1975): 75-77.

John Fletcher sets forth two opposing views: that of Paul Ramsey and Joseph Fletcher. Ramsey equetes genetically indicated abortion with infanticide, whereas, Joseph Fletcher not only equates the morality of abortion with selective euthanasia but also approves. To paraphrase the abstract, the author points out that though the two arguments are radically different, they are similar. Yet they are different moral features between the two--the postnatal existence has an opportunity for treatment, and parental support. Because of the different moral features, decision for abortion after prenatal diagnosis does not necessarily commit the parents to euthanasia in the management of a seriously damaged or deformed infant. John Fletcher would argue that if we hold to the Judeo-Christian view, we ought to care for the defective newborn as though our relationships with God depended on the outcome, and the basis of our dignity depended on the same.

238) Humphrey, Derek, and Ann Wickett. "Religion and Euthanasia." Chap. in The Right to Die. New York: Harper and Row, 1986.

This chapter briefly describes the views of the Roman Catholics, Jews, Lutherans, and others relative to euthanasia. There is also a list of religions and their beliefs which specifies whether or not each is opposed, accepts, or leaves it to individual decision on passive and active forms of the practice.

239) Hurley, Mark J. "The Value of Human Life: Challenge to a Brave New World." Hospital Progress 58 (February 1977): 70-73.

Two basic questions are addressed in this article on the value of life in the U.S.: 1) what premium is placed on human life in this country?; and 2) whose concept of values and whose perception of human life will assume ascendancy? Since there is so much difference in cultural practices, attitudes, and religious beliefs of the various peoples living in the United States, is there a danger of the standards and practices of one group being forced upon another? The author writes on how the value of human life has eroded in America. He traces the history of abuses of life, and points out that some philosophers advocate infanticide, while others still value life, and are undertaking heroic means to protect, preserve, and enhance it. The writer believes that there is a danger of one view being accepted to the detriment of others, however, he states that there is a line beyond which tolerance should not go, and appeals to the fact that history affirms the basic concepts of life, dignity, human value, and worth. Old Testament times are given as examples of what true human liberty means. Our two hundred year old Declaration of Independence is an example of how different peoples of different cultures come together under one covenant to form one society in which true freedom and liberty can be pursued with respect to each citizen's views and concepts.

240) Kantrowitz, Adrian, et al. Who Shall Live and Who Shall Die? New York: Union of American Hebrew Congregations (Pamphlet), 1968.

Discusses the ethical implications of the new medical technology, and its effect on society.

241) Kapusta, Morton Allan, and Solomon Frank. "The Book of Job and the Modern View of Depression." Annals of Internal Medicine 86 (May 1977): 667-672.

A recommended study of the book of Job and depression. The authors present the book as being an instrument to provide professionals of the day with a realistic approach to the problems of life. Its disclosure of depression is the same as the modern view of depression. There are clues throughout the book that distinguish between normal grief and deep depression. Kapusta and Frank are convinced that Job not only gives a good description and meaning of depression, but that it also provides solutions for dealing with modern depression. Chapter 30 of Job provides answers that are vital for results of depression. The authors say, ". . .part of the wisdom of the Book of Job is a timeless medical masterpiece that provides an unexcelled standard of clinical observation and medical intervention." While this study is not specifically on the subject of euthanasia, it provides insight into the depression that occurs as a result of grief on the part of those who deal with the problems of euthanasia. It is highly recommended for all who experience depression, regardless of the cause.

242) Lamm, Maurice. The Jewish Way in Death and Mourning. Flushing, N.Y.: Jonathan David, 1969.

On Jewish tradition in dealing with death and grief. For those who have little or no knowledge of Hebrew, a detailed glossary is included with transliterated Hebrew terms.

243) Mack, Arien, ed. Death in the American Experience. New York: Schocken Books, 1973.

A paperback book reprinted from the Fall issue of Social Research. A compilation of essays including: "Being and Becoming Dead," by Eric Cassell; "The Sacral Power of Death in ContemContemporary Experience," by William May; "Death in the Judaic and Christian Tradition," by Roy Eckhardt;, and Johannes Fabian writes on "How Others Die - Reflections on the Anthropology of Death."

244) Meier, Levi, ed. Jewish Values in Bioethics. New York: Human Sciences, 1986.

A collection of addresses on biomedical issues echoing the voices of many Jewish authorities; Orthodox and Conservative, legal and philosophical, medical and literary, and wrestles with modern dilemmas in the health care field.

245) Moberg, David C., ed. Spiritual Well-Being: Sociological Perspectives. Lanham, Md.: University Press of America, 1979.

A Judeo-Christian orientation on the religious beliefs of the aged. Death, preparation for death, and the right to die are presented with hope for immortality. Today, while many writers leave the dying without any hope, Moberg presents a positive outlook for those who must go beyond death's door. An excellent work.

246) Raab, Robert A. Coping with Death. New York: Richards Rosen, 1978.

Concentrates on all issues concerning death. A good work for those having interest in the Jewish way of death.

247) Riemer, Jack. Jewish Reflections on Death. New York: Schocken Books, 1974.

A collection of essays dealing with the laws of Judaism relative to bereavement, and explores the modern problems relating to death from the Jewish experience. A benefit for both Jewish and non-Jewish readers.

248) Rosner, Fred. "The Jewish Attitude Toward Euthanasia." New York State Journal of Medicine 67 (September 1967): 2499-2506.

Rosner gives a detailed account of Protestant, Catholic, and Jewish views of euthanasia, with emphasis on the Jewish. According to the Bible and Talmud, he can find no justification for active euthanasia, although there is, he believes, justification and support for passive euthanasia.

249) _____. Medicine in the Bible and the Talmud. New York: KTAV Publishing House, Yeshiva University Press, 1977.

While this work is not on euthanasia *per se*, it presents Biblical and Talmudic references to organs, diseases, manifestations of diseases, treatment, and other topics of medical interest. The essays are heavy on interpretation. A broad sketch of health and disease in ancient and medieval Jewish society. One may gather from these essays an understanding of death and dying in the Jewish community.

250) _____. "Judaism and Medical Ethics." Annals of Internal Medicine 101 (November 1984): 721, 722.

A physician writes to discuss Judaism's view that life is of infinite value, and that restoration of health and preservation of life is the physician's responsibility.

251) _____. Modern Medicine and Jewish Ethics. New York: Yeshiva University Press, 1986.

A compilation of essays on Jewish ethics as they pertain to issues such as: artificial insemination, in-vitro fertilization, genetic engineering, organ transplantation, and extraordinary life support measures. Jewish thought in other areas are brought forth which touch on contraception, abortion, euthanasia, and autopsy. Specific biomedical issues are dealt with in each chapter, and contain Biblical passages, interpretations, and codified Jewish laws on ethical issues. Modern day interpretations by rabbinical councils are also included. Anyone wanting to familiarize themselves with Jewish thought on the vital issues of health care and ethics will want to peruse this volume.

252) Rosner, Fred, and J. David Bleich, ed. Jewish Bioethics. New York: Sanhedrin, 1979.

In this volume, outstanding medical and rabbinic experts bring together discussions which deal with Jewish bioethics. On the subject of euthanasia, there is a section, "Death and Dying," which deals in depth with: The Jewish Attitude Toward Euthanasia; The Quinlan Case: A Jewish Perspective; Establishing Criteria of Death; The Halakhic Definition of Death; Neurological Death and Time of Death Statutes; and Suicide in Jewish Law. The reader who is interested in Jewish views on euthanasia will profit greatly from this edited work.

253) _____. "Organ Transplantation." In Jewish Boiethics. New York: Sanhedrin, 1979.

Two chapters dealing with organ transplantation reveals Jewish thinking on the subject: What is the Halakhah for Organ Transplants and Organ Transplantation in Jewish Law? The first mentioned chapter answers the question ". . . may one administer a treatment which will, if it fails, kill him immediately, but, if it succeeds, prolong his life?" The other chapter deals with theological, moral, ethical, social, legal, and philosophical problems surroundding heart transplantation; the halakhah in eye transplants; the halakhah in kidney transplants; and the halakhah in heart transplants. Each of these chapters has bearing on euthanasia--at least in the Jewish view.

254) Sherwin, Byron L. "Jewish Views of Euthanasia." In Beneficent Euthanasia, ed. Marvin Kohl, 3-11. Buffalo, N.Y.: Prometheus Books, 1975.

An attempt to explain Jewish ethics, specifically euthanasia, from historical Judaism. The writer contends that determination of Judaism's position on euthanasia should be by consultation of Jewish legal literature. He summarizes that (1) Jewish religio-moral-legal literature forbids active euthanasia of any kind but permits passive euthanasia, (2) the technology of refrigeration has become a choice and bypasses the problem of euthanasia, and (3) active euthanasia may have a case within the framework of Jewish law.

255) Tedeschi, G. "On Tort Liability for 'Wrongful Life'." ISR (Israel Law Review) 1 (1966): 513.

The article centers around the idea that certain circumstances of a patient's existence could be a misdeed or injury to the patient.

256) Tendler, Moshe D., Yashar Hirshant, Jacob Weinberg, and Abraham Twerski. The Mount Sinai Hospital and Medical Center Symposia on Medicine and Halacha (Jewish Law). Chicago: Mount Sinai Hospital 1975/1976.

A discussion in two parts: Part I took place in October of 1975 involving Tendler and Hirshan. The discussion centered on Halacha and the terminally ill. Part II: Halacha and Care of the Terminally Ill transpired in February 1976. The discussants were Weinberg and Twerski. Two cases are presented in each part. Part I discusses and eighty-year-old man with a history of diabetes mellitus, who had several strokes, was unable to speak, and had arterosclerotic heart disease complicated by a heart attack. The case in Part II involved a thirty-one-year-old Jewish woman who had ingested a large amount of aspirin because she was unhappy. Discussion centers around trying to help the woman and her family. A study of this book will give one a look inside the Jewish mind and its relationship to caring for others according to Jewish law.

257) Vaux, Kenneth. Biomedical Ethics: Morality for the New Medicine. New York: Harper and Row, 1974.

Dr. Vaux is a Presbyterian minister and professor of ethics, and brings a wealth of material out of his experience. He shares many insights on ethical problems. The book is a help for physicians and others who need assistance in making decisions in the sensitive area of health care. Dr. Vaux points out that disciplines which were at one time helpful are now outdated because they are pre-technological and , therefore, new disciplines need to be formulated. The first part of the book is a summary of historical roots of medical ethics. It discusses Judaism, Islam, Catholicism, Protestantism, and Marxism, and ends with some insight into the Nuremburg trials. The second half of the book centers on ethical concerns in biomedicine; genetic manipulation, organ transplantation, controlling man, and immortalizing man, which deals with death. Theological terms are used which should be appealing to the clergy, as well as to the theologians.

CHAPTER 7

EUTHANASIA:
THE SOCIOLOGICAL CHALLENGE

Economical Reaction

258) Beauchamp, Tom L., and LeRoy Walters. Contemporary
Issues in Bioethics. Encino and Belmont, Calif.:
Dickenson, 1978.

A co-edition by a theologian and philosopher at
the Kennedy Institute for Bioethics at Georgetown
University. Sections included are on moral and
conceptual foundations, patient-physician relationship, life and death, allocation of health resources,
human experimentation, and behavioral and biomedical technology. Important judicial documents
are included. The Hippocratic oath and the Quinlan
case are examined. Policy statements, such as the
Harvard Medical School Definition of Irreversible
Coma, and articles by professionals in other fields
go together to compile the anthology. Each essay is
well written, and taken together make a book that
is recommended for teachers who desire to inform
students of the issues confronting medical science.
The book is a major effort to address perplexing
problems.

259) Beecher, H. K. "Ethical Problems Created by the Hopelessly Unconscious Patient." New England Journal
of Medicine 278 (June 1968): 1425-1430.

A discussion of death and its criteria, and the
difference between ordinary and extraordinary
means. Problems of society and limited resources
are presented. Some important questions are raised
on an all important issue--cadaver transplants.

260) Bedell, Susanna E., Denise Delle, Patricia L. Maher, and Paul D. Cleary. "Do-Not-Resuscitate Orders for Critically Ill Patients in Hospitals: How Are They Used and What is Their Impact?" Journal of The American Medical Association 256 (July 1986): 233-237.

A study of DNR compliance orders at a university hospital. As a result, the data gathered suggest that changes be made in the use of DNR protocol if patients are to be participants in the decision not to undergo pulmonary resuscitation.

261) Beswick, David E. "Attitudes to Taking Human Life." The Australian and New Zealand Journal of Sociology 6 (1970): 120-130.

An exceptional survey which was taken by third-year psychology students. The interviews conducted in April and May, 1969 resulted in responses from various sections of the Canberra population. The study centers on attitudes to taking of human life.

262) Blaker, C. W. "Thanatopsis." Christian Century 83 (December 7 1966): 1503-1506.

An account of a patient who was kept alive by machines for eight years. A discussion of death, the definition of death, and the time when it is right for man to intervene into the situation. ". . .Man is justified in tampering with the transition between the two."

263) Brim, Orville G. The Dying Patient. New York: Russell Sage, 1970.

The book focuses on the social context of dying and discusses the legal, ethical, and economic factors in the termination of life.

264) Brodie, Howard. Ethical Decisions in Medicine. Boston: Little, Brown, 1976.

Presents methods for dealing with ethical problems, and examines key issues such as: informal consent, determination of scarce resources, euthanasia, and allowing to die. A benefit for all who read it.

265) Cameron, Daniel, and Mitchel Meznick. "Do-Not-Resuscitate Orders." Journal of The American Medical Association 256 (November 1986): 2677.

A letter briefly discussing a study done on patients who were unable--because of dementia, encephalopathy, or coma--to participate in the decision not to resuscitate. The results of the study encourage patients to enter into dialogue with their physician. They are encouraged to discuss, before hospitalization, whether they would want to be resuscitated in the event of cardiac arrest, so that the individual's desire is known to all concerned in cases of inability to communicate their wishes. A written statement concerning one's desires is also encouraged.

266) "Catholic Theologian (Reverend Gerald Kelly) Defends Man's Right to Die." Journal of The American Medical Association 180 (April 28 1962): 23-24.

Euthanasia is discussed from a materialistic point of view, along with the cost of terminal illness for the working man. Passive and active euthanasia are also argued.

267) Colen, B. D. "Nobody Looks at Cara Lynn." Chap. in Hard Choices. New York: G.P. Putnam's Sons, 1986.

Cara Lynn Bailey, an "anencephalic monster," born with no cerebral cortex and a skull that looks sawed off about two inches above eyelids that are fused shut, is the subject of this chapter. It is an account mostly about her parents, who care for her, suffer for her, and long for her death, yet look forward with sadness to her demise.

268) Colman, Hila. Hanging On. Atheneum, N.Y., 1977.

A wife's account of the pain and trials of caring for her dying husband, the ordeal of dealing with the high cost of medical bills, caring for him at home, and the injustice of health care costs.

269) "Euthanasia" New England Journal of Medicine 292 (April 1975): 863-867.

Fourteen letters which deal with the issue of euthanasia, discussed by Dr. James Rachel ("Active and Passive Euthanasia" New England Journal of Medicine 292 (1975): 78-80). Rachel draws little difference between passive and active euthanasia and, therefore, is taken to task in most of these letters which vent important attitudes of fourteen physicians on the subject. The reader will readily understand how individual doctors react to euthanasia by reading the letters.

270) Evans, Andrew L., and Baruch A. Brody. "The Do-Not-Resuscitate Order in Teaching Hospitals." Journal of The American Medical Association 253 (April 1985): 2236-2239.

After a study of DNR orders at three teaching hospitals, the authors conclude that DNR orders do not fulfill their major goals. Six proposals are offered for improving future DNR orders.

271) Fishbein, M. "When Life Is No Longer Life." Medical World News 15 (March 1974): 84.

Medical, legal, and moral questions have been debated relative to euthanasia by various professionals. In this article, Dr. Fishbein presents case studies and statistics involving the opinions of 250 Chicago internists and surgeons.

272) Fox, Renee C., and Judith P. Swazey. The Courage to Fail: A Social View of Organ Transplants and Dialysis. Chicago and London: The University of Chicago Press, 1978.

A paperback revised edition. An analysis of the emotional, social, and economic problems of heart and kidney transplantation besetting both patient and doctor.

273) Freund, Paul A. "Organ Transplants: Ethical and Legal Problems." In Ethics in Medicine: Historical Perspective and Contemporary Concerns, ed. Stanley Joel Reiser, Arthur J. Dyck, and William J. Curran, 173-177. Cambridge, Mass.: MIT, 1977.

Freund discusses problems concerning the allocation of resources; from whom they should come and to whom organs should be transferred. Implications raised by the questions concern moral, legal, and medical considerations. Each differs on removal of organs after death and during life. He briefly discusses the question of whether or not a dying patient should be allowed to consent to surgical intervention for the purpose of saving another's life.

274) Fuchs, Victor R. Who Shall Live? New York: Basic Books, 1974.

An excellent introduction for those who have had no formal training or background in economics. The discussion is limited almost exclusively to health services in the U.S.A., and deals with the problems besetting such services. It not only discloses what is presently confronting health care, but in the last chapter looks into the future and sees that few simple solutions exist. In fact, Fuchs believes that some health problems challenge solution. If the reader wants some idea as to how health care economics relate to euthanasia and other problems in society, a perusal of this work is a must.

275) Fulton, Robert. "Death and Dying: Some Sociologic Aspects of Terminal Care." Modern Medicine (May 1972): 74-77.

Fulton presents sociologic and demographic facts, along with dying in an institution, and the importance of recognizing the dignity of a person during the process of dying.

276) Gillon, Raanan. "Ordinary and Extraordinary Means." British Medical Journal 292 (January 1986): 259-261.

A scholarly discussion on the Roman Catholic view of ordinary and extraordinary means. The importance of the patient's permission is tantamount relative to withholding or discontinuing treatment. Burdensomeness of treatment (risks, cost, and other difficulties) is also taken into consideration, along with burdens on others. Withholding of nutritional support for infants with an encephaly, severe brain damage, and total necrotising enterocolitus would be appropriate because of prolonged treatment for the remainder of the infant's life.

277) Glover, Jonathan. Causing Death and Saving Lives. Harmondsworth: Penguin Books, 1977.

A lucid discussion presenting the arguments used in prohibiting or justifying the killing of others. It deals with: moral theory; autonomy and rights, ends and means; not striving to keep alive; abortion, infanticide, suicide, voluntary and involuntary euthanasia; choices between people in allocating resources; assassination; and war. A skillful work and highly recommended for those interested in euthanasia and problems surrounding it.

278) Gonda, Thomas Andrew, and John Edward Ruark. Dying Dignified: The Health Professional's Guide to Care. Menlo Park: Addison-Wesley, 1984.

Lucid case histories are presented at the beginning of the book, and are referred to throughout the discussion. Emphasis is placed on the fact that decision making for the most part resides in the hands of the patient. Broad issues are outlined, such as medical, social, and economic aspects of dying. Suicide and working with dying children comprise a part of the book. Each chapter has an annotated bibliography at its end.

279) Johnson, Dana E. "Life, Death, and the Dollar Sign." Journal of The American Medical Association 252 (July 1984): 223, 224.

A discussion on economical questions raised due to prolongation of life support. That the most important interest is on behalf of the patient, and not in the interest of the governmental or corporate entity who pays the bills.

280) Jonasson, Olga. "Organ Transplantation: Interview With Olga Jonasson," interview by Illinois Medical Journal 171 (May 1987): 301-310.

An outstanding dialogue on organ transplantation: costs, availability of donors, donor choice, and types of patients sought for donorship. While euthanasia is not discussed, the subject should be considered relative to imminent-death patients who may be candidates as donors.

281) Kane, Robert L., and Rosalie A. Kane. Long-Term Care in Six Countries: Implications for the United States. Washington, D.C.: U.S. Government Printing Office, n.d.

A comparative analysis of the extent and mechanisms for delivery of long-term care to the aged in England, Scotland, Sweden, Norway, The Netherlands, and Israel. Concluding section discusses common themes and problems, rising costs, and implications for the United States. Everyone in health care delivery for the elderly and other professionals should be aware of the information compiled in this report.

282) Katz, Jay, and Alexander Morgan Capron. Catastrophic Diseases: Who Decides What? New York: Russell Sage Foundation, 1975.

Two law professors, one of whom is a psychiatrist (Jay Katz), write on catastrophic diseases (a catastrophic disease is a disease for which expensive and unusual equipment must be made available for treatment, and which can sustain life for a period of time), and goals and values proposed to treat such diseases. A brief account is given of the state of the art of hemodialysis and organ transplantation. The definition of death, and the right to refuse life-sustaining treatment are examined thoroughly with reference to legal problems which surround the issues. The work is scholarly and merits extensive readership, especially among those who want to know who will be making decisions on the future use of equipment for those who are less fortunate than most of us.

283) Macklin, Ruth. Bioethics in Today's World. New York: Pantheon Books, 1987.

A pioneer in bioethics discusses problems and analyzes many real-life episodes relative to "mortal choices." She writes that these choices are made in the following areas: ethical dilemmas in medicine, applying moral principles, gaining informed consent, aggressive treatment, foregoing life-sustaining therapy, determining incompetency, deciding for others, the best interest of the child, treating the family, allocating scarce resources, conflicting obligations, experimenting on human subjects, harming and wronging patients, and resolving the issues. The book is well indexed, and her notes on each chapter suggest a cross-section of bibliographical material pertinent to each subject discussed.

284) Macneil-Lehrer Newshour (PBS) April 8, 1988. Discussion on bone marrow transplants and the cost involved.

In a very real sense, this report is a good example of both involuntary passive and involuntary, active euthanasia, in that two young children in dire need of bone marrow transplants were denied help by the State of Oregon. The state had money available, but due to policy refused to pay one hundred thousand dollars for each of the children. The result was tragic--both children died a very short time after the refusal.

285) Mannes, Marya. Last Rights. New York: William Morrow, 1974.

A humanist looks at the taboo issue of euthanasia. She shares accounts of discussions with the dying, their families, their doctors and attorneys, and those who witnessed the effects of high technological machines on worn out bodies. Human suffering and money are tallied and found to be a high cost for hypocritical attitudes toward the death of those who should be allowed to die. The book is frank and to the point.

286) May, A. E. "An Assessment of Homicidal Attitudes." The British Journal of Psychiatry 114 (April 1968): 479, 480.

An assessment of homicidal attitudes was made using three groups: normals, psychiatric patients, and homicidal patients. Inquiry into each of these groups was based on the attitude of a psychiatric patient who believed that anyone with physical or mental imperfections should be exterminated. The Respiratory-Grid technique was used on all three groups to see if the psychiatric patient's attitude was abnormal. In summary, "a high correlation between 'feeling love for the family' and 'being in favor of mercy killing' was predicted for a patient

with psychotic and sadistic idealtion. This prediction was confirmed."

287) Meyer, J. E. Death and Neurosis. Vol. 12, New York:
International Universities Press, 1975.

A theory that man's fear of death is the
beginning of neuroses. A presentation of theological and philosophical concepts about dying.

288) Ogg, Elizabeth. Facing Death and Loss. Lancaster, Pa.,
1985.

A sensitive book which considers the subject of
death and the individual's needs and concerns during the process of dying. The patient's right to
choose death in a hospice rather than a hospital and
its torturous machine-like technological life-sustaining practices is discussed, along with financing
terminal care.

289) Powills, Suzanne. "Coalition Asks 'Life At Any Price?'"
Hospital (May 1985): 110, 114.

A discussion on a report by The Minnesota
Coalition on Health Care Costs. The report was
prompted by the high cost of technological advances. "The report suggests that promoting the patient's
right of self-determination and reducing the emphasis on life-prolonging technology may significantly
reduce the resources consumed by terminally-ill
patients."

290) Riffer, Joyce. "Sharing Arrangements Proving Cost-
Effective." Hospital (May 1984): 56-58.

A "brief" on the merging of hospitals for certain treatments and tests in order to cut costs, especially with hemodialysis patients.

291) Rodin, C. M., J. Chmara, J. Ennis, S. Fenton, H. Locking, and K. Steinhouse. "Stopping LifeSustaining Medical Treatment: Psychiatric Considerations in the Termination of Renal Dialysis." Canadian Journal of Psychiatry 26 (December 1981): 540-544.

A presentation of data regarding the decision by medical staff and patients to discontinue renal dialysis. The patient's mental competence, motivations and psychiatric state are discussed. Medical factors involved in decision making are mentioned. The patient's active participation is emphasized.

292) Schulz, Richard. The Psychology of Death and Dying. Reading, Mass.: Addison-Wesley, 1978.

The text presents the following topics: research strategies, thinking about death, demography of death, the terminal phase of life, extending life, grief and bereavement, and death education.

293) Shanbrom, E. "Malthus, Morality and Miracle Drugs." Journal of The American Medical Association 182 (November 24 1962): 856-857.

A statement that with increased use of antibiotics, nature has not been allowed to take its course, and the result is that the number of aged and infirmed has increased. This leaves the question: not "whom should we kill?", but "whom should we let live?"

294) Somers, Ann. "NJ Hospitals React to the 'Geriatric Imperative'." Hospital (October 1986): 108.

A brief discussion on the importance of reacting to a cost-effective way of treating the elderly, otherwise, the increasing danger of societal pressure to "let them die."

295) Veatch, Robert M. Case Studies in Medical Ethics. Cambridge, Mass.: Harvard University Press, 1977.

Veatch employs the case method as a pedagogic tool for fastening abstract thought and intellectual theory into an operational unit relative to a particular problem. He incorporates such topics as abortion, contraception, allocation of resources, human experimentation, death and dying problems, and rights which have to do with accepting or refusing treatment. The book is most profitable, and makes one aware of the needs of the patient, family, and physician.

296) Weiss, Ann E. Bioethics: Dilemmas in Modern Medicine. Hillside, N.J.: Enslow, 1985.

Weiss makes difficult subjects comprehensible, such as right to life, organs for sale, the Baby Doe rule, experimenting on humans, who gets health care, genetic engineering, rights of patients, and the right to die. After reading this book, one will have a good understanding of what bioethics is all about.

297) Williamson, W. P. "Should the Patient Be Kept Alive?" Medical Economics 44 (January 1967): 60-63.

A discussion of the economics of keeping a patient alive in light of resources and financial costs.

Ethical Reaction

298) Ahern, Mary. "Biomedical Ethics Committees Confront Prickly Issues." Hospital (August 1984): 66, 68, 70.

Ahern presents the importance of ethics committees and the part they will play as a result of technological advances in the health care field. Causes of interest in ethics committees are shared together with the role of such committees. Legal cases on ethics committees are listed. All involve withdrawal of life-sustaining equipment, and the terminally ill and/or comatose patient.

299) Baron, Charles H. "Termination of Life Support Systems in the Elderly." Journal of Geriatric Psychiatry 14 (1981): 45-70.

This discussion was presented at a scientific meeting of The Boston Society for Gerontologic Psychiatry, April 12, 1980. It is a discussion of legal issues surrounding euthanasia and the elderly. A number of cases are presented which give examples of the courts' weaknesses and strengths. Judicial processes are contrasted with medical-ethical decisions.

300) Barry, Robert, Fenella Rouse, Fidel Dovila, and Nancy W. Dickey. "Withholding or Withdrawing Treatment." Journal of The American Medical Association 256 (July 1986): 469-471.

Letters written in opposition to the American Medical Association's (AMA) Council of Ethical and Judicial Affairs, which adopted a stand based on ethical considerations that allows withholding nutrition and fluids from patients under special clinical circumstances.

301) Barton, David, ed. Dying and Death: A Clinical Guide for Caregivers. Baltimore: Williams and Wilkins, 1977.

A look at current thoughts and views on clinical terminal care. A two-part work. Part I: "An Approach to Caring for Dying Persons" is done by the author. Various authors' works appear in Part II: Perspectives. Veatch writes on ethics. Van Eys writes on the dying child. Peak writes on the dying and the elderly. The thoughts, feelings, and reflections of a person with a life-threatening illness is dwelt upon by Gattis and Cummings. Commendable.

302) Basson, Marc D., ed., Ethics, Humanism and Medicine. New York: Alan R. Liss, 1980.

Proceedings of three conferences by the committee on ethics, humanism, and medicine at the University of Michigan, 1978-1979. The following discussions are included: 'under what circumstances should euthanasia be performed?'; 'moral principles relevant to euthanasia'; and 'the euthanasia problem.'

303) Battin, Pabst M. Ethical Issues in Suicide. Englewood Cliffs, N.J.: Prentice-Hall, 1982.

Margaret Battin is a philosopher who writes for an intelligent readership. The problems considered by her in this work are of widespread importance, and are treated effectively as well as intelligently. In the introduction, the current view of suicide is discussed, which incorporates: the scientific view, the treatment of suicide, the legal dilemma, and the suicide taboo.

Moving into the body of the book, arguments for and against the moral permissibility of suicide are presented. The arguments are arranged in two parts. Part I comprises traditional arguments concerning suicide, among which are: religious views of suicide, social arguments concerning suicide, and suicide and the value of life. Part II is contemporary in character and compiles up-to-date issues on suicide. Beginning with Chapter 4, the concept of rational suicide and its criteria is presented. Chapter 5 expounds paternalism and suicide, which deals with paternalistic intervention in suicide, and the facilitation thereof. Chapter 6 graphically sets forth the rights of suicide, together with suicide as being a right within itself, and the rights and roles of others who are involved.

After reading the book, one will discover that the author has an automist view of suicide, which sees the act as ". . . potentially rational and dignity-promoting. . ." Yet she ". . .applauds the sincere efforts of suicide-prevention workers and researchers to prevent suicide which is irrationally or pathologically chosen, and welcomes those voices who remind us of the value of life." (See page 195 in work cited.) This work is truly philosophical in content.

304) Beauchamp, T. L., and J. F. Childress. <u>Principles of Biomedical Ethics.</u> New York: Oxford University Press, 1979.

Explains basic ethical principles and shows how they are applied to major issues in bioethics, such as informed consent, risk-benefit assessments, confidentiality, and decisions to terminate therapy. Termination of therapy is in the realm of euthanasia.

305) Behnke, John, and Sissela Bok, ed. <u>The Dilemmas of Euthanasia.</u> Garden City, New York Anchor/ Doubleday, 1975.

This paperback incorporates seven chapters dealing with the historical, moral, ethical, legal, and diagnostic aspects of euthanasia. A good work for the general reader. There is enough detail on the subject to inform one quite satisfactorily. Legal and other documents are appended.

306) Campbell, A. V. <u>Moral Dilemmas in Medicine: A Course-book in Ethics for Doctors and Nurses.</u> 2nd Edition. Churchill Livingston, 1975.

A basic ethics coursebook dealing with theoretical and practical issues, among which are: abortion; resuscitation and euthanasia; human experimentation; and transplantation. Included is a limited bibliography.

307) Campbell, M., and R. Duff. "Moral and Ethical Dilemmas in the Special Care Nursery." New England Medical Journal 289 (October 1973): 890-894.

Moral and ethical issues surrounding decisions to allow certain babies to die are presented by Campbell and Duff. They believe it is perfectly alright to allow infants to die who have poor "quality of life" (withhold treatment). The family is taken into consideration as being the ultimate decision makers in allowing the infant to die. Special guidelines are suggested in order that the decision to withhold treatment should not be abused.

308) Caplan, Arthur L. "Ethical and Policy Issues in the Procurement of Cadaver Organs for Transplant-ation." New England Journal of Medicine 311 (October 1984): 981-983.

Questions are posed concerning availability, cost, and donors of organ transplantations. A policy of "required request" is discussed, which concerns patients whose situations are hopeless, and that no one on a respirator who might serve as a donor should be declared legally dead until a request for organ donation has been made of any available next of kin or legal proxy.

309) Crane, Diane. The Sanctity of Social Life: Physician's Treatment of Critically Ill Patients. New Bruns-wick, N.J.: Transactions Books, 1977.

Crane addresses social and ethical problems of the dying in America. A search for ethical guidelines is continued by a seven year research among physicians who are faced with decision making when confronted with terminally ill and severely handicapped infants. Criteria are investi-gated by which physicians treat critically ill patients. Circumstances are investigated under which physicians take part in active euthanasia. A social policy is sought in this work, i.e., a different criteria for establishing a person's worth to society other than that of meeting physical criteria of life.

310) Davis, John W., Barry Hoffmaster, and Sarah Shorten, eds. Contemporary Issues in Biomedical Ethics. Clifton, N.J.: Humana, 1978.

A compilation of comments and papers presented at a colloquium on biomedical ethics at the University of Western Ontario. Contained in the volume are issues such as rights and moral decisions, legalism, and the rights of the terminally ill. Among other issues brought to the reader's attention are issues in genetics, the role of the physician, informed consent and paternalism, and professional responsibility.

311) Dayringer, Richard. "Death Ethics." American Protestant Hospital Association Bulletin 44 (1980): 1-9.

"Death Ethics" seeks to answer such questions as: 'when does death occur?'; 'how long should life be prolonged?'; 'should death ever be allowed to occur?' These questions are answered to some degree by a discussion of the definition of death, the prolonging of life, and a brief historical survey of euthanasia and its forms. A case history is presented to illustrate some of the concepts set forth in the article. It is a quick survey of the ethics of death.

312) Death and Dying. Chicago, Ill.: 2 AudioCassettes Sale. American Health Congress. Teach'em Inc., 160 E. Illinois St. (60611)

Programs of the American Health Congress discussing personal and ethical issues centering on dying, the prolongation of life, and dying-patient rights.

313) Doherty, Dennis J. "Ethically Permissible." Archives of Internal Medicine 147 (August 1987): 1381-1384.

Doherty discusses questions in this article which have a direct bearing on both medical practice and ethics. As the author states: "What interests us here is the clinico-medical judgement that a given treatment modality is 'ethically permissible' or acceptable or, simply, ethical." Four questions for discussion are asked: (1) What does this assertion really mean?, (2) How is it arrived at?, (3) Who is entitled to make such a judgement?, and (4) Can contradictory approaches be equally permissible from an ethical standpoint? This article will be found helpful by those who are in a quandry as to how to make decisions in the area of life-and-death situations.

314) Duff, Raymond S., and A. G. M. Campell. "Moral and Ethical Dilemmas in Special Care Nursery." New England Journal of Medicine 289 (October 1973): 3890-3894.

A review of records in a special-care nursery found that over a two-and-one-half-year period, fourteen percent of the deaths were the result of withholding treatment from abnormal infants.

315) Englehardt, H. Tristram, Jr., and Stuart F. Spicker, eds. Philosophy and Medicine. Vol. 18, Medical Ethics in Antiquity: Philosophical Perspectives on Abortion and Euthanasia, by Paul Carrick. Boston: D. Reidel, 1985.

An exploration of the origins and development of medical ethics as practiced by the ancient Greek and Roman physicians together with their views on abortion and euthanasia. Infanticide and suicide are also examined. The Hippocratic oath is dissected relative to abortion, infanticide, euthanasia, and suicide. The book is in three parts. Part One explores the social setting of Greek medicine. Part Two specifically deals with the beginning of Greek medical ethics, and Part Three examines a variety of divergent Greco-Roman ethical views and opinions on abortion and euthanasia. An excellent work. Scholarly done, well indexed, and should be in the libraries of those who are interested in historical aspects of euthanasia and related subjects.

316) Englehardt, H. Tristram, Jr. The Foundations of Bioethics. New York: Oxford University Press, 1986.

A bold and provocative book which raises questions having to do with contemporary issues such as abortion, infanticide, and euthanasia.

317) Fletcher, George P. "Prolonging Life." In Bioethics, ed. Thomas A. Shannon, 189-206. Ramsey, N.J.: Paulist, 1976.

A legal analysis of the problem of a physician's decision not to prolong a terminally ill patient's life. Focus centers on the relationship of the physician and patient. Fletcher examines the ethical relationship of the two. As an Assistant Professor of Law at the University of Washington, Fletcher is found to be qualified to write on the subject from a legal point of view.

318) Fletcher, Joseph. Humanhood: Essays in Biomedical Ethics. Buffalo, N.Y.: Prometheus Books, 1979.

Perplexities confronting modern man, such as genetic engineering, transplantation, fetal research, recombinant DNA, abortion, suicide, and euthanasia are discussed by this well-known ethicist. In the early chapters he establishes standards of humanhood, and chooses progress and rationalism over the rights and loving concern of individuals. These essays are well written.

319) _____. Stopping Treatment With or Without Consent. 62 min. B&W Videocassette. Rental. Georgia Regional Medical TV Network, Emory University.

Dr. Joseph Fletcher discusses the ethics of euthanasia followed by a 30 minute lecture on its medical aspects.

320) Gift of Life/Right to Die. 15 min., B&W. Rental, EMC No. 7320. Champaign, Ill.: Indiana University Audio-Visual Center and Visual Aids Service, Division of University Extension, University of Illinois (61822), 1968.

A short film discussing one person's death and another who becomes an organ recipient of the former. Other ethical issues are mentioned, such as euthanasia for infants who are malformed, and individuals who suffer from catastrophic disease.

321) Goldberg, J. H. "The Dying Patient: Tackling the New Ethical and Legal Questions." Hospital Physician 36 (June 1968): 41-45.

Because of new medical techniques, Goldberg stresses the importance of new death definitions. The age of transplants requires such. Doctors should be given more freedom in forming opinions, and allowed to implement them, depending on each case.

322) Heifetz, Milton D. and Charles Mangel. The Right to Die: A Neurosurgeon Speaks of Death with Candor. New York: Putnam's Sons, 1975.

A discussion of the euthanasia controversy by a physician. Heifetz contends for the right of the patient to die, dealing with the legal and ethical aspects of euthanasia.

323) Hook, Sidney. "The Ethics of Suicide." In Beneficent Euthanasia, ed. Marvin Kohl, 57-69. Buffalo, N.Y.: Prometheus Books, 1975.

An attempt by the author through the method of moral and philosophical analysis to show that any system of thought that absolutely refuses to condone suicide as a rational possibility is irresponsibly optimistic or utterly immoral. He classifies the major arguments against suicide: (1) suicide is against society, (2) suicide is cowardly, (3) suicide is a violation of our duty to God, (4) suicide is unnatural, (5) suicide is an insult to human dignity, and (6) suicide is cruel in that it inflicts pain upon one's family and friends. Hook counters each argument. Whether or not he is successful is left to the reader for judgement.

324) Horan, Dennis J., and David Mall, eds. Death, Dying and Euthanasia. Washington, D.C.: University Publications of America, 1977.

Controversial aspects of euthanasia are discussed, such as: involuntary euthanasia of the defective newborn; ethical, moral, and legal aspects of "mercy killing"; the feasibility of legalized euthanasia; and the right of the individual to reject treatment.

325) Kantoi, George, Maria R. Silver, and Stuart J. Younger. A Closer Look at the Institutional Ethics Committee. 27 min. Videocassette; VHS and Beta; $90, Ohio: University of Akron, 1985.

This tape looks at many problems which beset ethical committees, such as; the committee's effects on the institution, medical staff, decision processes, and legal liabilities. A hypothetical case is presented in which a physician is faced with the problem of whether to withdraw ventilator support from a patient who had been comatose for four days. The patient's family plays a large role in the tape. Anyone may profit from the production in that some insight into the workings of an ethics committee will be gained, and along with it some understanding of what pressures are brought to bear on those who are involved in decision making on life and death issues.

326) Kohl, Marvin, ed. Infanticide and the Value of Life. Buffalo, N.Y.: Prometheus Books, 1978.

Examined are the religious, medical, legal, and ethical issues surrounding infanticide. Familiar personalities writing are: Joseph Fletcher, Arval A. Morris, Glanville Williams, Joseph Margolis, Richard Brandt, Peter Black, Immanuel Jababovits, and Leonard Weber. Indexed, with bibliography.

327) Ladd, John, ed. Ethical Issues Relating to Life and Death. New York and Oxford: Oxford University Press, 1979.

Nine essays which are concerned with euthanasia from the philosophical and ethical points of view. References to the essays are mostly non-medical literature.

328) Lamb, David. Death, Brain Death and Ethics. Albany: State University of New York Press, 1985.

"What is considered so essential to human life, such, that when it is lost we consider the individual dead?" This question sets one's thinking for the author's discussion on death, the brain, and ethics. A series of lectures inquiring into what death is relative to the brain. Lamb's thesis is that death of the brain stem is death of the individual organism. He provides a philosophical framework for criteria for determining death. The book is well written, up to date, and more philosophical than practical. Good for anyone looking for a definition of death.

329) Lo, Bernard. "Behind Closed Doors." New England Journal of Medicine 317 (July 1987): 46-49.

Dr. Lo deals with three important questions relative to ethics committees: (1) are such committees ethical?, (2) is agreement by ethics committees always desirable?, and (3) are ethics committees effective? He discusses promises and pitfalls in ethics committees, goals and procedures of ethics committees, pitfalls of committee discussions, and evaluating ethics committees.

330) Lynn, Joanne, ed. By No Extraordinary Means: The Choice to Forgo Life-Sustaining Food and Water. Bloomington: Indiana University Press, 1986.

The authors present the medical, moral, ethical, social, and legal perspectives of the nutrition and hydration issue. Situations discussed have to do with the newborn, terminally ill, unconscious persons (permanently), and the chronically ill but not terminal patient who has decided to refuse food and water. This collection of papers was prepared for the Society for Health and Human Values and should be purchased by all who are interested in the subject, because it compiles the views of different authors.

331) McCormick, Richard A. How Brave A New World?: Dilemmas in Bioethics. Garden City, N.Y.: Doubleday, 1951.

The issues which continually make headlines are brought forth in McCormick's How Brave A New World. Birth control, abortion, fetal and genetic research, test-tube reproduction, human experimentation, and euthanasia are thoroughly discussed. Much, if not all of the book, is a compilation of articles which have appeared in different periodicals and other publications.

332) Nelson, Leonard J., ed. The Death Decision. Ann Arbor, Mich.: Servant Books, 1984.

A collection of essays from the Fourth Annual Christianity and Law Seminar presented November 11-13, 1982 at the City of Faith Continuing Education Center in Tulsa, Oklahoma, sponsored by the O.W. Coburn School of Law of Oral Roberts University. The contributors are composed of such men as Harold O. J. Brown, John Eidsmore, Leonard J. Nelson III, John T. Noonan, Walter Probert, Charles E. Rice, Peter J. Riga, and George Huntston Williams. The above experts address the legal and ethical issues emerging on the frontier of today's new biology, including abortion, euthanasia, treatment of newborns, genetic screening, bioengineering, and reproductive techniques. "Who decides when it's time for someone to die?" is what the book is all about. A book which presents the Christian stand on important issues.

333) Nevins, Madeline M., ed. A Bioethical Perspective on Death and Dying: Summaries of the Literature. Rockville, Md.: Information Planning Associates, 1977.

This work contains 217 abstracts from the first 12 issues of the Bioethics Digest. Such issues explore the following: attitudes toward death, death education, definitions of death, euthanasia, care of the dying, bereavement, and suicide. The annotations are satisfactory.

334) President's Commission for the Study of Ethical Problems in Medicine and Biomedical and Behavioral Research. Defining Death: A Report on the Medical, Legal and Ethical Issues in the Determination of Death. Washington, D.C.: U. S. Government Printing Office, 1984.

This is a report to the President on the "definition" of death, and a recommendation of a statute by Congress to provide a clear and socially accepted basis for making determinations of death. Chapter one deals with the question, "Why 'update' death?" Chapter two presents the 'state of the art' in medicine. 'Understanding the meaning of death' is the topic of chapter three. "Who ought to define death?" is answered in chapter four, and chapter five inquires, "What 'definition' ought to be adopted?" The book is a must for professionals.

335) Ramsey, Paul. The Ethics of Fetal Research. New Haven and London: Yale University Press, 1975.

The ethics of fetal research distinguishes between fetal research and fetal politics. First, Ramsey outlines various types of fetal research, and acknowledges their potential benefits. He then presents a description of the development of proposed American guidelines up to the National Research Act, passed by Congress in 1974, with a comparison to England's "Peel Report." Moral and ethical problems involved in fetal research are considered, along with how medical policy is formulated in America. The book is a guideline for those who want to know how to think about fetal research.

336) Reiser, Stanley Joel, Arthur J. Dyck, and William J. Curran, eds. Ethics in Medicine: Historical Perspectives and Contemporary Concerns. Cambridge, Mass.: MIT, 1977.

This text was developed while teaching graduate and undergraduate courses at Harvard University. It is practical for practitioners and students in medicine, law, ethics, counselling, and for individual patients and groups who are concerned with medical care. The volume is separated into eight sections: (1) Ethical Dimensions of the Physician - Patient Relationship, (2) Moral Basis of Medical Ethics, (3) Regulation, Compulsion, and Consumer Protection in Clinical Medicine and Public Health, (4) Truth-Telling in the Physician-Patient Relationship, (5) Medical Experimentation on Human Subjects, (6) Procreative Decisions, (7) Suffering and Dying, and (8) Rights and Priorities in the Provision of Medical Care. Each section contains articles, essays, and class lectures. An excellent textbook.

337) Restak, Richard M. Pre-Meditated Man: Bioethics and the Control of Future Human Life. New York: Viking, 1973.

A three-part book discussing the issues raised in psychosurgery. The most dramatic form of behavior modification in use is discussed in part one. Part two explores the implications of genetic engineering of different kinds. The third part analyzes experiences, and the frightful lesson of the past and present having to do with human experimentation.

338) Rosner, Fred. "Withholding or Withdrawing Treatment." Archives of Internal Medicine 147 (January 1947).

A disagreement with the position of the American Medical Association Council on Ethical Affairs that, under certain very limited circumstances, "it is not unethical to discontinue all means of life-prolonging medical treatment." Rosner's view is that the physician is responsible to heal, and should not assist in hastening death.

339) Rosner, Fred and J. David Bleich, ed. "Organ Transplantation". In Jewish Bioethics. New York: Sanhedrin, 1979.

Two chapters dealing with organ transplantation reveal Jewish thinking on the subjects: "What is the Halakhah for Organ Transplants?" and "Organ Transplantation in Jewish Law." The first mentioned chapter answers the question ". . . may one administer a treatment which will, if it fails, kill him immediately, but, if it succeeds, prolong his life?" The other chapter deals with theological, moral, ethical, social, legal, and philosophical problems surrounding heart transplantation; the halakhah in eye transplants; the halakhah in kidney transplants; and the halakhah in heart transplants. Each of these chapters has bearing on euthanasia--at least in the Jewish view.

340) Scully, Thomas, and Celia Scully. Playing God: The New World of Medical Choices. New York: Simon and Schuster, 1987.

A collaboration by husband and wife, with whom the reader feels an affinity because of their compassion and care for patients and families alike. Their concern is revealed through the subject content of Playing God. One learns how to make choices relative to health care while reading this work: the right choice of physician for one's self and family; building the right relationship with one's physician; patients' rights and how to exercise them; "living will" and the power of attorney; transplantation of human organs; different ways of making babies; dilemmas in treatment and non-treatment; who should be the spokesperson for a child who has a disabling, life-threatening, or terminal illness; making life-and-death decisions for another adult; how to get action when you have been wronged through malpractice and billing fraud. A very important feature of the book is the appendices, which are "packed" with information on bills of rights in most areas of health care. The Scullys state, "The whole purpose of this book is to help you understand the issues and their ethical underpinnings, how to protect yourself, and where to go for help." Having researched many "how to" books, I put this one at the top of my list, and recommend it highly to be read and digested by all who are interested in the subject of euthanasia, in order to make the right decisions in the area of health care. It is well indexed, and would be a handy tool for discussion groups.

341) Sherwin, Byron L. "Jewish Views of Euthanasia." In Beneficent Euthanasia, ed. Marvin Kohl, 3-11. Buffalo, N.Y.: Prometheus Books, 1975.

An attempt to explain Jewish ethics, specifically euthanasia, from historical Judaism. The writer contends that determination of Judaism's position on euthanasia should be by consultation of Jewish legal literature. He summarizes that (1) Jewish religio-moral-legal literature forbids active euthanasia of any kind, but permits passive euthanasia, (2) the technology of refrigeration has become a choice and bypasses the problem of euthanasia, and (3) active euthanasia may have a case within the framework of Jewish law.

342) Simmons, Roberta G. and Julie Fulton. "Ethical Issues in Kidney Transplantation." In Is It Moral to Modify Man?, ed. Claude A. Frazier 171-188. Springfield, Ill.: Charles C. Thomas, 1973.

Simons addresses serious ethical issues, and treats such vital questions as: what are the criteria by which potential recipients should be selected for transplantation and others refused life-saving treatment? How can a donor be protected against premature termination of his life (a practice of euthanasia is implied here)? What is an acceptable definition of death? Should living donors be used? Other vital issues are treated. Excellent!

343) Suffolk University Law Review 11 (Spring 1977): 919-973. Three addresses on mental incompetents and the right to die.

Jones V. Saikewicz, No. 711 (Mass., Sup. Jud. Ct., July 6, 1976) is discussed. A retarded man who was dying from leukemia was denied life-prolonging chemotherapy. Substituted consent, hospital ethics committees, the courts, and the patient's right to life are reviewed.

344) The Patient's Right to Die. Videotape Library, 60 min. B&W, Videocassette. Walter Reed Army Medical Center, Washington, D.C., 20307, n.d.

Discusses moral and ethical dilemmas on preservation of life, and active and passive euthanasia. Theological in approach.

345) "Thesis Abstracts." Calvin Theological Journal 20 (1985): 355.

"The Moral Revolution: Humanism vs. Christianity", by Clifford Earl Bajema, "presents the contrast between two ethical approaches to the issue of treatment termination decisions. The first, that of euthanasia, defends indirect or direct mercy killing and suicide . . . the second (endorsed) approach, that of benemortasia, works within the moral parameters of patient consent and imminence of death to determine when a person should be allowed to die and be provided only with palliative care, while life supports are withheld or even withdrawn." (Thesis Abstracts 1985)

346) Thomson, A. R. A Dictionary of Medical Ethics and Practice. Bristol: John Wright and Sons, 1977.

Among other things, the author gives accounts of bereavement, moment of death, brain death, suicide, and euthanasia. There is also a piece on "care of the dying." One will find the work moralistic and sincere.

347) van den Berg, Jan H. Medical Power and Medical Ethics. New York: W.W. Norton, 1978.

The brief work comprises 91 pages and was originally published in The Netherlands. The author is a psychiatrist and brings into question the Hippocratic Oath that all human lives must be saved or prolonged by whatever means available. The author believes that a new and fundamental code of ethics should be required because of the technological advances in the science of medicine. Although the work is short, the case histories presented are well worth the reading time.

348) Vaux, Kenneth, ed. Powers That Make Us Human: The Foundations of Medical Ethics. Urbana, Ill.: University of Illinois Press, 1985.

These essays are brought together to give the reader insight into the complex problems of health and illness. They deal with reason, hope, virtue, feeling, honor, and mortality. Two essays by Leon Kass and William May are well worth purchasing the book. They are on mortality (to what extent is longer life no good for individuals), and honor (a critique of medical and social attitudes toward care for the aged).

349) Veatch, Robert M., "Saying 'No' To Hemodialysis: Should A Minor's Decision Be Respected?" Hastings Center Report (September 1974): 8-10.

A case study in bioethics reflecting the attitudes of a 16 year-old girl who underwent transplant surgery. After receiving her father's kidney, it eventually failed to function, resulting in deep depression for both Karen and her parents. A shunt was placed in Karen's arm for dialysis, and soon became infected. It was judged that other transplantations would also fail, and the decision was made by Karen and her parents to discontinue hemodialysis. Two professionals study her case and give some interesting comments. I would encourage those, who may be undergoing serious decisions concerning life-and-death situations confronting teenage children, to read Karen's case.

350) _____. Death, Dying, and the Biological Revolution: Our Last Quest for Responsibility. New Haven: Yale University Press, 1976.

A well-knit view of developments in ethical and legal aspects regarding the care of dying persons. He deals with topics such as the definition of death, life-prolonging care of the moribund, the patient's right to refuse treatment, and the medical use of bodily parts. Dr. Veatch proposes a statutory definition of death, and a bill which would permit the refusal of medical treatment. He believes that legal provision is the best manner in which to handle death and dying issues, and has a mistrusting attitude toward physicians in the matter. He is critical of the ways in which physicians handle the matter of informing the patient who has serious progressive illness. Veatch defends his position skillfuly.

351) _____. Case Studies in Medical Ethics. Cambridge: Harvard University Press, 1977.

A collection of case studies in the field of bioethics. One hundred and twelve problems in the area of medical ethics are discussed. A case history is presented for each. There are also commentaries on the cases by other parties. The topics covered are: values in health and illness, problems in health care delivery, confidentiality, truth telling, abortions, sterilizations, contraceptives, genetics, transplantations, the allocation of scarce resources, psychiatry and control of human behavior, experimentation on human beings, consent and the right to refuse treatment, and death and dying problems. The book is easy to read and is a good case book for anyone concerned with ethical problems in the health care field. Veatch is rated as one of the best, if not the best, in the field of ethics.

352) _____. "Deciding Against Resuscitation: Encouraging Signs and Potential Dangers." Journal of The American Medical Association 253 (January 1985): 77-78.

A brief discussion on a study done which gave evidence that the decision against resuscitation is having an important impact on the care of critically and terminally-ill patients.

353) Visscher, Maurice B. Humanistic Perspectives in Medical Ethics. Buffalo: Prometheus Books, 1972.

A collection of essays written by leading physicians, psychiatrists, social scientists, and philosophers. This edition comprises the following contents:

1) The Humanistic Tradition in the Health Professions - Chauncey D. Leake
2) Medical Ethics in Philosophical Perspective - Patrick Romanell
3) The Sanctity of Life Principle - Marvin Kohl
4) The Right to Die - Walter C. Alvarez
5) The Evolution of the Right-to-Health Concept in the U.S. - Carleton B. Chapman and John M. Talmadge
6) The Fee-for-Service System - H. Roy Kaplan
7) The Ethics of the Physician in Human Reproduction - Howard C. Taylor
8) Birth Defects - Leroy Augenstein
9) Human Experimentation - Louis Lasagna
10) Medical Ethics and Psychotropic Drugs Mervin F. Silverman and Deborah B. Silverman
11) Prison Doctors - Tom Murton
12) Medicine and The Military - Gordon Livingston
13) Beyond Atrocity - Robert J. Litton
14) Social Ethics for Medical Educators - John G. Bruhn and Douglas C. Smith

354) Weiss, Ann E. Bioethics: Dilemmas in Modern Medicine. Hillside, N.J.: Enslow, 1985.

Weiss makes difficult subjects comprehensible, such as right to life, organs for sale, the Baby Doe rule, experimenting on humans, who gets health care, genetic engineering, rights of patients, and the right to die. After reading this book, one will have a good understanding of what bioethics is all about.

355) Williams, P., ed. To Live and Die: When, Why and How. New York: Springer-Verlag, 1973.

Covers a wide range of topics dealing with current important and vital issues such as: genetic engineering, contraception, abortion, euthanasia, transplant ethics, marriage, and other issues.

356) Winkenwerder, William, Jr. "Ethical Dilemmas for House Staff Physicians: The Care of Critically Ill and Dying Patients." Journal of The American Medical Association 254 (December 1985): 3454-3457.

This article addresses the issue of ethical dilemma faced by residents who care for critically ill patients. A case study is presented.

Familial Reaction

357) Baylor Law Review 27 (Winter 1975). Symposium Issue on Euthanasia.

The symposium dealt with the following: "Euthanasia: Why No Legislation"; "The Physician's Dilemma: A Doctor's View: What the Law Should Be"; "Death? When Does it Occur?"; "Medical Death"; "Bill of Rights for the Dying Patient"; "Medical Technology as It Exists Today"; "The Family Deals with Death"; "The Living Will, Coping with the Historical Event of Death"; "The Physician's Criminal Liability for the Practice of Euthanasia"; "Euthanasia: The Three-In-One Issue"; "Euthanasia v. The Right to Live"; "Euthanasia, Medical Treatment and the Mongoloid Child: Death as a Treatment of Choice"; and "Death With Dignity: The Physician's Civil Liability."

358) Christie-Seely, Janet, ed. Working With the Family in Primary Care: A Systems Approach to Health and Illness. New York: Praeger Studies, Praeger Scientific, 1984.

The book stresses the importance of the family in light of drastic changes in medicine, as well as other fields. The family systems approach is presented in such a way that anyone who reads this work will appreciate the work done by the editor and authors. Specific problems besetting the family, such as acute and chronic illness, terminal illness, and death, as well as other problems, are discussed in detail. An annotated bibliography is included, along with a subject index.

359) Colen, B. D. "A Time to Die." Washington Post (March 10-12, 1974).

A series of three newspaper articles dealing with actual cases on decisions to die. Doctors and relatives of dying patients were interviewed. The March issue deals with traumatic victims. Neonates (newborns) are dealt with in the March 11 edition. The copy of March 12 deals with patients who are terminally ill.

360) _____. "Nobody Looks at Cara Lynn." Chap. in Hard Choices. New York: G. P. Putnam's Sons, 1986.

Cara Lynn Bailey, an "anencephalic monster," born with no cerebral cortex and a skull that looks sawed off about two inches above eyelids that are fused shut, is the subject of this chapter. It is an account mostly about her parents, who care for her, suffer for her, and long for her death, yet look forward with sadness to her demise.

361) Collin, V. J. "Limits of Medical Responsibility in Prolonging Life." Journal of The American Medical
Association 206 (October 1968): 389-392.

That medicine is obligated to enhance life as
much as possible is reason enough not to maintain
mere biological life, if that life is poor quality and
beyond recovery. To discontinue treatment or
therapy is not morally wrong if biological existence
is all that is to be hoped for, Collin maintains.
The author leaves the responsibility to the physician
and his expertise in determining the condition and
state of the patient who is to be denied therapy or
life-sustaining treatment. Collin contends that the
doctor need only be concerned with the patient. The
family's best interests will follow.

362) Colman, Hila. Hanging On. Atheneum, N.Y., 1977.

A wife's account of the pain and trials of caring
for her dying husband, the ordeal of dealing with
the high cost of medical bills, caring for him at
home, and the injustice of health care costs.

363) Corbet, Thomas E. "Withholding or Withdrawing Life-
Prolonging Medical Treatment." Journal of The
American Medical Association 256 (November 1986):
2673.

This is an appeal to allow the patient the right
to die should he or she desire, and not endeavor to
maintain life. Mr. Corbet's wife was in a vegetative
state for three years. He appeals to physicians who
advocate keeping a person alive--thus prolonging
their suffering--that they put themselves in the
same position and ask themselves, "Would I want
myself or my loved ones in the same situation?"

364) Death Be Not Proud. New York: 99 min. Color; Rental/
Long-Term Lease. CBS: Westfall Productions Learning Corporation of America, 1976.

Based on the book Death Be Not Proud. The
account of John Gunther's son, who had a brain
tumor at 16. A family's ordeal during the dying
process of their son, his quality of life, and the grief
involved. Robby Benson, who starred as Johnny was
nominated for an Emmy. A very impacting movie.

365) "Doctor at the Bar." Newsweek 35 (January 16 1950): 20.

Dr. Herman Sander is accused of administering
a fatal injection of air (40cc) into the vein of his
cancer patient, Abbie Borroto. At the request of
Mr. Borroto, Dr. Sander complied with four injec-
tions--10cc each injection.

366) Evans, Jocelyn. Living With A Man Who Is Dying.
N.Y.: Taplinger, 1971.

On the death of Aron Evans (husband of the
author), who died at 33 years of age of abdominal
cancer. Apart from poor care by the medical
profession, a dignified and peaceful death was
accomplished at home by a loving and caring
family. A good book.

367) "Father Killer." Newsweek 35 (February 13, 1950): 21.

The story of Carol Paight, whose father was
cancer-ridden, and how she shot him in an act of
mercy.

368) Feifel, Herman. New Meanings of Death. New York:
McGraw Hill, 1977.

A companion book to Feifel's The Meaning of
Death. A collection that brings together various
issues related to death. Subjects covered are:
death and the developmental cycle; clinical
management; problems faced by survivors; and

cultural responses to death. Included are personal accounts of living with terminal illness, and family relationships during such a trying time. Among the articles in the volume are: "Dying They Live"; "Death and the Continuity of Life"; and "Make Today Count."

369) Freeman, J. "Is There a Right to Die--Quickly?" Journal of Pediatrics 80 (May 1972): 904-905.

According to Freeman, infants who have serious birth defects should be killed rather than have their lives prolonged indefinitely, prolongation would result in much suffering, not only for them, but also for their parents and those who serve their health care needs.

370) Gariepy, G. "Euthanasia and Death." Catholic Hospital, Canada 2 (March-April 1974): 131-133.

An examination of euthanasia and death relative to the position of the Catholic Church, the family, and health care professionals.

371) Gullo, Steven Viton, ed. Death and Children: A Guide for Educators, Parents and Caregivers. Dobbs Ferry, N.Y.: Tappan, 1985.

This book focuses on the death of children. It is broad in its scope in that it deals with three areas: education, parenthood, and those who are directly related to care for dying children. The child's reactions to death and others are examined, along with how parents themselves accept and react to the death of their children. Pointed out is the fact that dying children grieve just as adults, and adults will profit greatly as they gain an insight into the thinking of dying children.

372) Gustafson, J. "Mongolism, Parental Desires and the Right to Life." Perspectives in Biology and Medicine (Summer 1973): 529-557.

A different version of the famous Johns Hopkins cases of the mongoloid infant who was allowed to die at its parents request and insistence. All issues involved in the case are examined, and the author gives his views, but respects the opinions of others.

373) Hall, William T. "Legalized Suicide." Delaware State Medical Journal 40 (February 1968): 50-51.

Dr. Hall's conclusion - - after discussing the process of dying with his family and patients - - is that they would approve of legalized suicide.

374) Hiscoe, S. "Awesome Decision to Stop Heroic Measures." American Journal of Nursing 73 (February 1973): 291-293.

The family of a patient whose vegetative existence would continue is helped by a nurse who answers their questions honestly with to-the-point frankness. She helped them arrive at a decision to discontinue life-supporting machinery.

375) Hofling, C. K. "Life-Death Decisions May Undermine M.D.'s Mental Health." Frontiers In Hospital Psychiatry 5 (March 1968): 3

Hofling is emphatic in believing that decision making with regard to euthanasia should be a team effort composed of a group effort. The expertise of the physician, clergyman, family, and friends should be brought to bear on the decision.

376) Horan, Dennis J. Death, Dying and Euthanasia. Washington, D.C.: University Publications of America, Inc., 1977.

An impressive collection of works by authors from various fields: physicians, attorneys, ethicists, clergy, philosophers, and others who write with conviction on euthanasia. The works, most of which are reprints from periodicals, are classified under seven headings: (1) Death: When Does It Occur and How Do We Define It?; (2) Death as a Treatment of Choice?: Involuntary Euthanasia of the Defective Newborn; (3) Euthanasia: Ethical, Religious, and Moral Aspects; (4) Euthanasia: The Legal Aspects of "Mercy Killing"; (5) How Should Medicine and Society Treat the Dying?; (6) Legalized Euthanasia: Social Attitudes and Governmental Policies; and (7) Suicide and the Patient's Right to Reject Medical Treatment. The editors list the contributors in the back of the book. Good for research.

377) Humphrey, Derek. Jean's Way. London: Quartet Books, 1978.

An individual author-journalist's contribution to euthanasia literature. His account of his wife's death, and the issue.

378) "Interpreted Letter: Euthanasia Act." Lancet 2 (July 3, 1971): 39.

A discussion of how a physician deals with the family of a euthanasia participant. It is a painful process for the family, the patient, and doctor.

379) Jury, Mark and Dan Jury. Gramp. New York: Viking, 1976.

Concerns the dying of Frank Tugend and his family's support of him during his last days. He removed his false teeth and announced, at age 81, he would not eat or drink. Respecting his wishes, his family did not hospitalize him. He died at home three weeks later. A moving account of voluntary euthanasia.

380) Kantoi, George, Maria R. Silver, and Stuart J. Younger. A Closer Look at the Institutional Ethics Committee. 27 min. Videocassette; VHS and Beta; $90, Ohio: University of Akron, 1985.

This tape looks at many problems which beset ethical committees, such as: the committee's effects on the institution, medical staff, decision processes, and legal liabilities. A hypothetical case is presented in which a physician is faced with the problem of whether to withdraw ventilator support from a patient who had been comatose for four days. The patient's family plays a large role in the tape. Anyone may profit from the production in that some insight into the workings of an ethics committee will be gained, and along with it some understanding of what pressures are brought to bear on those who are involved in decision making on life-and-death issues.

381) Kraut, Melvin. Death and Dignity: The Meaning and Control of Personal Death. Springfield, Ill., 1974.

Written by an oncologist who explores meaningful and self-controlled dying. Presents some ways in which the health care team, family, and community can be supportive of the patient.

382) Lack, Sylvia, and Robert W. Buckingham. First American Hospice: Three Years of Home Care. New Haven, Conn.: Hospice Inc., 1978.

A manual giving detail on patient and family needs during terminal illness. It deals with different aspects of death and dying.

383) <u>Learning To Live With The Dying</u>. 39 min. Color.
Videocassette. Rental.

A National Continuing Medical Education tape
sharing management of the terminally ill patients
with patients and family. A discussion involving
medical students, physicians, and a minister. For use
by NCME subscribers only. Write to: 15 Columbus
Circle, New York, NY 10023.

384) "Let's Respect Death, Too." <u>Journal of The Kansas
Medical Society</u> 69 (June 1968): 328.

Tells of the plight of the parents of a thirteen-
year-old son who suffered total brain damage which
resulted from an accident. Possible solutions and
arguments for compassion are shared.

385) London, Jack. "The Law of Life." In <u>Best Short Stories of Jack London</u>. Garden City, N.Y.: Doubleday, 1953.

A perfect example of euthanasia as practiced
among the Indians. Old Koskoosh is left behind by
his tribe to die in the snow, during which time he
thinks about life and death. Although he tells them
all is well, he is resentful in that they left him to
die all alone.

386) McHugh, James T., ed. <u>Death, Dying and The Law</u>.
Huntington, Ind.: Our Sunday Visitor, Inc., and
Bishop's Committee for Pro-Life Activities, National
Conference of Catholic bishops, 1976.

Helps people to understand how to make
decisions respecting life-and-death situations in
terms of the Gospel and Christian-moral principals.
Stresses how respect for life should be protected by
the law. It also sets forth how the dying patient and
family members may be assisted by the medical and
nursing professions. A listing of films on the
subject is also provided.

387) Mannes, Marya. Last Rights. New York: William Morrow, 1974.

A humanist looks at the taboo issue of euthanasia. She shares accounts of discussions with the dying, their families, their doctors and attorneys, and those who witnessed the effects of high technological machines on worn out bodies. Human suffering and money are tallied and found to be a high cost for hypocritical attitudes toward the death of those who should be allowed to die. The book is frank and to the point.

388) Martinson, Ida Marie. The Dying Child, The Family and The Health Professionals: An Annotated Professional Bibliography. St. Paul, Minn.: 2303 Doswell St. (55108), 1976.

Management and care of the dying child. Some 80 items are listed. A helpful work, although limited.

389) "Mercy Killing Debated: Chicago Wesley Memorial Hospital." AMA News 10 (August 28 1967): 9.

The account of the murder of a mother by her son, Robert Waskin. After much suffering, she wished to die. He shot and killed her in an act of mercy.

390) Nash, Irwin. "An ICU Death: A Gordian Knot in Search of Alexander." New England Journal of Medicine 311 (December 1984): 1705

A physician relates a visit with his seventy-three-year-old uncle who was terminally ill in an intensive care unit of a major medical center, and how he was somewhat neglected by those who could have relieved his suffering by an act of active euthanasia.

391) Oden, Thomas C. Should Treatment Be Terminated? Moral Guidelines for Christian Families and Pastors. New York: Harper and Row, 1976.

Arguments which favor and oppose ending treatment of the terminally ill are addressed, along with problems having to do with truth telling, organ donation, home care, and legal limits. Disagreements between families and physicians are discussed, with other issues such as "living wills" and refusal of medical treatment.

392) Parham, Allan M., Donald J. Higby, Jean-Pierre Kaufmann, and Sharon Murphy. "Last Rights." New England Journal of Medicine 295 (November 1976): 1139-1142.

Ten letters written by physicians, both pro and con, on views which have bearing on terminating life-support systems for terminal patients. Patients' families are also discussed.

393) Ricci, Lawrence R. "A Death in the Family." Journal of The American Medical Association 257 (May 1987): 2485.

A touching account of the death of a doctor's father, and the son's hurt because of the cold and callous care given during the course of his father's hospitalization.

394) Robertson, John A., and Norman Fost. "Passive Euthanasia of Defective Newborn Infants: Legal Considerations." The Journal of Pediatrics 88 (May 1976): 883-889.

The reason for this article is to consider legal ramifications in light of the fact that little mention has been made in reports on passive euthanasia of defective infants. The authors feel that parents, physicians, nurses, and administrators are liable on several grounds; homicide by omission, child neglect, and failure to report child neglect. Increasing publicity of passive euthanasia practices is thought to increase the probability of prosecution. The appeal of this writing is to persuade open discussion and debate to change existing laws, not to try and subvert them through private action. Two alternative policies are described: (1) establishment of criteria for a class of infants who can be allowed to die, and (2) a better process of decision making. Their conclusion is that a commitment to process would be preferable.

395) Scully, Thomas, and Celia Scully. Playing God: The New World of Medical Choices. New York: Simon and Schuster, 1987.

A collaboration by husband and wife, whom the reader feels an affinity because of their compassion and care for patients and families alike. Their concern is revealed through the subject content of Playing God. One learns how to make choices relative to health care while reading this work: the right choice of physician for one's self and family; building the right relationship with one's physician; patients' rights and how to exercise them; "living will" and the power of attorney; transplantation of human organs; different ways of making babies; dilemmas in treatment and non-treatment; who should be the spokesperson for a child who has a disabling, life-threatening, or terminal illness; making life-and-death decisions for another adult; how to get action when you have been wronged through malpractice and billing fraud. A very important feature of the book is the appendices, which are "packed" with information on bills of rights in most areas of health care. The Scullys state, "The whole purpose of this book is to help you understand the issues and their ethical underpinnings, how to protect yourself, and where to go for help." Having researched many "how to" books, I put this one at the top of my list, and recommend it highly to be read and digested by all who are interested in the subject of euthanasia, in order to help make the right decisions in the area of health care. It is well indexed, and would be a handy tool for discussion groups.

396) Sempos, Christopher, and Richard Cooper. "Passive Euthanasia." Archives of Internal Medicine 143 (July 1983): 1492.

A letter written to oppose the thought that parents may be justified in allowing their children with profound mental retardation to be killed, which is incompatible with social experiences.

397) Simmons, Paul D. "Euthanasia: The Person and Death." Chap. in Birth and Death: Bioethical Decision-Making. Philadelphia: The Westminster Press, 1983.

In this chapter, the author examines matters having to do with life and death and endeavors to answer the question: Does one have a moral right to die well or experience a "good death" that is rooted in Christian theology? In his defense of a more liberal approach to euthanasia he discusses the following: ancient and modern views of euthanasia, types of elective death, Biblical perspectives on elective death, and killing vs. allowing to die. Simmons believes that the traditional approach to euthanasia which leaves death and dying issues in the hands of God has been outdated due to the scientific revolution, i.e. machines and drugs now keep people alive beyond the point of natural normal death; that family members and health care personnel should be responsible for determining the manner in which one may die and the right to decide, within limits, the circumstances under which one dies. "What is of ultimate importance" says the author "is not the manner of one's death but the responsibility one accepts for dealing with death in the light of the victory of Christ."

398) Simpson, Michael A. "Brought in Dead." Omega 7 No. 3, 1976): 243-248.

The author presents social factors which are influential as determinants on whether or not to resuscitate in emergency rooms.

399) Tendler, Moshe D., Yashar Hirshant, Jacob Weinberg, and Abraham Twerski. The Mount Sinai Hospital and Medical Center Symposia on Medicine and Halacha (Jewish Law). Chicago: Mount Sinai Hospital, 1975/1976.

A discussion in two parts: Part I took place in October of 1975 involving Tendler and Hirshaut. The discussion centered on Halacha and the terminally ill. Part II: Halacha and Care of the Terminally Ill transpired in February 1976. The discussants were Weinberg and Twerski. Two cases are presented in each part. Part I discusses an eighty year-old man with a history of diabetes mellitus who had several strokes, was unable to speak, and had arterosclerotic heart disease complicated by a heart attack. The case in Part II involved a thirty one year-old Jewish woman who had ingested a large amount of aspirin because she was unhappy. Discussion centers around trying to help the woman and her family. A study of this book will give one a look inside the Jewish mind and its relationship to caring for others according to Jewish law.

400) Troup, Stanley B., and William A. Greene, ed. The Patient, Death, and The Family. New York: Charles Scribner's Sons, 1974.

A compilation of twelve essays that grew out of a conference sponsored by Rochester General Hospital in New York. Medicine, nursing, philosophy, the chaplaincy, and sociology are represented, and relate effectively because each participant had the opportunity to read and review the others' essays before sharing his or her thoughts on the theme of the conference. The central thought throughout the book is that the dying patient goes through the process of relating to two systems: the hospital or institution which provides the care, and the family, each of which assumes that the other is meeting the patient's needs. Historical, symbolical, and philosophical views of death are treated. The physician is seen as one who has difficulty in grappling with the issues facing the dying patient, and it is pointed out that the chaplain and/or clergy can be of tremendous help and assistance with the terminally ill patient, if trained correctly. This book will be especially helpful for the family, as well as health care personnel.

401) U.S. House of Representatives. Discursive Dictionary of Health Care. Washington, D.C.: Prepared by the staff for the use of the Subcommittee on Health and the Environment of The Committee on Interstate and Foreign Commerce. U.S. Government Printing Office, 1976.

This dictionary was prepared for legislators and the public due to unfamiliar terms which have become part of the National Health Insurance debate. The work defines such terms as "audit," "peer review," "third party," "kitting," "me-to-drug," and "ping-ponging" (the practice of passing a patient from one physician to another for the purpose of spreading out health care business--for unnecessary examinations and tests). Many terms used through out this dictionary would be beneficial to those who are involved in counselling situations. A great help for $2.40 from the Government Printing Office.

402) Veatch, Robert M. "Saying 'No' To Hemodialysis: Should A Minor's Decision Be Respected?" Hastings Center Report (September 1974): 8-10.

A case study in bioethics reflecting the attitudes of a 16-year-old girl who underwent transplant surgery. After receiving her father's kidney, it eventually failed to function, resulting in deep depression for both Karen and her parents. A shunt was placed in Karen's arm for dialysis, and soon became infected. It was judged that other transplantations would also fail, and the decision was made by Karen and her parents to discontinue hemodialysis. Two professionals study her case and give some interesting comments. I would encourage those, who may be undergoing serious decisions concerning life-and-death situations confronting teenage children, to read Karen's case.

403) Wertenbaker, Lael T. Death of a Man. Toronto: Beacon Press, Boston and Saunders, 1974.

"Death of a Man" is written about death in the family. Wertenbaker writes about his last 60 days after discovering he had cancer. His wife completed the book.

404) Whitelaw, Andrew. "Death as Option in Neonatal Intensive Care." Lancet 8502 (August 1986):328-331.

According to Whitelaw, many physicians believe there are circumstances in which infants should be allowed to die without having their lives prolonged. He mentions that seventy-five infants were so seriously ill that withdrawal of treatment was considered. Criteria for withdrawal of treatment from a particular infant had to be based on certainty of total incapacity and a unanimous decision among the nursing staff caring for the child. Treatment was withdrawn from fifty-one of the seventy-five patients. The parents of forty-seven infants accepted the decision, and all the infants died. Parents of four chose continued intensive care, and two infants survived with disabilities. Treatment of twenty-four cases was continued. Seventeen survived and seven died. Agreement was unanimous among staff and parents that treatment should be withdrawn, and that treatment on purely legal grounds is not justifiable.

405) <u>Who Speaks for the Baby?</u> New York, N.Y.: 20 min., color. 3/4" Videocassette. 15 Columbus Circle (10023).

Parents of a mongoloid baby are reluctant to give consent for surgery to solve life-saving problems for the infant. The pediatrician proceeds to seek a court order to operate. Should he? Should the child be allowed to live or die?--a difficult question which the content of the tape seeks to answer. A National Continuing Medical Education tape. Subscribers only.

406) Wright, H. T. <u>The Matthew Tree</u>. New York: Pantheon Books, 1975.

The author writes on the death of her father and his last seven years of living with multiple strokes. An example of a "very easy death." Honest and sincere.

Individual Reaction

407) Adams, Gerald R., Nancy Bueche, and Jay D. Schvaneveldt. "Contemporary Views of Euthanasia: A Regional Assessment." <u>Social Biology</u> 25 (1983): 62-68.

Abstract of the above piece is as follows: "Abstract: A survey of euthanasia attitudes of 245 college students at six universities in three regions of the United States. . . using two scales which assessed idealogical position toward and behavioral endorsement of euthanasia actions. Geographical region, religious participation, mass media, class rank, socioeconomic status, and personality (locus control) were associated in various ways with the scales employed. In addition, the attitudinal and behavioral dimensions were moderately associated."

408) Alsop, Stewart. <u>Stay of Execution</u>. Lippincott, 1973.

The author was told that he had leukemia and as a result of living with it, had varied experiences. His

appraisal of his situation is that "a dying man needs
to die, as a sleepy man needs sleep, and there comes a
time when it is wrong, as well as useless, to resist."

409) _____. "The Right to Die with Dignity." Good
Housekeeping 179 (August 1974): 130-132.

Alsop, a distinguished journalist, shares his
viewpoints on euthanasia, and believes that a
terminal patient has the right to decide his or her
fate, and be allowed to receive pain-killing medication, including heroin, if necessary.

410) Austin, Alfred. "Euthanasia - A Poem." Temple Bar 3
(1861): 472.

For the individual who is awaiting death, this
poem appeals to the individual's patience while
waiting for death's arrival. The poem states that
death will come in its own good time.

411) Bacon, Francis. The Historie of Life and Death with
Observations Naturall and Experimentall for the
Prolonging of Life. New York.: Arno, 1976.

Bacon's treatise on death, prolongation of life,
euthanasia, transfusion, and transplantation. The
first edition of the work: London, 1638.

412) Barton, David, ed. Dying and Death: A Clinical Guide
for Caregivers. Baltimore: Williams and Wilkins,
1977.

A look at current thoughts and views on clinical
terminal care. A two-part work. Part I: An
Approach to Caring for Dying Persons is done by the
author. Various authors' works appear in Part II:
Perspectives. Veatch writes on ethics. Van Eys
writes on the dying child. Peak writes on the dying
and the elderly. The thoughts, feelings, and
reflections of a person with a life-threatening illness
is dwelt upon by Gattis and Cummings. Commendable.

413) <u>Baylor Law Review</u> 27 (Winter 1975). Symposium Issue on Euthanasia.

The symposium dealt with the following: "Euthanasia: Why No Legislation"; "The Physician's Dilemma: A Doctor's View: What the Law Should Be"; "Death? When Does it Occur?"; "Medical Death"; "Bill of Rights for the Dying Patient"; "Medical Technology as It Exists Today"; "The Family Deals with Death"; "The Living Will, Coping with the Historical Event of Death"; "The Physician's Criminal Liability for the Practice of Euthanasia"; "Euthanasia: The Three-In-One Issue"; "Euthanasia v. The Right to Live"; "Euthanasia, Medical Treatment and the Mongoloid Child: Death as a Treatment of Choice"; and "Death With Dignity: The Physician's Civil Liability."

414) Bender, David L. <u>Problems of Death: Opposing View-points</u>. Anoka, Minn.: Greenhaven, 1974.

A selection of readings on vital issues of the day: abortion, euthanasia, capital punishment, suicide, and American funeral practices. Chapter two deals with euthanasia. Readings are: I Favor Mercy; Euthanasia and the New Ethic; My Views on Euthanasia; The American Way of Death; The Case for Euthanasia; and The Case Against Euthanasia. A major emphasis of this book is on critical thinking skills. Discussion exercises follow each reading in order to stimulate discussion and critical thinking. The book is published for use in classrooms, and would be effective with the high school age group.

415) Bok, Sissela. "Personal Directions for Care at the End of Life." <u>New England Journal of Medicine</u> 295 (August 1976): 367-369.

A review of how one would like to be treated should terminal illness ensue, together with a discussion of how "living wills" should be worded.

416) Brand, Paul. Escape From Pain. London: Christian Medical Fellowship, 1975.

Dr. Paul Brand discusses the puzzle of pain relative to God, and the person who must endure it. He believes that it is a definite gift from God and is for man's benefit rather than his undoing. While this is a short pamphlet of 15 pages, those holding to the Christian faith will appreciate it.

417) Breo, Dennis. Extraordinary Care: The Medical Treatment of Adolph Hitler, Howard Hughes, Elvis Presley, President Ronald Reagan, Barney Clark.... Chicago: Review, 1986.

A not-so-serious examination of the issues facing society today. A collection of interviews which shed light on outstanding personalities and their patientphysician relationship. The interview format touches on perplexing issues, such as surrogate motherhood, the right to choose forms of cancer therapy, and the subject which has real bearing on all our lives--euthanasia. The discussions involving the author and VIPs will interest all who care to read the assemblage.

418) Butler, Robert N. Why Survive? Being Old in America. New York: Harper and Row, 1975.

Informative on the "right to die" and death management. Problems of growing old in America are highlighted.

419) Cantor, Normal L. "A Patient's Decision to Decline Life-Saving Medical Treatment: Bodily Integrity Versus the Preservation of Life." Rutgers' Law Review 26 (Winter 1972): 228-264.

Pointed out are the arguments of constitutional principles, and common law standards which argue for the right to refuse life-saving measures. Other issues discussed are preservation of society, respect for sanctity of life, and third-party protection.

420) Caroline, N. L. "Dying in Academe." The New Physician 21 (November 1972): 655-657.

A prize-winning essay about a man who chose to die rather than linger in "life" on a respirator. The author has little to support her claim that it is wrong to sustain patients on life-support systems, but is to be congratulated on her stand.

421) Cavanagh, J. R. "Bene Mori: The Right of the Patient to Die With Dignity." Linacre Quarterly (May 1963).

Cavanagh says that it is the doctor's responsibility to see that his patients are not kept alive against obvious signs that he or she will not recover, and that privacy and human company are of more benefit than being kept on machines. That dying with dignity is of the utmost concern to Cavanagh goes without question.

422) Choron, J. Death and Western Thought. New York: Collier, 1963.

If one is interested in what the great western philosophers thought about death and dying, this is a classic which should not be avoided. It incorporates pre-Socratic views to the present day. Highly recommended.

423) Clark, Brian. Whose Life Is It, Anyway? 53 min. Color. Rental/Sale. University of Michigan, 1975.

A paraplegic desires to die, which sets up conflict between doctors and the patient. Well done and effective.

424) Colen, B. D. "A Time to Die." Washington Post (March 10-12, 1974).

A series of three newspaper articles dealing with actual cases on decisions to die. Doctors and relatives of dying patients were interviewed. The March 10 issue deals with trauma victims. Neonates (newborns) are dealt with in the March 11 edition. The March 12 copy deals with patients who are terminally ill.

425) Corbet, Thomas E. "Withholding or Withdrawing Life-Prolonging Medical Treatment." Journal of The American Medical Association 256 (November 1986): 26-73.

This is an appeal to allow the patient the right to die should he or she desire, and not endeavor to maintain life. Mr. Corbet's wife was in a vegetative state for three years. He appeals to physicians who advocate keeping a person alive--thus prolonging their suffering--that they put themselves in the same position and ask themselves, "Would I want myself or my loved ones in the same situation?"

426) Crane, Diane. The Sanctity of Social Life: Physician's Treatment of Critically Ill Patients. New Brunswick, N.J.: Transactions Books, 1977.

Crane addresses social and ethical problems of the dying in America. A search for ethical guidelines is continued by a seven-year research among physicians who are faced with decision making when confronted with terminally ill and severely handicapped infants. Criteria are investigated by which physicians treat critically ill patients. Circumstances are investigated under which physicians take part in active euthanasia. A social policy is sought in this work, i.e., a different criteria for establishing a person's worth to society other than that of meeting physical criteria of life.

427) Davis, John W., Barry Hoffmaster, and Sarah Shorten, eds. Contemporary Issues in Biomedical Ethics. Clifton, N.J.: Humana, 1978.

A compilation of comments and papers presented at a colloquium on biomedical ethics at the University of Western Ontario. Contained in the volume are issues such as rights and moral decisions, legalism, and the rights of the terminally ill. Among other problems brought to the reader's attention are: issues in genetics; the role of the physician; informed consent and paternalism; and professional responsibility.

428) Death and Dying. Chicago, Ill.: 2 Audiocassettes. Sale. American Health Congress. Teach'em Inc., 160 E. Illinois St. (60611).

Programs of the American Health Congress discussing personal and ethical issues centering on dying, the prolongation of life, and dying patient rights.

429) Death Be Not Proud. New York: 99 min. Color; Rental/Long-Term Lease. CBS: Westfall Productions-Learning Corporation of America, 1976.

Based on the book Death Be Not Proud. The account of John Gunther's son, who had a brain tumor at 16. A family's ordeal during the dying process of their son, his quality of life, and the grief involved. Robby Benson, who starred as Johnny, was nominated for an Emmy. A very impacting movie.

430) Dempsey, David. The Way We Die: An Investigation of Death and Dying in America Today. New York: MacMillan, 1975.

A competent work on death, transplants, longevity, the right to die, the experience of dying, mourning, and burial. Another book pointing out the process of dying in the U.S.

431) Desmond, Stewart. Socrates and the Soul of Man. Boston: Beacon, 1951.

The work incorporates a fresh translation of Plato's Phaedo, in which Plato describes the last hours of Socrates. The book documents the fact that man during Plato's and Socrates' period became aware that man is a personality (soul). It is more or less a memorial to Socrates. A very emotional account of the death of one of the greats of philosophical thinking.

432) Evans, Jocelyn. Living With A Man Who Is Dying. New York: Taplinger, 1971.

On the death of Aron Evans (husband of the author), who died at 33 years of age of abdominal cancer. Apart from poor care by the medical profession, a dignified and peaceful death was accomplished at home by a loving and caring family. A good book.

433) Feifel, Herman. "Older Persons Look at Death." Geriatrics 11 (March 1956): 127-130.

The data in this article is presented to demonstrate the attitudes of individuals 65 years and older regarding death and dying. Forty white males at a Veteran's Administration home are subjects of the article.

434) _____. New Meanings of Death. New York: McGraw Hill, 1977.

A companion book to Feifel's The Meaning of Death. A collection that brings together various issues related to death. Subjects covered are: death and the developmental cycle; clinical management; problems faced by survivors; and cultural responses to death. Included are personal accounts of living with terminal illness, and family relationships during such a trying time. Among the articles in the volume are: "Dying They Live,"; "Death and the Continuity of Life,"; and "Make Today Count."

435) Fletcher, Joseph. "Voluntary Euthanasia: The New Shape of Death." Medical Counterpoint (June 1970): 13.

Fletcher's pro-euthanasia arguments are presented, along with sanctity of human life, and mercy as an attribute which responds to one's fellow man.

436) _____. "Euthanasia: Our Right to Die." Chap. in Morals and Medicine. Princeton, N.J.: Princeton University Press, 1979.

An examination of the practice of euthanasia in its medical form, and is limited to cases in which the patient chooses euthanasia with the understanding that the physician sees little hope of recovery or relief by any other means. Fletcher's hope is--along with Maeterlinck--that ". . .there will come a day when science will protest its errors and will shorten our sufferings." As one will be able to see after reading this chapter, Fletcher, as always, is in favor of euthanasia--sometimes to the extreme.

437) Flew, A. "The Principle of Euthanasia." In Euthanasia and the Right to Die. A. B. Downing, ed. New York: Humanities, 1970.

In defense of a legal right to voluntary euthanasia. The author believes that one's freedom is curtailed by legislating against a person's right to voluntary euthanasia.

438) Fox, Renee C., and Judith P. Swazey. The Courage to Fail: A Social View of Organ Transplants and Dialysis. Chicago: The University of Chicago Press, 1974.

A very detailed study of the different aspects of the transplant and dialysis situation. The section on the right to give life and the right to die should be of interest to those who are pro and con on the issue of euthanasia.

439) Freund, Paul A. "Organ Transplants: Ethical and Legal Problems." In Ethics in Medicine: Historical Perspectives and Contemporary Concerns, ed. Stanley Joel Reiser, Arthur J. Dyck, and William J. Curran, 173-177. Cambridge, Mass.: MIT, 1977.

Freund discusses problems concerning the allocation of resources--from whom they should come and to whom organs should be transferred. Implications raised by the questions concern moral, legal, and medical considerations. Each differs in removal of organs after death and during life. He briefly discusses the question of whether or not a dying patient should be allowed to consent to surgical intervention for the purpose of saving another's life.

440) Gift of Life/Right to Die. 55 min., B&W. Rental, University Audio-Visual Center and Visual Aids Service, sity Extension, University of Illinois (61822), 1968.

A short film discussing one person's death and another who becomes an organ recipient of the former. Other ethical issues are mentioned, such as euthanasia for infants who are malformed, and individuals who suffer from catastrophic disease.

441) Gilman, C. P. "Right to Die." Forum 94 (November 1935): 297-300.

This article was publicized in August of 1935, after the suicide of Mr. Gilman, wherein he appeals for a more positive attitude toward euthanasia and suicide.

442) Goff, W. "How Can a Physician Prepare His Patient for Death?" Journal of The American Medical Association 201 (July 1967): 280.

Goff believes that children should never be told they are going to die unless they ask. Adults, he believes, should have hope for a cure of their ills and hope of eternal life. This article should be read together with Friedman's "Serious Gap Between Theory and Practice Seen in Physicians' Management of Terminal Patients." For annotation on Friedman, (see Citation 662).

443) Green, M. "Care of the Dying Child." Pediatrics 40 (September 1967): 492-497.

Green discusses management of the terminally ill child and the child's concept of death. He feels that the child's physician should be available at all times, otherwise, a competent substitute should be available. Dr. Thomas Sculley has a good discussion on the physician/patient relationship in his Playing God (see Citation 19).

444) Gruman, Gerald. "An Historical Introduction to Ideas About Voluntary Euthanasia: With a Bibliographical Survey and Guide for Interdisciplinary Studies." Omega: Journal of Death and Dying 4 (Summer 1973): 87-138.

An examination of the evolution of modern ideas about euthanasia. The views of individual death of great thinkers are put into historical context relative to the circumstances and mood of the time in which they lived. A bibliography is included in the piece.

445) Hackett, T. P. "An Understanding of Death." Episcopal Theological School Bulletin LXIV (September 1971): 1.

Dr. Hackett reveals that many patients know when they are going to die, and even predict their death prior to surgery. It is the dying process they fear, not death itself. He also includes some first-hand accounts of what it is like to be dead. An interesting article.

446) Heifetz, Milton D. and Charles Mangel. The Right to Die: A Neurosurgeon Speaks of Death with Candor. New York: Putnam's Sons, 1975.

A discussion of the euthanasia controversy by a physician. Heifetz contends for the right of the patient to die, dealing with the legal and ethical aspects of euthanasia.

447) Hendin, D. Death As A Fact Of Life. New York: W. W. Norton, 1973.

This book covers many aspects of the subject; criteria of death, euthanasia, and cryonics. One will find this a compilation from many sources, and helpful.

448) Higgins, Colin. Harold and Maude. New York: Avon Books, 1975.

A humorous book about Harold and Maude, two people who enjoy attending funerals for pastime and amusement. Harold attempts suicide many times, and Maude finally commits suicide in order to have some control over her own death--a form of euthanasia.

449) Hinton, John. Dying. Harmondsworth and Baltimore: Pelican Books, 1967.

An update on the knowledge of death, and existing attitudes toward dying. The author tells what it is like to die, relative to terminal illness and mourning. His own experience is shared with the reader.

450) Horan, Dennis J., and David Mall, eds. Death, Dying and Euthanasia. Washington, D. C.: University Publications of America, 1977.

Controversial aspects of euthanasia are discussed, such as: involuntary euthanasia of the defective newborn; ethical, moral, and legal aspects of "mercy killing"; the feasibility of legalized euthanasia; and the right of the individual to reject treatment.

451) Humphrey, Derek. Jean's Way. London: Quartet Books, 1978.

An individual author-journalist's contribution to euthanasia literature. His account of his wife's death, and the issue of mercy killing.

452) Humphrey, Derek, and Ann Wickett. The Right to Die. New York: Harper and Row, 1986.

Husband and wife, who are leading authorities in the field of euthanasia, give a complete history of the subject. From Greek and Roman attitudes to the present day active and passive euthanasia issues, they discuss up front problems surrounding the subject. The book does well in evaluating such an important subject. It should be read by doctors, lawyers, ministers, and families in order to get a comprehensive understanding of "the right to die." The appendixes include a listing of films and organizations which deal with death.

453) Imbus, Sharon H., and Bruce E. Zawacki. "Autonomy for Burned Patients When Survival is Unprecedented." New England Journal of Medicine 297 (August 1977): 308-311.

While in the state of lucidity, severely burned patients were asked if they wished maximal therapeutic measures or ordinary medical treatment. In either case, they were assured of every concern for their well-being. Their mortality rate was neither improved nor diminished as the result of the approach.

454) "Interpreted Letter: Euthanasia Act." Lancet 2 (July 3 1971): 39.

A discussion of how a physician deals with the

family of a euthanasia participant. It is a painful process for both the family, the patient, and doctor.

455) Jackson, Douglas M. Human Life and Human Worth. Christian Medical Fellowship, 1970.

What a Christian surgeon thinks of life, death, and the value of human life.

456) Johnson, Dana E. "Life, Death, and the Dollar Sign." Journal of The American Medical Association 252 (July 1984): 223, 224.

A discussion on economical questions raised due to prolongation of life-support. That the most important interest is on behalf of the patient and not in the interest of the governmental or corporate entity who pays the bills.

457) Johnson, Eric W. Older and Wiser. New York: Walker, 1987.

A moving account of how the elderly feel about growing older, eventually meeting with man's last experience--Death. They express their feelings about dying with dignity, the right to die, the senselessness of prolonging a painful death, the right of choosing how to die, and living wills. Much of the book is composed of questions and answers. It is very easy to read, and would probably lend itself to discussion groups.

458) Jury, Mark and Dan Jury. Gramp. New York: Viking, 1976.

Concerns the dying of Frank Tugend and his family's support of him during his last days. He removed his false teeth and announced, at age 81, that he would not eat or drink. Respecting his wishes, his family did not hospitalize him. He died at home three weeks later. A moving account of voluntary euthanasia.

459) Kapusta, Morton Allan, and Solomon Frank. "The Book of Job and the Modern View of Depression." Annals of Internal Medicine 86 (May 1977): 667-672.

A recommended study of the book of Job and depression. The authors present the book as being an instrument to provide professionals of the day with a realistic approach to the problems of life. Its disclosure of depression is the same as the modern view of depression. There are clues throughout the book that distinguish between normal grief and deep depression. Kapusta and Frank are convinced that Job not only gives a good description and meaning of depression, but that it also provides solutions for dealing with modern depression. Chapter 30 of Job provides answers that are vital for results of depression. The authors say, ". . .part of the wisdom of the Book of Job is a timeless medical masterpiece that provides an unexcelled standard of clinical observation and medical intervention." While this study is not specifically on the subject of euthanasia, it provides insight into the depression that occurs as a result of grief on the part of those who deal with the problems of euthanasia. It is highly recommended for all who experience depression, regardless of the cause.

460) Keleman, Stanley. Living Your Dying. New York: Random House, 1976.

A psychological viewpoint on man's traditional images of death. Keleman's belief is that man should be free to die his own death.

461) Kolff, W. J. Artificial Organs. New York: Halsted, 1976.

This work is "tops" in its field because it was done by the "father" of artificial organs. With his vast experience behind him, he discusses three major areas having to do with artificial organs. Much of the book describes artificial organ research, especially that having to do with the artificial heart, artificial hearts driven by atomic energy, and significant research surrounding the artificial heart. Dr. Kolff developed and demonstrated clinical effectiveness of hemodialysis for the treatment of patients with chronic renal failure early in his career, and in the present volume describes the future of the dialysis, and the costs of dialysis. This book would benefit pastors, psychologists, and those who are interested in specifics which have to do with transplants and artificial organs, especially in light of the fact that counsellors are called upon more often to advise in the area of death and dying.

462) Kraut, Melvin. Death and Dignity: The Meaning and Control of Personal Death. Springfield, Ill., 1974.

Written by an oncologist who explores meaningful and self-controlled dying. Presents some ways in which the health care team, family, and community can be supportive of the patient.

463) Kubler-Ross, Elizabeth. On Death and Dying. New York: MacMillan, 1969.

Kubler-Ross gives a classic statement of the five stages of dying: denial, anger, bargaining, depression, and acceptance. Dr. Kubler-Ross wrote this book as a result of 200 interviews with terminally ill patients. The book is certainly an eye opener to the reactions of terminal patients during the dying process.

464) Lack, Sylvia, and Robert W. Buckingham. First American Hospice: Three Years of Home Care. New Haven, Conn.: Hospice Inc., 1978.

A manual giving detail on patient and family needs during terminal illness. It deals with different aspects of death and dying.

465) Learning To Live With The Dying. New York, N.Y.: 39 min. Color. Videocassette. Rental. 15 Columbus Circle (10023).

A National Continuing Medical Education tape sharing management of the terminally ill patients with patients and family. A discussion involving medical students, physicians, and a minister. For use by NCME subscribers only.

466) Letourneau, C. W. "Dying With Dignity." Hospital Management 109 (June 1970): 27.

Dr. Letourneau discusses whether or not life after eighty is good or bad for society. He argues the issue, and presents the pros and cons of voluntary euthanasia for those who suffer from an incurable condition.

467) London, Jack. "The Law of Life." In Best Short Stories of Jack London. Garden City, N.Y.: Doubleday, 1953.

A perfect example of euthanasia as practiced among the Indians. Old Koskoosh is left behind by his tribe to die in the snow, during which time he thinks about life and death. Although he tells them all is well, he is resentful in that they left him to die all alone.

468) McHugh, James T., ed. Death, Dying and The Law. Huntington, Ind.: Our Sunday Visitor, Inc., and Bishop's Committee for Pro-Life Activities, National Conference of Catholic Bishops, 1976.

Helps people to understand how to make decisions respecting life-and-death situations in terms of the Gospel and Christian-moral principals. Stresses how respect for life should be protected by the law. It also sets forth how the dying patient and family members may be assisted by the medical and nursing professions. A listing of films on the subject is also provided.

469) McKengney, F. and P. Lange. "The Decision To No Longer Live On Chronic Hemodialysis." American Journal of Psychiatry 128 (September 1971): 267-274.

A discussion of four hemodialysis patients and their attitude toward death. The authors stress that there is a life not worth living.

470) Mannes, Marya. Last Rights. New York: William Morrow, 1974.

A humanist looks at the taboo issue of euthanasia. She shares accounts of discussions with the dying, their families, their doctors and attorneys, and those who witnessed the effects of high technological machines on worn out bodies. Human suffering and misery are tallied and found to be a high cost for hypocritical attitudes toward the death of those who should be allowed to die. The book is frank and to the point.

471) Mead, Margaret. "Individuals Should Have A Choice Of Euthanasia." In Problems Of Death: Opposing Viewpoints, ed. David L. Bender, 27-30. St. Paul, Minn., Greenhaven, 1981.

Views on the individual's choice of euthanasia are presented by the world renowned anthropologist. While she believes in protecting the rights of older people to live as long as possible, she defends their right to die, and the means to do so, whenever they deem it necessary.

472) Montange, Charles H. "Informed Consent and The Dying Patient." Yale Law Journal 83 (July 1974): 1632-1664.

An article which, indeed, stresses the importance of informed consent. The author emphasizes that if the patient has a right to consent, he also has a right to refuse, if he is competent to do so. The courts should recognize the right of the patient to forego treatment. Keeping this in mind, the courts should establish proper tests for competency through mitigation.

473) Moos, R. H., ed. Coping With Physical Illness. New York: Plenum Medical Book, 1977.

Reprinted articles from the literature of the 70's dealing with serious physical illness. Chapters dealing with the subject are: chronic grief, stillbirth, birth defects, cancer, infarct, stroke, burns, hospital environments, transplants, staff stresses, and terminal care. Insight into individual experience is enhanced.

474) Novak, Nina. "Natural Death Acts Let Patients Refuse Treatment." Hospital (August 1984): 71-73.

The piece defines NDAs (natural death acts) as being statutes enacted by a state legislature, which allow the creation of documents that provide a legally recognized way for competent adults to express, in advance, their desires regarding life-crucial medical decisions, in the event they become terminal and death is imminent. Difficult questions arising under NDAs are dealt with. Those states which have NDAs are identified by a graph.

475) Ogg, Elizabeth. Facing Death and Loss. Lancaster, Pa., 1985.

A sensitive book which considers the subject of death and the individual's needs and concerns during the process of dying. The patient's right to choose death in a hospice rather than a hospital and its torturous machine-like technological life-sustaining practices is discussed, along with financing terminal care.

476) O'Rourke, Kevin D. "Christian Affirmation of Life." Hospital Progress 55 (July 1974): 65-67.

For the Christian who is interested in signing a "living will." An expression of the Christian's faith relative to death as being the last act upon entrance to everlasting life.

477) Pattison, Mansell E., ed. The Experience of Dying. New York: Prentice-Hall, 1976.

A clinically relevant work dealing with the malformed and burned child, childhood leukemia, middle childhood and hemophilia, trauma, and cancer; adolescence and cardiac pacemakers, renal transplants, and cancer; young adults and M.S., trauma, and leukemia; middle age and the I.C.U., cancer, leukemia, and hemodialysis; the elderly and euthanasia; and two chapters which review different styles of dying.

478) _____. The Experience of Dying. Englewood Cliffs, N.Y.: Prentice-Hall, 1977.

An in-depth study of the dying process at different stages of life. Examples are taken from clinical reports of caring for the dying. A bibliography is included.

479) Platt, Michael. "Commentary on Asking to Die." Hastings Center Report 5 (December 1975): 9-12.

The account of a young man who was severely burned, and his plea to die. The author discusses "should he be allowed to die?" A videotape describes an interview between the patient and his physician, together with the legal problems they both face.

480) Please Let Me Die. Galveston, Tex.: 30 min. Color. Videocassette. Rental/Sale. Library of Clinical Psychiatric Syndromes; Dr. Robert B. White, Department of Psychiatry, University of Texas Medical Branch (77550).

A twenty-seven-year-old man is interviewed, who wants to be allowed to die as a result of being severely burned and handicapped. His argument for being allowed to die is compelling.

481) "Right to Die - Opinion of Physicians, Church-Men and Press." Literary Digest 120 (November 23 1935): 17.

Can an individual who is racked with pain, who is incurable, choose to die mercifully? The issue is discussed from various viewpoints.

482) Rynearson, E. H. "You Are Standing at the Bedside of a Patient Dying of Untreatable Cancer." CA 9 (May/June 1959): 85-87.

Rynearson is definitely in favor of euthanasia for those patients whose poor "quality of life" indicates it. It is his contention that there is no point in prolonging such a life, and finds support in the fact that no church requires that heroic measures be taken.

483) Sanes, Samuel. A Physician Faces Cancer in Himself. Albany: State University of New York Press, 1979.

Dr. Samuel Sanes, a pathologist, found that he had reticulum cell carcinoma. He lived a little longer than five years after the diagnosis, during which time he wrote a series of articles on which this book is based. He contends that female physicians tend to care for cancer patients better than male physicians, and he emphasizes that physicians have had some failures in caring for cancer patients in that they do not know what the patients need. His message is clear: patients need to know what they have, and what can be expected and predicted. They need support. Sanes advises how physicians can and should communicate with their patients. Dr. Sanes is not only one who knows the body, but he also knows how a cancer patient feels. This book is written from first-hand experience.

484) Sarton, May. A Reckoning. New York: W. W. Norton, 1978.

The death of sixty-year-old Laura Spelman, and her condition of lung cancer are shared in this moving account. She is elated in that she is allowed to have her own death. A moving book about letting go of the non-essentials of life and dying.

485) Scully, Thomas, and Celia Scully. Playing God: The New World of Medical Choices. New York: Simon and Schuster, 1987.

A collaboration by husband and wife, with whom the reader feels an affinity because of their compassion and care for patients and families alike. Their concern is revealed through the subject content of Playing God. One learns how to make choices relative to health care while reading this work: the right choice of physician for one's self and family; building the right relationship with one's physician; patients' rights and how to exercise them; "living will" and the power of attorney; transplantation of human organs; different ways of making babies; dilemmas in treatment and non-treatment; who should be the spokesperson for a child who has a disabling, life-threatening, or terminal illness; making life-and-death decisions for another adult; how to get action when you have been wronged through malpractice and billing fraud. A very important feature of the book is the appendices, which are "packed" with information on bills of rights in most areas of health care. The Scullys state, "The whole purpose of this book is to help you understand the issues and their ethical underpinnings, how to protect yourself, and where to go for help." Having researched many "how to" books, I put this one at the top of my list, and recommend it highly, to be read and digested by all who are interested in the subject of euthanasia. It is well indexed, and would be a handy tool for discussion groups.

486) Schwartzenberg, L., and P. Viansson-Ponte. <u>Changer La Mort</u>. Paris: Albin-Michel, 1977.

A review of the current French views of euthanasia. Cases of active euthanasia are presented. Anyone interested in how the French view euthanasia would profit from this volume.

487) Selzer, Richard. <u>Letters to a Young Doctor</u>. New York: Simon and Schuster, 1982.

In his chapter on "Mercy," page 70, Dr. Selzer gives a vivid description of his involvement in actively participating in the attempted death of a patient by injection, all of which was requested by the patient and family members. A good example of active euthanasia.

488) Slater, E. "Case for Voluntary Euthanasia." <u>Contemporary Review</u> 219 (August 1971): 84-88.

Slater believes that every individual should be allowed to choose between life and death. Human rights, old age, medical ethics, and dying itself are dealt with, along with who should have a right to die, and when. The ultimate responsibility of who is responsible for a patient's death is considered.

489) Snow, Lois Wheeler. <u>A Death With Dignity</u>. New York: Random House, 1974.

This work describes the care, concern, and sensitivity of a Chinese medical team for a journalist during his last days.

490) Steinfels, Peter, and Robert M. Veatch, eds. <u>Death Inside Out</u>. New York: Harper and Row, 1975.

Being the result of a continuing interest in the problems of death and dying, these articles present a clarification of death attitudes during the past eight centuries. They show the change in the relationship of medicine and the dying. The "death with dignity" issue is also discussed. An impressive collection of articles.

491) Stratton, R. W. "Controversial Euthanasia Bill Introduced in Maryland." Hospital Progress 55 (April 1974): 21.

A bill introduced in the Maryland General Assembly by Senator Julian L. Lapides, which would give legal power to an individual's request that no heroic measures be used to prolong his or her life. This bill is opposed by Archbishop Lawrence Cardnal Shehan because it does not make provision for those who have not signed the document.

492) Strauss, Anselm and Barney Glaser. Anguish. California: Sociology, 1970.

A description of the dying trajectory of a patient. Some clear insight into the dying experience of a patient.

493) Strauss, Anselm L. Chronic Illness and The Quality of Life. St. Louis: C. V. Mosby, 1975.

A study on how chronic illness effects the quality of life. The psycho-social aspects of living with chronic illness focuses on the patient and the family. Renal failure and dying in the hospital are discussed, along with how to gather information from such patients in order to better understand their needs. An informative piece of literature.

494) Summer, F. B. "Biologist Reflects on Old Age and Death." Scientific Monthly 61 (August 1945): 143-149.

Summer stresses that a curious fact about old age is that everyone clings to life as long as possible. No one wants to die, and fights for life until the very last.

495) Taylor, Jeremy. The Rule and Exercises of Holy Dying: In Which Are Described the Means and Instruments of Preparing Ourselves and Others Respectfully for a Blessed Death. New York: Arno, 1976.

Written by the chaplain to King Charles I of England, in which he stresses death education and preparation for death. Taylor also proposes suggestions for helping the dying. A historically significant book.

496) The Literature of Death and Dying. New York: Arno, 1977.

The Literature of Death and Dying is a forty-volume collection on the subject of death, the content of which is extremely varied. It deals with the subject from the seventeenth century through the 1960s. Included are anthropological studies, religious essays, suicide, immortality, funerals, and history. Volumes can be ordered separately. More information can be obtained from the publisher.

497) The Mercy Killers. 30 min. B&W. Film/Rental. University of Illinois, Visual Aids Department, n.d.

Physicians, clergymen, and four terminally-ill patients discuss euthanasia.

498) The Right to Die. 56 min. Color. Rental/Sale. EMC No. 9193. University of Michigan: MacMillan Films, 1974.

An ABC-TV documentary presenting a well-done production on actual cases of life prolongation by machines, and suffering patients who want to die. Euthanasia is explored effectively and efficiently.

499) Tordella, Mary A., and James J. Newtens. "An Instrument
to Appraise Attitudes of College Students Toward
Euthanasia." The Journal of School Health (June
1979): 351, 352.

After reviewing literature, no instrument was
found to measure attitudes relative to euthanasia.
These two pages present the purpose, procedures,
and findings relative to such an instrument. The
instrument is an attitude scale--How I Feel About
Euthanasia--with directions both to teachers and
students. It was found to be valid, and capable of
appraising the attitudes of college students.

500) Turpin, Joe P. "Some Psychiatric Issues of Euthanasia."
In Beneficent Euthanasia, ed. Marvin Kohl, 193-203.
Buffalo, N.Y.: Prometheus Books, 1975.

Turpin begins with the assumption that a person
has a right to consent to his or her demise. He
proceeds to discuss important practicalities relative
to the exercise of that right. Informed consent,
competence, and pain are factors which determine
the right of a patient to exercise freedom to die.

501) van den Berg, Jan H. Medical Power and Medical
Ethics. New York: W. W. Norton, 1978.

The brief work comprises 91 pages and was
originally published in The Netherlands. The author
is a psychiatrist and brings into question the
Hippocratic Oath that all human lives must be
saved or prolonged by whatever means available.
The author believes that a new and fundamental
code of ethics should be required because of the
technological advances in the science of medicine.
Although the work is short, the case histories
presented are well worth the reading time.

502) Veatch, Robert M. "Saying 'No' To Hemodialysis: Should A Minor's Decision Be Respected?" Hastings Center Report (September 1974): 8-10.

A case study in bioethics reflecting the attitudes of a 16-year-old girl who underwent transplant surgery. After receiving her father's kidney, it eventually failed to function, resulting in deep depression for both Karen and her parents. A shunt was placed in Karen's arm for dialysis, and soon became infected. It was judged that other transplantations would also fail, and the decision was made by Karen and her parents to discontinue hemodialysis. Two professionals study her case and give some interesting comments. I would encourage those, who may be undergoing serious decisions concerning life-and-death situations confronting teenage children, to read Karen's case.

503) _____. Case Studies in Medical Ethics. Cambridge: Harvard University Press, 1977.

A collection of case studies in the field of bioethics. One hundred and twelve problems in the area of medical ethics are discussed. A case history is presented for each. There are also commentaries on the cases by other parties. The topics covered are: values in health and illness, problems in health care delivery, confidentiality, truth telling, abortions, sterilizations, contraceptives, genetics, transplantations, the allocation of scarce resources, psychiatry and control of human behavior, experimentation of human beings, consent and the right to refuse treatment, and death and dying problems. The book is easy to read, and is a good case book for anyone concerned with ethical problems in the health-care field. Veatch is rated as one of the best, if not the best, in the field of ethics.

504) _____. Death, Dying, and the Biological Revolution: Our Last Quest for Responsibility. New Haven: Yale University Press, 1976.

A well-knit view of developments in ethical and legal aspects regarding the care of dying persons. Veatch deals with topics such as the definition of death, life-prolonging care of the moribund, the patient's right to refuse treatment, and the medical use of bodily parts. Dr. Veatch proposes a statutory definition of death and a bill which would permit the refusal of medical treatment. He believes that legal provision is the best manner in which to handle death and dying issues, and has a mistrusting attitude toward physicians in the matter. He is critical of the ways in which physicians handle the matter of informing the patient who has serious progressive illness. Veatch defends his position very well, and contributes a work worth the reader's attention.

505) Waltzer, Herbert. "People Who Choose to Die." In Is It Moral to Modify Man?, ed. Claude A. Frazier, 102-110. Springfield, Ill.: Charles C. Thomas, 1973.

An excellent discussion on people who choose to die, specifically by suicide. Individuals who succeed, whether conscious or unconscious, are considered. The right to suicide by euthanasia practices is mentioned, but only briefly; however, what is written is thoughtful.

506) Weir, Robert F., ed. Death in Literature. New York: Columbia University Press, 1980.

A rich sampling of stories, poems, and passages about death taken from great literature written over the ages. The inevitability of death; death personified; personal views of the dying; death scenes; children, youth, and death; death by killing; suicide; funeral and burial customs; bereavement; perspectives on immorality; and the death of Ivan Ilych are all combined to make an excellent volume on the subject. The section: Death by Killing, features a poem "To The Mercy Killers," in which one begs for life even though the quality is too poor to continue living--opposition to active euthanasia.

507) Wertenbaker, Lael T. Death of a Man. Toronto: Beacon Press, Boston and Saunders, 1974.

Death of a Man is written about death in the family. Wertenbaker writes about his last 60 days after discovering he had cancer. His wife completed the book.

508) West, Jessamyn. The Woman Said Yes: Encounters With Life and Death. New York: Fawcett Book Group, 1977.

West gives an account of her own fight for life, and supports her sister's desire for death rather than a drug-dominated existence. She also gives an account of assist suicide, whereby she helped her sister commit suicide rather than face a prolonged dying-process resulting from cancer of the bowel.

509) Whiter, Walter. Dissertation on the Disorder of Death: Or, That State of The Frame Under The Signs of Death Called Suspended Animation. New York: Arno, 1976.

A description of resuscitation experiences. Whiter believes that society fails to revive individuals because death, according to popular belief, is inevitable. A good work on the importance of life-prolongation.

510) Williams, Phillip G. The Living Will Source Book. Oak Park, Ill.: The P. Gaines, 1986.

A must for all who are interested in the subject of euthanasia. Dr. Williams has done a thorough work on the "living will." In this book he covers about everything there is to know about living wills. Chapter I defines living will. Chapter 2 lists specific state laws governing execution of a living will. Appendices A and B cover state-mandated living-will forms and instructions, and forms to execute a living will in states with specific natural death laws. A truly helpful work.

511) Williams, Samuel D. "Euthanasia." The Popular Science Monthly 3 (July 1872): 90-96.

This is the sixth article of seven, published by The Speculative Club in 1870, wherein, the author defends the administration of chloroform for the relief of pain. Williams states: "'That in all cases of hopeless and painful illness it should be the recognized duty of the medical attendant, whenever so desired of the patient, to administer chloroform, or such other anaesthetic as may by-and-by supersede chloroform, so as to destroy consciousness at once, and put the sufferer at once to a quick and painless death;   all needful precautions being adopted to prevent any possible abuse of such duty; and means being taken to establish, beyond the possibility of doubt or question, that the remedy was applied at the express wish of the patient.'" He also believes that such action demonstrates respect for the sacredness of life. Other articles and publications are mentioned in order to present opposing views to that of Mr. Williams. Since this article was written in 1870, it is important in that it reveals the thinking of society on the subject of euthanasia at that time. Interesting and highly recommended for reading.

512) Wright, H. T. The Matthew Tree. New York: Pantheon Books, 1975.

The author writes on the death of her father and his last seven years of living with multiple strokes. An example of a "very easy death." Honest and sincere.

Legal Reaction

513) Ahern, Mary. "Biomedical Ethics Committees Confront Prickly Issues." Hospital (August 1984): 66, 68, 70.

Ahern presents the importance of ethics committees and the part they will play as a result of technological advances in the health care field. Causes of interest in ethics committees are shared, together with the role of such committees. Legal cases on ethics committees are listed. All involve withdrawal of life-sustaining equipment, and the terminally ill and/or comatose patient.

514) Allred, V. C. "Euthanasia - Legal Aspects." Linacre Quarterly 14 (April 1947): 1-15.

Legal aspects of euthanasia are treated. Cases explained are: mercy killings, suicide pacts, abortion, and duelling. The legal guild involved in each case is explained. Legal definitions and statutes are quoted. Discussions of natural and divine laws are incorporated.

515) Ayd, F. Jr. "Voluntary Euthanasia: The Right To Be Killed." Medical Counterpoint (June 1970): 12.

Arguments against legalization of euthanasia are presented effectively throughout by Ayd. He is positive that under certain circumstances it is good medicine to withdraw treatment and allow nature to take its course. He also contends that euthanasia is not necessary in light of pain-killing drugs given in large doses.

516) Bandman, Elsie L., and Bertram Bandman, eds. Bioethics and Human Rights. Boston: Little, Brown, 1978.

The volume comprises fifty-two essays by professionals in philosophy, medicine (doctors and nurses), educators, and attorneys. Listed under four topics are: foundations of human rights in health care; the right to life; the right to live as persons and the responsibilities for changing behavior; and health care rights. Opposing views are presented on a number of subjects.

517) Baron, Charles H. "Termination of Life Support Systems in the Elderly." Journal of Geriatric Psychiatry 14 (1981): 45-70.

This discussion was presented at a scientific meeting of The Boston Society for Gerontologic Psychiatry, April 12, 1980. It is a discussion of legal issues surrounding euthanasia and the elderly. A number of cases are presented which give examples of the courts' weaknesses and strengths. Judicial processes are contrasted with medical-ethical decisions.

518) Barry, Robert, Fenella Rouse, Fidel Dovila, and Nancy W. Dickey. "Withholding or Withdrawing Treatment." Journal of The American Medical Association 256 (July 1986): 469-471.

Letters written in opposition to the American Medical Association's (AMA) Council of Ethical and Judicial Affairs, which adopted a stand based on ethical considerations that allows withholding nutrition and fluids from patients under special clinical circumstances.

519) Bartlett, Robert H., Walter M. Whitehouse, Jr., and Jeremiah G. Turcotte, eds. Life Support Systems in Intensive Care. Chicago: Year Book Medical, 1984.

This volume is for practitioners in intensive care. The contributors cover a wide range of professionals from departments of surgery, physiologists, internists, engineers, and physicians who are oriented in biomedical engineering and legal/ethical fields. There are four sections to the book. Section one deals with the monitoring of artificial organs. Sections two and three cover the basic pathophysiology of disease states and organ failure. Section four, "Ethics and Values," written by a physician and a professor of religion, discusses ethical considerations associated with the terminally ill. This section would probably be of the most interest to clergy personnel; however, the material presented would benefit anyone interested in health care.

520) <u>Baylor Law Review</u> 27 (Winter 1975). Symposium Issue on Euthanasia.

The symposium dealt with the following: "Euthanasia: Why No Legislation"; "The Physician's Dilemma: A Doctor's View: What the Law Should Be"; "Death? When Does it Occur?"; "Medical Death"; "Bill of Rights for the Dying Patient"; "Medical Technology as It Exists Today"; "The Family Deals with Death"; "The Living Will, Coping with the Historical Event of Death"; "The Physician's Criminal Liability for the Practice of Euthanasia"; "Euthanasia: The Three-In-One Issue"; "Euthanasia v. The Right to Live"; "Euthanasia, Medical Treatment and the Mongoloid Child: Death as a Treatment of Choice"; and "Death With Dignity: The Physician's Civil Liability."

521) Behnke, John, and Sissela Bok, ed. <u>The Dilemmas of Euthanasia</u>. Garden City, N.Y.: Anchor/Doubleday, 1975.

This paperback incorporates seven chapters dealing with the historical, moral, ethical, legal, and diagnostic aspects of euthanasia. A good work for the general reader. There is enough detail on the subject to inform one quite satisfactorily. Legal and other documents are appended.

522) Bishop's Committee for Pro-Life Activities. <u>Euthanasia: Legislative Packet</u>. 1312 Massachusetts Ave., N.W., Washington, D.C. 20005, n.d.

This packet contains copies of select euthanasia bills which have been introduced into state legislatures during recent years.

523) Brim, Orville G. The Dying Patient. New York: Russell Sage, 1970.

The book focuses on the social context of dying, and discusses the legal, ethical, and economic factors in the termination of life.

524) Cantor, Norman L. "A Patient's Decision to Decline Life-Saving Medical Treatment: Bodily Integrity Versus the Preservation of Life." Rutgers' Law Review 26 (Winter 1972): 228-264.

Pointed out are the arguments of constitutional principles and common law standards which argue for the right to refuse life-saving measures. Other issues discussed are preservation of society, respect for sanctity of life, and third-party protection.

525) Caplan, Arthur L. "Ethical and Policy Issues in the Procurement of Cadaver Organs for Transplantation." New England Journal of Medicine 311 (October 1984): 981-983.

Questions are posed concerning availability, cost, and donors of organ transplantations. A policy of "required request" is discussed, which concerns patients whose situations are hopeless, and that no one on a respirator who might serve as a donor should be declared legally dead until a request for organ donation has been made of any available next of kin or legal proxy.

526) Cohen, Douglas. "To Live or Let Die?" Australian and New Zealand Journal of Surgery 56 (March 1986): 429-432.

This article examines the history of infanticide and some motivating reasons for infanticide. Personhood is discussed relative to abortion and infanticide. Selective non-treatment, such as no surgery, nutrition, fluids, and drugs is mentioned along with legal liability.

527) Colen, B. D. "Premies and Politics." Chap. in Hard Choices. New York: G.P. Putnam's Sons, 1986.

An excellent treatment of infanticide. The author reviews early accounts of killing defective newborns and brings the reader up to date on the latest cases having to do with treating or not treating the defective infant. Discussion of parental responsibility regarding deformed children recalls such cases as "Baby Doe," Roe vs. Wade, and Baby Andrew.

528) Curran, William J. "Defining Appropriate Medical Care: Providing Nutrients and Hydration for the Dying." New England Journal of Medicine 313 (October 1985): 940-942.

Dr. Curran cites different medical-legal cases which relate to nutrition and fluids in terminal patient care. He states that the high court in New Jersey issued a sensible opinion in the Karen Ann Quinlan case, by allowing her parents to use discretion in removing life support from her. However, the court's decision which obligated nursing homes to provide nutrition and water to patients, did not seem wise to him. He further cites the case of Claire Conroy, on whose behalf the court viewed removal of a nasogastric tube to be the same as other medical and nursing treatment. Removal of the tube was found to be proper in all respects. He highlights the case. Curran was encouraged by the court's decision in the Conroy case.

529) Damme, Catherine. "Infanticide: The Worth of an Infant Under Law." Medical History 22 (1978): 1-24.

An examination of medieval values and customs relating to the neonate, and the low status in which the infant was held by society. The position has been institutionalized in English laws, which the American jurisprudential system has inherited, evidenced in Roe v. Wade. Highly recommended for the study of infanticide.

530) "Doctor at the Bar." Newsweek 35 (January 16 1950): 20.

Dr. Herman Sander is accused of administering a fatal injection of air (40cc) into the vein of his cancer patient, Abbie Borroto. At the request of Mr. Borroto, Dr. Sander complied with four injections - 10cc each injection.

531) Dworkin, R. "Death in Context." Indiana Law Journal 48 (Summer 1973): 623-639.

Dworkin discusses brain death in context--that brain death should be defined relative to each individual case rather than a blanket definition.

532) Englehardt, H. Tristram, Jr. "Euthanasia and Children: The Injury of Continued Existence." Journal of Pediatrics 83 (July 1973): 170-171.

A presentation of legal cases which have bearing on the "quality of life" rated below normal. According to the author a person's "quality of life", if below normal, could be used negatively to deny his or her right to live. In this case, vulnerable children are at risk. Englehardt believes that the moral right would bring great pressure to bear on physicians involved.

533) "Euthanasia." Spectator 88 (February 1902): 175-176.

A series of letters putting forth various views on euthanasia. Euthanasia and legislation, and euthanasia and suicide are discussed relative to the Christian ethic.

534) "Euthanasia: A Study in Comparative Criminal Law." University of Pennsylvania Law Review 103 (December 1954): 350-389.

Suicide and mercy killing are discussed, defined, and compared with criminal law.

535) "Euthanasia: No Present Future." Medical World News 14 (March 23 1973): 5-6.

An account of opposing views of a positive euthanasia bill introduced into the state of Oregon's legislature. The views are explained and reveal where legislation relative to euthanasia is headed.

536) Evans, F. J. "Death With Dignity Legislation: It Really Isn't Necessary." Journal of The Florida Medical Association 61 (May 1974): 363-365.

Sets forth the argument that the Florida euthanasia legislative bill would be ineffective. Professional judgement cannot be legislated. Evans emphasizes that the bill is confusing and enhances the chance of malpractice suits.

537) Filbey, E. E., and K. E. Reed. "Some Overtones of Euthanasia." Hospital Topics 43 (September 1965): 55-58.

The different forms of euthanasia are discussed, along with two questions raised: (1) can anyone be justified in deciding when to kill?, and (2) would all the necessary legal machinery further depersonalize the hospital room?

538) Fishbein, M. "When Life Is No Longer Life." Medical World News 15 (March 15, 1974): 84.

Medical, legal, and moral questions have been debated relative to euthanasia by various professionals. In this article, Dr. Fishbein presents case studies and statistics involving the opinions of 250 Chicago internists and surgeons.

539) Fletcher, George P. "Prolonging Life." In Bioethics, ed. Thomas A. Shannon, 189-206. Ramsey, N.J.: Paulist, 1976.

A legal analysis of the problem of a physician's decision not to prolong a terminally-ill patient's life. Focus centers on the relationship of the physician and patient. Fletcher examines the ethical relationship of the two. As an Assistant Professor of Law at the University of Washington, Fletcher is found to be qualified to write on the subject from a legal point of view.

540) Flew, A. "The Principle of Euthanasia." In Euthanasia and the Right to Die. A. B. Downing, ed. New York: Humanities, 1970.

In defense of a legal right to voluntary euthanasia. The author believes that one's freedom is curtailed by legislating against a person's right to voluntary euthanasia.

541) Freund, Paul A. "Organ Transplants: Ethical and Legal Problems." In Ethics in Medicine: Historical Perspectives and Contemporary Concerns, ed. Stanley Joel Reiser, Arthur J. Dyck, and William J. Curran, 173-177. Cambridge, Mass.: MIT, 1977.

Freund discusses problems concerning the allocation of resources--from whom they should come and to whom organs should be transferred. Implications raised by the questions concern moral, legal, and medical considerations. Each differs on removal of organs after death and during life. He briefly discusses the question of whether or not a dying patient should be allowed to consent to surgical intervention for the purpose of saving another's life, which borders on euthanasia practices.

542) Fried, Charles. "Terminating Life Support: Out of the Closet." New England Journal of Medicine 295 (August 12, 1976): 390, 391.

An attorney comments on the publicity given to changing attitudes of hospital administrators who promulgate and discuss, openly, policies about deliberate withdrawal or non-application of life-prolonging measures.

543) Goldberg, J. H. "The Dying Patient: Tackling the New Ethical and Legal Questions." Hospital Physician 36 (June 1968): 41-45.

Because of new medical techniques, Goldberg stresses the importance of new death definitions. The age of transplants requires such. Doctors should be given more freedom in forming opinions, and allowed to implement them, depending on each case.

544) Gould, J., and Lord Craigmyle. Your Death Warrant? New Rochelle, New York: Arlington House, 1971.

A history of euthanasia legislation in England, and arguments against such laws.

545) Gregg, W. W. "Right to Kill." North American Review 237 (March 1934): 239-249.

Active and passive euthanasia are discussed, along with abortion, infanticide, and capital punishment. An analysis of legal and moral implications is offered.

546) Guideline for Consent: The Uniform Anatomical Gift Act. New York, N.Y.: 15 min. B&W, 3/4" Videocassette. 15 Columbus Circle (10023).

A National Continuing Medical Education tape dealing with medical and legal aspects of transplantation. For subscribers' use only.

547) Hall, William T. "Legalized Suicide." Delaware State Medical Journal 40 (February 1968): 50-51.

Dr. Hall's conclusion--after discussing the process of dying with his family and patients--is that they would approve of legalized suicide.

548) Halley, M. and W. Harvey. "Medical vs. Legal Definitions of Death." Journal of The American Medical Association 204 (May 6, 1968): 423-425.

A discussion of both legal and medical definitions of death. Physicians and lawyers are appealed to in order to arrive at a reasonable criteria for death.

549) Harvard, J. D. J. "Legal Regulation of Medical Practice - Decisions of Life and Death: A Discussion Paper." Journal of The Royal Society of Medicine 75 (May 1982): 351-355.

An examination of the reasons why the medical profession has serious doubts about the role of Anglo-Saxon law regulating certain decisions which doctors have to make in the course of medical practice. The paper discusses legal protection of the child between implantation of the fertilized ovum through the completion of the birth process. Life-threatening abnormalities are presented as a problem now that technological advances have been made which increase the ability to keep such infants alive. The author shows throughout the discussion that Anglo-Saxon law has not been impressive in its ability to keep pace with technological developments in medical science.

550) Harwood, Ann L., ed. Cardiopulmonary Resuscitation. Baltimore and London: Williams and Wilkins, 1982.

Topics for discussion include: ventilation during cardiopulmonary resuscitation; perfusion in cardiopulmonary cardiac arrest; pharmacology of resuscitation; defibrillation; pre-hospital management of cardiac arrest; pediatric resuscitation; liability aspects of cardiopulmonary resuscitation and emergency cardiac care; and traumatic cardiac arrest.

551) Heifetz, Milton D. and Charles Mangel. The Right to Die: A Neurosurgeon Speaks of Death with Candor. New York: Putnam's Sons, 1975.

A discussion of the euthanasia controversy by a physician. Heifetz contends for the right of the patient to die, dealing with the legal and ethical aspects of euthanasia.

552) Holder, Angela Roddey. Legal Issues in Pediatrics and Adolescent Medicine. New York: Wiley, 1977.

A handbook for the physician who is interested in combating those who are opposed to his rights as he operates within the confines of the medical profession. Holder identifies many legal issues confronting pediatricians, neonatologists, and others who treat minors. Among the problems she discusses are genetic counselling, genetic screening, fetal research, and the physician's liability to treat deformed newborns. Discussion of allowing the malformed infant to die is presented with the fact that it cannot be swept under the rug, but must be openly addressed. Moral issues are also treated which pediatricians are faced with as they must come to terms with the question of whether to treat or not to treat severely deformed infants.

553) Horan, Dennis J., and David Mall, eds. Death, Dying and Euthanasia. Washington, D.C.: University Publications of America, 1977.

Controversial aspects of euthanasia are discussed, such as: involuntary euthanasia of the defective newborn; ethical, moral, and legal aspects of "mercy killing"; the feasibility of legalized euthanasia; and the right of the individual to reject treatment.

554) Humber, James and Robert F. Almeder, eds. Biomedical Ethics and The Law. New York: Plenum, 1976.

This work covers social problems brought about by the revolution of medical technology, such as: abortion mental illness, human experimentation, NIH guidelines on research with human subjects, human genetics, and dying. Capron and Katz have a thoughtful discussion on definitions of death, (see Citation 282).

555) Humphrey, Derek, and Ann Wickett. "Significant Developments Late 1970s to 1985." Chap. in The Right to Die. New York: Harper and Row, 1986.

A discussion of the Karen Ann Quinlan case, "living wills", and NDRs (Natural Death Acts) of the United States. Also included is a checklist chart of 36 living-will laws enacted between 1976 and 1985 which legally recognize the individual's right to die with dignity. One will find this chapter very informative.

556) In The Matter of Karen Quinlan. Vol. I, Washington, D.C.: University Publications of America, Inc., 1977.

An integration of all the legal briefs, court proceedings, and decisions in the Superior Court of New Jersey. A helpful volume for those pursuing legal issues in euthanasia.

557) Jackson, E. "Is Euthanasia Christian?" Christian Century 67 (March 8, 1950): 300-301.

This article is divided into three parts: medical, theological, and legal. Each of these aspects are discussed relative to Christianity.

558) Katz, Jay, and Alexander Morgan Capron. Catastrophic
Diseases: Who Decides What? New York: Russell Sage
Foundation, 1975.

Two law professors, one of whom is a psychiatrist (Jay Katz), write on catastrophic diseases (a
catastrophic disease is a disease for which expensive and unusual equipment must be made available
for treatment, and which can sustain life for a
period of time), and goals and values proposed to
treat such diseases. A brief account is given of
the state of the art of hemodialysis and organ
transplantation. The definition of death, and the
right to refuse life-sustaining treatment are examined thoroughly with reference to legal problems
which surround the issues. The work is scholarly,
and merits extensive readership, especially among
those who want to know who will be making decisions on the future use of equipment for those who
are less fortunate than most of us.

559) Karnofsky, David A. "Treating Incurables." Science Newsletter 80 (November 4, 1961): 300.

Dr. Karnofsky states that the doctor's responsibility is to keep the patient living as long as
possible. Not only is the physician responsible
medically, but also legally.

560) Kohl, Marvin, ed. Infanticide and the Value of Life.
Buffalo, N.Y.: Prometheus Books, 1978.

Examined are the religious, medical, legal, and
ethical issues surrounding infanticide. Familiar
personalities writing are: Joseph Fletcher, Arval A.
Morris, Glanville Williams, Joseph Margolis, Richard
Brandt, Peter Black, Immanuel Jababovits, and
Leonard Weber. Indexed, with bibliography.

561) Lamb, David. Death, Brain Death and Ethics. Albany: State University of New York Press, 1985.

"What is considered so essential to human life, such, that when it is lost we consider the individual dead?" This question sets one's thinking for the author's discussion on death, the brain, and ethics. A series of lectures inquiring into what death is relative to the brain. Lamb's thesis is that death of the brain stem is death of the individual organism. He provides a philosophical framework for criteria for determining death. The book is well written, up to date, and more philosophical than practical. Good for anyone looking for a definition of death.

562) Lantos, John. "Baby Doe Five Years Later." New England Journal of Medicine 317 (August 1987): 444-447.

The author reviews the unfortunate case of Baby Doe and the Supreme Court decision legalizing abortion. For additional reference see "The Story of Baby Doe." New England Journal of Medicine 309 (1983):644.

563) Legislative Manual 1977. New York: The Society for the Right to Die, 1978.

Legislative activity on the "right to die" in 1977. Includes eight new laws with a commentary on each, and gives a chart of 1977's bills in 47 states. Good for legal reference.

564) Levisohn, A. A. "Voluntary Mercy Deaths." Journal of Forensic Medicine 8 (April/June 1961): 57-79.

This article is pro-euthanasia. Court cases are cited throughout. Legal language about murder is analyzed. Levisohn states that relative to euthanasia there are laws which deal with other areas in technology, but none for medicine. He feels that laws should be made to deal specifically with doctors who want to practice euthanasia--laws to help them in their decision making. The author believes that the anti-euthanasia view is religious in nature and, therefore, should not be written into law.

565) "License to Live." Christianity Today 18 (July 1974): 22-23.

An editorial warning against the acceptance of legalized abortion in that it would result in forced sterilization, passive euthanasia, and eventually active euthanasia. An alarm for Christians to speak out in opposition.

566) Lo, Bernard. "The Death of Clarence Herbert: Withdrawing Care Is Not Murder." Annals of Internal Medicine 101 (August 1984): 248251.

Discussion of a case where two physicians were charged with murder of a comatose patient for discontinuing a ventilating machine and intravenous fluids.

567) "The Case of Claire Conroy: Will Administrative Review Safeguard Incompetent Patients?" Annals of Internal Medicine 104 (June 1986): 869-73.

A review by the New Jersey Supreme Court in the case of Claire Conroy, who was an 84-year-old resident of a nursing home, and an incompetent. A review of ordinary and extraordinary treatment.

568) Lynn, Joanne, ed. By No Extraordinary Means: The Choice to Forgo Life-Sustaining Food and Water. Bloomington: Indiana University Press, 1986.

The authors present the medical, moral, ethical, social, and legal perspectives of the nutrition and hydration issue. Situations discussed have to do with the newborn, terminally ill, unconscious persons (permanently), and the chronically ill but not terminal patient who has decided to refuse food and water. This collection of papers was prepared for the Society for Health and Human Values and should be purchased by all who are interested in the subject because it compiles the views of different authors.

569) Maguire, Daniel C. "A Catholic View of Mercy Killing." In Beneficent Euthanasia, ed. Marvin Kohl, 34-43. Buffalo, N.Y.: Prometheus Books, 1975.

Maguire's position is that in a medical context, it may be moral and should be legal to speed up the death process by active euthanasia through overdose of drugs, etc., and that the use of extraordinary means is optional. He attempts to justify his position by showing that it is relatively in line with historical Catholic ethical theory.

570) McHugh, James T., ed. Death, Dying and The Law. Huntington, Ind.: Our Sunday Visitor, Inc., and Bishop's Committee for Pro-Life Activities, National Conference of Catholic Bishops, 1976.

Helps people to understand how to make decisions respecting life-and-death situations in terms of the Gospel and Christian-moral principals. Stresses how respect for life should be protected by the law. It also sets forth how the dying patient and family members may be assisted by the medical and nursing professions. A listing of films on the subject is also provided.

571) "Make It Legal." Time 48 (November 18, 1946): 70.

An attempt by Dr. Robert Latou Dickinson was made to have euthanasia legalized. The public's reaction is recorded in this article--furious!

572) Matheson, J. C. M. "Infanticide." Medico-Legal and Criminological Review 9 (July 1941): 135-152.

A look at medical questions involving infanticide. Also presents several case histories of abortions.

573) Medicine, Morality and The Law: Euthanasia. 30 min.
B&W. Rental/Sale. University of Michigan T.V.
Center, n.d.

A panel discussion of the legal and moral aspects of three case studies on the subject of
euthanasia.

574) Meier, Levi, ed. Jewish Values in Bioethics. New York:
Human Sciences, 1986.

A collection of addresses on biomedical issues
echoing the voices of many Jewish authorities:
Orthodox and Conservative; legal and philosophical;
medical and literary; and wrestles with modern
dilemmas in the health care field.

575) Meyers, David W. "The Legal Aspects of Medical
Euthanasia." Bioscience 23 (August 1973): 467-470.

The term "euthanasia" is analyzed and defined.
A discussion of withholding treatment and the
termination of ordinary medical treatment is
presented. Extraordinary means of keeping a patient alive is also part of the discussion

576) _____. "Legal Aspects of Withdrawing Nourishment From an Incurably Ill Patient." Archives of
Internal Medicine 145 (January 1985): 125-128.

A well-thought-through discussion presenting
a list of arguments for and against the practice, with
a number of court cases decided to date (the time of
the article's publication).

577) Milbauer, Barbra and Bert N. Oberentz. The Law
Giveth: Legal Aspects of the Abortion Controversy.
Atheneum, N.Y.: McClelland and Stewart Ltd., 1983.

The facts on abortion are well summarized in
this book. The reader is taken on a journey through
case law and pertinent American history. Social,
medical, religious, and moral aspects of the abortion

debate are discussed. The book assists greatly in helping to understand abortion in our time. The bearing of the book on euthanasia is simply this: if abortion is allowed to be performed on the healthy unborn, the "green light" for aborting the deformed is certainly a permissive sign.

578) Milunsky, Aubrey and George J. Annas, eds. Genetics and The Law. New York: Plenum, 1976.

In this book, a distinguished faculty of scientists, physicians, lawyers, and ethicists explore the major issues in modern genetics which confront the law. Topics discussed are: the legal rights of the fetus; the xyy controversy; law and pre-natal diagnosis of hereditary disorders; informed-consent requirements in genetic counselling; legal implications of genetic screening; legal aspects of artificial insemination; sterilization of the mentally handicapped; malpractice risks in genetic counselling; and governmental and social restriction of experiments involving gene manipulation, cloning, and in vitro fertilization. A thorough discussion of the medical and legal aspects of the non treatment of defective newborns is set forth. This book is a must for all professionals and anyone concerned about the effects of genetics on society.

579) Montange, Charles H. "Informed Consent and The Dying Patient." Yale Law Journal 83 (July 1974): 1632-1664.

An article which indeed stresses the importance of informed consent. The author emphasizes that if the patient has a right to consent, he also has a right to refuse, if he is competent to do so. The courts should recognize the right of the patient to forego treatment. Keeping this in mind, the courts should establish proper tests for competency through mitigation.

580) Mueller, Daniel Mark. "Involuntary Passive Euthanasia of Brain-Stem-Damaged Patients: The Need for Legislation - An Analysis and A Proposal." San Diego Law Review 14 (July 1977): 1277-1297.

Mueller points out the deficiency of physician guides to terminate treatment of brain-stem-damaged patients. Medical practices and maintaining or withdrawing treatment are examined regarding such patients. A proposal is introduced which would legalize withholding treatment from brainstem-damaged patients.

581) Munkithick, R. K. "Bill to Kill: Poem." Harper's Weekly 50 (May 19 1906): 709.

In the legal vein, a poem is injected, which ends in the words: "Tis very rough/And quite enough/To kill the bill to kill."

582) Nelson, Leonard J., ed. The Death Decision. Ann Arbor, Mich.: Servant Books, 1984.

A collection of essays from the Fourth Annual Christianity and Law Seminar presented November 11-13, 1982 at the City of Faith Continuing Education Center in Tulsa, Oklahoma, sponsored by the O. W. Coburn School of Law of Oral Roberts University. The contributors are composed of such men as Harold O. J. Brown, John Eidsmore, Leonard J. Nelson III, John T. Noonan, Walter Probert, Charles E. Rice, Peter J. Riga, and George Huntston Williams. The above experts address the legal and ethical issues emerging on the frontier of today's new biology, including abortion, euthanasia, treatment of newborns, genetic screening, bioengineering, and reproductive techniques. "Who decides when it's time for someone to die?" is what the book is all about. A book which presents the Christian stand on important issues.

583) Novak, Nina. "Natural Death Acts Let Patients Refuse Treatment." Hospital (August 1984): 71-73.

The piece defines NDAs (natural death acts) as being statutes enacted by a state legislature which allow the creation of documents that provide a legally recognized way for competent adults to express in advance, their desires regarding life-crucial medical decisions, in the event they become terminal and death is imminent. Difficult questions arising under NDAs are dealt with, and those states which have NDAs are identified by a graph.

584) Oden, Thomas C. Should Treatment Be Terminated? Moral Guidelines for Christian Families and Pastors. New York: Harper and Row, 1976.

Arguments which favor and oppose ending treatment of the terminally ill are addressed, along with problems having to do with truth-telling, organ donation, home care, and legal limits. Disagreements between families and physicians are discussed, with other issues such as "living wills," and refusal of medical treatment.

585) Paris, John J., and Frank E. Reardon. "Court Responses to Withholding or Withdrawing Artificial Nutrition and Fluids." Journal of The American Medical Association 253 (April 1945): 2243-2245.

A presentation and review of different court cases and decisions which effect health care personnel who withhold artificial nutrition and fluids from terminally ill and comatose patients.

586) Platt, Michael. "Commentary on Asking to Die." Hastings Center Report 5 (December 1975): 9-12.

The account of a young man who was severely burned, and his plea to die. The author discusses "should he be allowed to die?" A videotape describes an interview between the patient and his physician, together with the legal problems they both face.

587) Portwood, Doris. Common-Sense Suicide. New York: Dodd-Mead, 1978.

Portwood puts forward straight facts in defense of what she terms "rational" suicide. She calls for the legalization of suicide for those who are in a pitiable state of health. Those who are in favor of her argument would indeed feel comfortable while reading her book.

588) President's Commission for the Study of Ethical Problems in Medicine and Biomedical and Behavioral Research. Defining Death: A Report on the Medical, Legal and Ethical Issues in the Determination of Death. Washington, D.C.: U.S. Government Printing Office, 1984.

This is a report to the President on the "definition" of death, and a recommendation of a statute by Congress to provide a clear and socially accepted basis for making determinations of death. Chapter one deals with the question, "Why 'update' death?" Chapter two presents the 'state of the art' in medicine. 'Understanding the meaning of death' is the topic of chapter three. "Who ought to define death?" is answered in chapter four, and chapter five inquires, "What 'definition' ought to be adopted?" The book is a must for professionals.

589) Rachels, James. "Active and Passive Euthanasia." New England Journal of Medicine 292 (January 1975): 78-80.

Dr. Rachels takes issue with the conventional view that there is a difference between active euthanasia and passive euthanasia. He challenges the doctrine for several reasons: (1) active euthanasia in many cases is more humane than passive euthanasia, (2) the conventional doctrine leads to decisions concerning life and death on irrelevant grounds, (3) the doctrine rests on a distinction between killing and letting die and that in itself has no moral importance and (4) the most common arguments favoring the doctrine are invalid. The doctor illustrates his arguments by presenting some hypothetical cases of actively taking part in the deaths of individuals, and passively standing by and allowing someone to die. He concludes in the article above: "So, whereas doctors may have to discriminate between active and passive euthanasia to satisfy law, they should not do any more than that. In particular, they should not give the distinction any added authority and weight by writing it into official statements of medical ethics."

590) Ramsey, Paul. Ethics at the Edge of Life: Medical and Legal Interactions. New Haven, Conn.: Yale University Press, 1978.

A serious study of the medical, legal and moral issues which come together in a depressing society. Ramsey, one of the more conservative theologians and ethicists of the present, addresses moral issues at the "first of life." These issues involve the Supreme Court decision regarding a Missouri statute which regulates abortion. The last six chapters which address the "last of life" discuss "dying well enough," the care of infants, and the Quinlan case, followed by a study of treatment withdrawn from a mentally incompetent man. Throughout Ramsey's study, discouragement and distress is obvious due to the fact that he sees very little hope in society's attempt to better the situation, i.e., take a stand against the low respect and regard for life. Those who share Ramsey's views will be encouraged to know that there are still those who stand in the gap for human dignity and right to life.

591) Reilly, Philip. Genetics, Law, and Social Policy. Cambridge, Mass.: Harvard University Press, 1977.

Reilly succeeds in pulling together material in the broad and diverse areas of genetics, law, and policy making. Section one of the book deals with human genetics and technology, with commentary on legal ramifications. Genetic legislation is discussed in section two, and provides comprehensive treatment of genetic screening legislation and its future. Reilly favors that genetic screening be modeled after the law passed by the State of Maryland, in which a Commission on Hereditary Diseases was created. Important issues on applied human genetics, and advances in reproductive technology are raised in section three. For those interested in how laws on human genetics in the present and future are being affected, the book is recommended.

592) Reiser, Stanley Joel, Arthur J. Dyck, and William J. Curran, eds. Ethics in Medicine: Historical Perspectives and Contemporary Concerns. Cambridge, Mass.: MIT, 1977.

This text was developed while teaching graduate and undergraduate courses at Harvard University. It is practical for practitioners and students in medicine, law, ethics, counselling, and for individual patients and groups who are concerned with medical care. The volume is separated into eight sections: (1) Ethical Dimensions of the Physician-Patient Relationship, (2) Moral Basis of Medical Ethics, (3) Regulation, Compulsion, and Consumer Protection in Clinical Medicine and Public Health, (4) Truth-Telling in the Physician-Patient Relationship, (5) Medical Experimentation on Human Subjects, (6) Procreative Decisions, (7) Suffering and Dying, and (8) Rights and Priorities in the Provision of Medical Care. Each section contains articles, essays, and class lectures. An excellent textbook.

593) Reverence For Life--Father John Powell. Allen, Tex.: 90 min., (30 min. each part), color, $94.50 with study guide, Video VHS or Beta; Argus Communications, P.O. Box 7000, One DLM Park (75002).

An expose on the historical and present day attempt to destroy our reverence for life. He describes the legal and medical efforts to replace it with the pragmatic "Quality of Life" ethic. He projects the consequences if we fail to stand up now and be counted for life. Part I: Reenactment of the Nazi Nightmare; Part II: Contemporary American Scene; Part III: Challenge to Conviction: The Call to Action.

594) Robertson, John A., and Norman Fost. "Passive Euthanasia of Defective Newborn Infants: Legal Considerations." The Journal of Pediatrics 88 (May 1976): 883-889.

The reason for this article is to consider legal ramifications in light of the fact that little mention has been made in reports of passive euthanasia of defective infants. The authors feel that parents, physicians, nurses, and administrators are liable on several grounds; homicide by omission, child neglect, and failure to report child neglect. Increasing publicity of passive euthanasia practices is thought to increase the probability of prosecution. The appeal of this writing is to persuade open discussion and debate to change existing laws, not to try and subvert them through private action. Two alternative policies are described: (1) establishment of criteria for a class of infants who can be allowed to die, and (2) a better process of decision making. Their conclusion is that a commitment to process would be preferable.

595) Rosner, Fred and J. David Bleich, ed. "Organ Transplantation." In Jewish Bioethics. New York: Sanhedrin, 1979.

Two chapters dealing with organ transplantation reveals Jewish thinking on the subject: "What is the Halakhah for Organ Transplants?" and "Organ Transplantation in Jewish Law." The first mentioned chapter administer a treatment which will, if it fails, kill him immediately, but, if it succeeds, prolong his life?" The other chapter deals with theological, moral, ethical, social, legal, and philosophical problems surrounding heart transplantation; the halakhah in eye transplants; the halakhah in kidney transplants; and the halakhah in heart transplants. Each of these chapters has bearing on euthanasia--at least in the Jewish view.

596) Rosner, Fred. "Withholding Therapy and Anti-Cruelty Policies." Annals of Internal Medicine 105 (September 1986): 468-469.

A comment by Dr. Rosner on the New Jersey Supreme Court decision in the case of Claire Conroy--that all involved in the case of a patient are obligated to provide care, including psychological and supportive care.

597) Russell, Ruth O. Freedom to Die: Moral and Legal Aspects of Euthanasia. New York: Human Sciences, 1975.

An articulate presentation of a pro-euthanasia view. The author leaves the impression that those in antiquity who held anti-euthanasia views were superstitious and religiously inflexible. On page 283, she writes: "It seems certain that it is only a matter of time until laws will be passed that will permit the administration of painless death when the only alternative is an agonizing or meaningless existence. It is a challenge to every citizen to hasten that day." The author won the Humanist Pioneer Award as a result of this work.

598) Sackett, W. W., Jr. "Death with Dignity." Medical Opinion and Review 5 (June 1969): 25-31.

Proposal by a member of the Florida House of Representatives to amend to the Florida constitution the right to die with dignity. In the bill, he pointed out the difference between the ability to keep patients alive, and the skills sufficient for making their lives meaningful and useful.

599) Steinfels, Peter, and Robert M. Veatch, eds. Death Inside Out. New York: Harper and Row, 1975.

Being the result of a continuing interest in the problems of death and dying, these articles present a clarification of death attitudes during the past eight centuries. They show the change in the relationship of medicine and the dying. The "death with dignity" issue is also discussed. An impressive collection of articles.

600) Stratton, R. W. "Controversial Euthanasia Bill Introduced in Maryland." Hospital Progress 55 (April 1974): 21.

A bill introduced in the Maryland General Assembly by Senator Julian L. Lapides, which would give legal power to an individual's request that no heroic measures be used to prolong his or her life. The bill is opposed by Archbishop Lawrence Cardinal Shehan because it does not make provision for those who have not signed the document.

601) Suffolk University Law Review 11 (Spring 1977): 919-973. Three addresses on mental incompetents and the right to die.

Jones v. Saikewicz, No. 711 (Mass., Sup. Jud. Ct., July 6, 1976) is discussed. A retarded man who was dying from leukemia was denied life-prolonging chemotherapy. Substituted consent, hospital ethics committees, the courts, and the patient's right to life are reviewed.

602) Tedeschi, G. "On Tort Liability for 'Wrongful Life'." ISR (Israel Law Review) 1 (1966): 513.

The article centers around the idea that certain circumstances of a patient's existence could be a misdeed or injury to the patient.

603) Temkin, Owsei, William K. Frankena, and Sanford H. Kadish. Respect for Life in Medicine, Philosophy, and the Law. Baltimore: The Johns Hopkins University Press, 1976.

Respect for life is approached from different perspectives which shed light on the subject in different ways. Temkin discusses the history of medicine and how early medicine understood respect for life. The philosophical approach by William Frankena interprets respect for life and how moral philosophy should define it. Kadish presents how the law treats different cases of taking human life. Euthanasia, abortion, infanticide, and other means of taking life are interwoven throughout the book.

604) The Right to Die. Chatsworth, Calif.: Filmstrip and Audiocassette. Sale. Career Aids Inc., 20417 Nord-hoss (91311).

A discussion on the moral, legal, and practical implications of life-extending technology.

605) U.S. House of Representatives. Discursive Dictionary of Health Care. Washington, D.C.: Prepared by the staff for the use of the Subcommittee on Health and the Environment of The Committee on Interstate and Foreign Commerce. U.S. Government Printing Office, 1976.

This dictionary was prepared for legislators and the public due to unfamiliar terms which have become part of the National Health Insurance debate. The work defines such terms as "audit,"; "peer review,"; "third party,"; "kitting,"; "me-to-drug,"; and "ping-ponging" (the practice of passing a patient from one physician to another for the purpose of spreading out health care business--for unnecessary examinations and tests). Many terms used throughout this dictionary would be beneficial to those who are involved in counselling situations. A great help for $2.40 from the Government Printing Office.

606) Veatch, Robert M. Death, Dying, and the Biological
Revolution: Our Last Quest for Responsibility. New
Haven: Yale University Press, 1976.

A well-knit view of developments in ethical
and legal aspects regarding the care of dying
persons. He deals with topics such as the definition
of death, life-prolonging care of the moribund, the
patient's right to refuse treatment, and the medical
use of bodily parts. Dr. Veatch proposes a statutory
definition of death, and a bill which would permit
the refusal of medical treatment. He believes that
legal provision is the best manner in which to
handle death and dying issues, and has a mistrusting
attitude toward physicians in the matter. He is
critical of the ways in which physicians handle the
matter of informing the patient who has serious
progressive illness. Veatch defends his position very
skillfuly, and contributes a work worth the reader's
attention.

607) Walker, Earl A., ed. Cerebral Death. Baltimore: Urban
and Schwarzenberg, 1985.

The author served on the President's Committee to evaluate guidelines for the determination of
death. He is a neurosurgeon, and in this work he
attempts to define brain death. Walker reviews the
history of brain death (medical views of brain
death), and the reaction of medical professions
throughout the world to brain death definition,
along with religious reaction. Legal problems which
present themselves in brain death situations are also
discussed.

608) Wallace, Samuel E., and Albin Eser, eds. Suicide and
Euthanasia. Knoxville: The University of Tennessee Press, 1981.

An edited work by a professor of sociology at
the University of Tennessee and a professor of
criminal and comparative law at the University of
Tubingen in West Germany. The essays address a

wide variety of issues related to suicide and euthanasia: social suicide, suicide among cancer patients, defending suicide, the right to live and the right to die, voluntary euthanasia, "sanctity" and "quality" of life in a historical-comparative view, and legal structure of the "living will." Collectively, the essays apply a variety of perspectives on unexplored areas relating to the study of death. The book provides a very helpful bibliography citing works which directly relate suicide and euthanasia, and is highly recommended.

609) Wecht, Cyril H., ed. Legal Medicine. Philadelphia: W.B. Saunders, 1982.

   While the book covers many areas in legal medicine by different authors, the one entitled "Death: Defining and Determining" by a physician and attorney, Dr. McCarthy DeMere, is excellent. Its fifteen pages chronicle an eight year battle between The American Bar Association, The American Medical Association, and The National Conference of Commissioners on Uniform State Laws, out of which came a compromise on a death definition--the Uniform Determination of Death Act. For those interested in the question, "When is one really dead?", this article is most appropriate.

610) Whitelaw, Andrew. "Death as Option in Neonatal Intensive Care." Lancet 8502 (August 1986):328-331.

   According to Whitelaw, many physicians believe there are circumstances in which infants should be allowed to die without having their lives prolonged. He mentions that seventy-five infants were so seriously ill that withdrawal of treatment was considered. Criteria for withdrawal of treatment from a particular infant had to be based on certainty of total incapacity and a unanimous decision among the nursing staff caring for the child. Treatment was withdrawn from fifty-one of the seventy-five patients. The parents of forty-seven infants accepted the decision, and all the infants died. Parents of four chose continued intensive care, and two infants survived with disabilities. Treatment of twenty-four cases was continued. Seventeen survived and seven died. Agreement was unanimous among staff and parents that treatment should be withdrawn, and that treatment on purely legal grounds is not justifiable.

611) "Who Should Decide? The Case of Karen Quinlan." Christianity and Crisis 35 (January 1976): 322-331.

Robert Veatch, the distinguished ethicist, along with others, comments on the Quinlan case and its disposition. For the most part, they are opposed to the decision. They are reluctant in allowing the medical profession to decide such issues.

612) Who Should Survive? Berkeley, Calif.: 26 min., color. Rental/Sale, Joseph P. Kennedy Foundation. Media Center, University Extension, University of California (94720).

Issues surround a mongoloid infant who is allowed to die. Experts discuss the legal, scientific, and ethical aspects of the case. For those who want to explore this aspect of euthanasia.

613) Wilson, Jerry B. Death By Decision: The Medical, Moral, and Legal Dilemmas of Euthanasia. Philadelphia: Western, 1975.

An attempt to shed light on the euthanasia debate. A well organized study of the subject which traces ancient practices of euthanasia to the present day. The author examines the medical, moral, and legal aspects of the subject, and presents pros and cons on its different forms. He has a tendency to support limited practices of euthanasia. The book is easy to read, and has an extensive bibliography.

614) Williams, Phillip G. The Living Will Source Book. Oak Park, Ill.: P. Gaines, 1986.

A must for all who are interested in the subject of euthanasia. Dr. Williams has done a thorough work on the "living will." In this book he covers about everything there is to know about living wills. Chapter I defines living will. Chapter 2 lists specific state laws governing execution of a living will. Appendices A and B cover state-mandated living-will forms and instructions, and forms to execute a living will in states with specific natural death laws. A truly helpful work.

Medical Reaction

615) Ahern, Mary. "Biomedical Ethics Committees Confront Prickly Issues." Hospital (August 1984): 66, 68, 70.

Ahern presents the importance of ethics committees and the part they will play as a result of technological advances in the health care field. Causes of interest in the role of such committees. Legal cases on ethics committees are listed. All involve withdrawal of life-sustaining equipment, and the terminally ill and/or comatose patient.

616) Alexander, L. "Medical Science Under Dictatorship." New England Journal of Medicine 241 (July 1949): 39-47.

An analysis of Nazi medicine and its evils. An expression of wonder as to how doctors and others could condone such practice--a practice which is nothing short of cold-blooded murder. Alexander believes that the Nazi view of life, and its disrespect for life no matter what the "quality," is a logical step toward euthanasia.

617) Amulree, Lord, et. al. On Dying Well: An Anglican Contribution To The Debate On Euthanasia. London: Church Information Office, 1975.

Euthanasia from the Anglican point of view. Argues against voluntary euthanasia, and emphasizes care and compassion for the dying person. Focuses on good quality terminal care. Moral, legal, and theological aspects are considered. A commendable work, well done by a distinguished working party from the field of medicine and theology.

618) Aring, C. D. "Intimations of Mortality." Annals of Internal Medicine 69 (July 1968): 137-152.

On death and its different aspects, and how it is dealt with by physicians. Because of the fact that doctors are, or seem to be, fearful of death, and feel that dying persons are something less than human, the author appeals to doctors for more sensitivity when dealing with the dying. The dignity of man is stressed throughout the article.

619) Ayd, F. Jr. "Voluntary Euthanasia: The Right To Be Killed." Medical Counterpoint (June 1970): 12.

Arguments against legalization of euthanasia are presented effectively. Under certain circumstances, he believes it is good medicine to withdraw treatment and allow nature to take its course. He also contends that euthanasia is not necessary in light of pain-killing drugs given in large doses.

620) Bandman, Elsie L., and Bertram Bandman, eds. Bioethics and Human Rights. Boston: Little, Brown, 1978.

The volume comprises fifty-two essays by professionals in philosophy, medicine (doctors and nurses), educators, and attorneys. Listed under four topics are: foundations of human rights in health care, the right to life; the right to live as persons and the responsibilities for changing behavior; and health care rights. Opposing views are presented on a number of subjects.

621) Barry, Robert, Fenella Rouse, Fidel Dovila, and Nancy W. Dickey. "Withholding or Withdrawing Treatment." Journal of The American Medical Association 256 (July 1986): 469-471.

Letters written in opposition to the American Medical Association's (AMA) Council of Ethical and Judicial Affairs, which adopted a stand based on ethical considerations that allows withholding nutrition and fluids from patients under special clinical circumstances.

622) Bartlett, Robert H., Walter M. Whitehouse, Jr., and Jeremiah G. Turcotte, eds. Life Support Systems in Intensive Care. Chicago: Year Book Medical, 1984.

This volume is for practitioners in "intensive care." The contributors cover a wide range of professionals from departments of surgery, physiologists, internists, engineers, and physicians who are oriented in biomedical engineering and legal/ethical fields. There are four sections to the book. Section one deals with the monitoring of artificial organs. Sections two and three cover the basic patho-physiology of disease states and organ failure. Section four, "Ethics and Values," written by a physician and a professor of religion, discusses ethical considerations associated with the terminally ill. This section would probably be of the most interest to clergy personnel, however, the material presented would benefit anyone interested in health care.

623) Basson, Marc D., ed., Ethics, Humanism and Medicine. New York: Alan R. Liss, 1980.

Proceedings of three conferences by the committee on ethics, humanism, and medicine at the University of Michigan, 1978-1979. The following discussions are included: "under what circumstances should euthanasia be performed?", "moral principles relevant to euthanasia", and "the euthanasia problem."

624) Baum, Michael. "Do We Need Informed Consent?" Lancet 8512 (October 1986): 911, 912.

   The problem of whether to inform a patient of his or her illness is presented. Relative to euthanasia, it is important that the patient know so a decision can be made as to whether or not one should refrain from treatment.

625) Bayles, Michael D., and Dallas M. High, eds. Medical Treatment of the Dying: Moral Issues. Cambridge, Mass.: G. K. Hall-Schenkman, 1978.

   Mostly consists of a collection of papers presented at a symposium which was held in October 1974. Moral issues concerning medical treatment of the dying are brought to the fore.

626) Baylor Law Review 27 (Winter 1975). Symposium Issue on Euthanasia.

   The symposium dealt with the following: "Euthanasia: Why No Legislation"; "The Physician's Dilemma: A Doctor's View: What the Law Should Be"; "Death? When Does it Occur?"; "Medical Death"; "Bill of Rights for the Dying Patient"; "Medical Technology as It Exists Today"; "The Family Deals with Death"; "The Living Will, Coping with the Historical Event of Death"; "The Physician's Criminal Liability for the Practice of Euthanasia"; "Euthanasia: The Three-In-One Issue"; "Euthanasia v. The Right to Live"; "Euthanasia, Medical Treatment and the Mongoloid Child: Death as a Treatment of Choice"; and "Death With Dignity: The Physician's Civil Liability."

627) Beauchamp, T. L., and J. F. Childress. Principles of Biomedical Ethics. New York: Oxford University Press, 1979.

Explains basic ethical principles, and shows how they are applied to major issues in bioethics, such as informed consent, risk-benefit assessments, confidentiality, and decisions to terminate therapy. Termination of therapy is in the realm of euthanasia.

628) Bedell, Susanna E., Denise Delle, Patricia L. Maher, and Paul D. Cleary. "Do-Not-Resuscitate Orders for Critically Ill Patients in Hospitals: How Are They Used and What is Their Impact?" Journal of The American Medical Association 256 (July 1986): 233-237.

A study of DNR compliance orders at a university hospital. As a result, the data gathered suggest that changes be made in the use of DNR protocol if patients are to be participants in the decision not to undergo pulmonary resuscitation.

629) Behnke, John and Sissela Bok, eds. The Dilemmas of Euthanasia. New York: Doubleday, 1975.

A work which contains selected works on euthanasia, together with different views, and the text of the Harvard Report on Irreversible Coma.

630) Bell, Nora K., ed. Who Decides? Conflicts of Rights in Health Care. Clifton, N.J.: Humana, 1982.

Included are sixteen essays by outstanding personalities in the field of philosophical and medical ethics: Tristam Engelhardt, Guenter Risse, Daniel Callahan, Ruth Macklin, and Thomas Szasz, along with others. Of interest are four controversial areas: the limits of professional autonomy, refusing and withdrawing treatment, "heroic measures" for the dying patient, and reproductive technology.

631) Braithwaite, Susan, and David C. Thomasma. "New Guidelines on Foregoing Life-Sustaining Treatment in Incompetent Patients: An Anti-Cruelty Policy." Annals of Internal Medicine 104 (May 1986): 711-715.

A proposal of an anti-cruelty policy which is in favor of foregoing life-sustaining equipment, thus preventing untimely death, and thereby relieving suffering.

632) Brodie, Howard. Ethical Decisions in Medicine. Boston: Little, Brown, 1976.

Presents methods for dealing with ethical problems, and examines key issues such as: informal consent, determination of scarce resources, euthanasia, and allowing to die. A benefit for all who read it.

633) Brody, M. "Compassion for Life and Death." Medical Opinion and Review 3 (January 1967): 108-113.

Brody differentiates between the basic meaning of euthanasia and that of "mercy killing," and points out that while doctors should ease the pain of the dying, they should not prolong the dying of persons with flat EEGs.

634) Bryant, D'Orsay D., III. "The Doctor and Death." Journal of The National Medical Association 78 (March 1986): 221-235.

A well-thought-through article. Emphasis is placed on the fact that doctors need to discuss death with their patients, and that communication is vital in order to help them during the process. Bryant also emphasizes that death comes to all, even Americans, who have a tendency to deny it more than other peoples around the world. He mentions that technological devices abound throughout the health-care industry for the purpose of prolonging death, all by which man attempts to play God. God will remove man according to his own good time. Importance is placed on Christ's death, resurrection, and return. Hope for the Christian is anchored in these.

635) Cameron, Daniel, and Mitchel Meznick. "Do-Not-Resuscitate Orders." Journal of The American Medical Association 256 (November 1986): 2677.

A letter briefly discussing a study done on patients who were unable--because of dementia, encephalopathy, or coma--to participate in the decision not to resuscitate. The results of the study encourage patients to enter into dialogue with their physician. They are encouraged to discuss before hospitalization, whether they would want to be resuscitated in the event of cardiac arrest so that the individual's desire is known to all concerned in cases of inability to communicate their wishes. A written statement concerning one's desires is also encouraged.

636) Campbell, A. V. Moral Dilemmas in Medicine: A Coursebook in Ethics for Doctors and Nurses. 2nd Edition. Churchill Livingston, 1975.

A basic ethics coursebook dealing with theoretical and practical issues, among which are: abortion; resuscitation and euthanasia ; human experimentation; and transplantation. Included is a limited bibliography.

637) Charlson, Mary E., Frederic L. Sax, C. Ronald Mackenzie, Suzanne D. Fields, Robert L. Graham and R. Gordon Douglas, Jr. "Resuscitation: How Do We Decide?" Journal of The American Medical Association 255 (March 1986): 1316-1322.

A prospective study of physicians preferences, and the clinical course of hospitalized patients. An imperative for physicians to address the question of the measures to be taken should a patient's condition deteriorate after admission to the hospital.

638) Clements, Colleen D. Medical Genetics Casebook: A
Clinical Introduction to Medical Ethics. Clifton,
N.J.: Humana, 1982.

The author maintains that ethicists approach
problems in medical ethics with theories that ignore
realities of medical practice. They make little
allowances for feedback from medical experience.
She follows 130 cases which involve problems such
as: working with information, trial and reality
testing , self-image , experimental research and
procedures, selective abortion, and societal and
individual interest conflicts. She reviews basic
principles of moral and ethical philosophy.
Clements also recommends that her book be used
as a source for prenatal diagnosis. Her book should
be a significant help for all who are concerned for
life and the impact of medical technology on that
life.

639) Cohen, Douglas. "To Live or Let Die?" Australian and
New Zealand Journal of Surgery 56 (March 1986):
429-432.

This article examines the history of infanticide
and some motivating reasons for the practice. Person hood is discussed relative to abortion and
infanticide. Selective non-treatment such as: no
surgery, nutrition, fluids, and drugs is mentioned
along with legal liability.

640) Collin, V. J. "Limits of Medical Responsibility in
Prolonging Life." Journal of The American Medical
Association 206 (October 1968): 389-392.

That medicine in obligated to enhance life as
much as possible is reason enough for Collin's
opinion not to maintain mere biological life; if that
life is poor quality and beyond recovery. To
discontinue treatment or therapy is not morally
wrong if biological existence is all that is to be hoped
for, Collin maintains. The author leaves the
responsibility to the physician and his expertise in

determining the condition and state of the patient who is to be denied therapy or life-sustaining treatment. Collin contends that the doctor need only be concerned with the patient. The family's best interests will follow.

641) Comfort, A. "A Vote for Humanity." Medical Opinion and Review 7 (February 1971): 28-29.

The possibility of a better life for the aged has been made by Geriatrics, however, according to Comfort, even though he feels that being old and chronically ill is not good reason for euthanasia, there are nevertheless occasions where treatment should be withheld. The doctor's "good judgement" seems to be his criteria.

642) Curran, William J. "Defining Appropriate Medical Care: Providing Nutrients and Hydration for the Dying." New England Journal of Medicine 313 (October 1985): 940-942.

Dr. Curran cites different medical-legal cases which relate to nutrition and fluids in terminal patient care. He states that the high court in New Jersey issued a sensible opinion in the Karen Ann Quinlan case, by allowing her parents to use discretion in removing life-support from her. However, the court's decision which obligated nursing homes to provide nutrition and water to patients did not seem wise to him. He further cites the case of Claire Conroy, on whose behalf the court viewed removal of a nasogastric to be the same as other medical and nursing treatment. Removal of the tube was found to be proper in all respects. He highlights the case. Curran was encouraged by the court's decision in the Conroy case.

643) Dessner, Fisher, Fredrick Port, John Paul Brady and Steven Neu, eds. "Stopping Long-Term Dialysis." New England Journal of Medicine 314 (May 1986): 1449-1451.

Pro-and-con views expressed in letters by physicians on the subject of dialysis, and some psychological results affecting dialysis patients.

644) "Doctor at the Bar." Newsweek 35 (January 16 1950): 20.

Dr. Herman Sander is accused of administering a fatal injection of air (40cc) into the vein of his cancer patient, Abbie Borroto. At the request of Mr. Borroto, Dr. Sander complied with four injections - 10cc each injection.

645) Doherty, Dennis J. "Ethically Permissible." Archives of Internal Medicine 147 (August 1987): 1381-1384.

Doherty discusses questions in this article which have a direct bearing on both medical practice and ethics. As the author states: "What interests us here is the clinico-medical judgement that a given treatment modality is 'ethically permissible' or acceptable or, simply, ethical." Four questions for discussion are asked: (1) What does this assertion really mean?, (2) How is it arrived at?, (3) Who is entitled to make such a judgement?, and (4) Can contradictory approaches be equally permissible from an ethical standpoint? This article will be found helpful by those who are in a quandry as to how to make decisions in the area of life-and- death situations.

646) Dresser, Rebecca S., and Eugene V. Boisaubin. "Ethics, Law, and Nutritional Support." Archives of Internal Medicine 145 (January 1985): 122, 123.

The authors discuss the feeding of unconscious patients, and view nutrition as a medical intervention guided by considerations similar to those governing other treatment methods. Feeding techniques are also discussed. A case report is presented, with comments.

647) Duff, Raymond S., and A. G. M. Campell. "Moral and Ethical Dilemmas in Special Care Nursery." New England Journal of Medicine 289 (October 1973): 3890-894.

A review of records in a special-care nursery found that over a 2-1/2 year period, 14 percent of the deaths were the result of withholding treatment from abnormal infants.

648) Elliott, Barbara A., Thomas W. Day, John L. A. Puma, Jack E. Zimmerman, William A. Knaus and Elizabeth A. Draper. "Do-Not-Resuscitate Orders." Journal of The American Medical Association 255 (June 1986): 3114, 3115.

A discussion of the inferences, differences, and meaning of do-not-resuscutate orders relative to cardiac or respiratory arrest.

649) Englehardt, Tristram H., Jr., and Stuart F. Spicker, eds. Philosophy and Medicine. Vol. 18, Medical Ethics in Antiquity: Philosophical Perspectives on Abortion and Euthanasia, by Paul Carrick. Boston: D. Reidel, 1985.

An exploration of the origins and development of medical ethics as practiced by the ancient Greek and Roman physicians together with their views on abortion and euthanasia. Infanticide and suicide are also examined. The Hippocratic Oath is dissected relative to abortion, infanticide, euthanasia, and suicide. The book is in three parts. Part One explores the social setting of Greek medicine. Part Two specifically deals with the beginning of Greek medical ethics, and Part Three examines a variety of divergent Greco-Roman ethical views and opinions on abortion and euthanasia. An excellent work. Scholarly done, well indexed, and should be in the libraries of those who are interested in historical aspects of euthanasia and related subjects.

650) "Euthanasia." New England Journal of Medicine 292 (April 1975): 863-867.

Fourteen letters which deal with the issue of euthanasia, discussed by Dr. James Rachel "Active and Passive Euthanasia" New England Journal of Medicine 292 (1975): 78-80. Rachel draws little difference between passive and active euthanasia and, therefore, is taken to task in most of these letters, which vent important attitudes of fourteen physicians on the subject. The reader will readily understand how individual doctors react to euthanasia by reading these letters.

651) Evans, Andrew L., and Baruch A. Brody. "The Do-Not-Resuscitate Order in Teaching Hospitals." Journal of The American Medical Association 253 (April 1985): 2236-2239.

After a study of DNR orders at three teaching hospitals, the authors conclude that DNR orders do not fulfill their major goals. Six proposals are offered for improving future DNR orders.

652) Farber, Neil J., Sallyann M. Brawman, David A. Major, and Willard P. Green. "Cardiopulmonary Resuscitation (CPR): Patient Factors and Decision Making." Archives of Internal Medicine 144 (November 1984): 2229-2232.

A study performed to analyze the effect of patient factors on the decision to initiate or withhold CPR, using residents as subjects.

653) Feldman, David M. Health and Medicine in the Jewish Tradition: L'Hayyim - To Life. New York: Crossroad, 1986.

This book is among others which grew out of Project X: Health/Medicine and Faith Traditions.

This particular one explores health and medicine in the Jewish tradition involving ten themes: well-being, sexuality, passages, morality, dignity, madness, healing, caring, suffering, and dying.

654) Fishbein, M. "When Life Is No Longer Life." Medical World News 15 (March 15, 1974): 84.

Medical, legal, and moral questions have been debated relative to euthanasia by various professionals. In this article, Dr. Fishbein presents case studies and statistics involving the opinions of two hundred fifty Chicago internists and surgeons.

655) Fletcher, George P. "Prolonging Life." In Bioethics, ed. Thomas A. Shannon, 189-206. Ramsey, N.J.: Paulist, 1976.

A legal analysis of the problem of a physician's decision not to prolong a terminally-ill patient's life. Focus centers on the relationship of the physician and patient. Fletcher examines the ethical relationship of the two. As an Assistant Professor of Law at the University of Washington, Fletcher is found to be qualified to write on the subject from a legal point of view.

656) Fletcher, Joseph. "Euthanasia: Our Right to Die." Chap. in Morals and Medicine. Princeton, N.J.: Princeton University Press, 1979.

An examination of the practice of euthanasia in its medical form, and is limited to cases in which the patient chooses euthanasia, with the understanding that the physician sees little hope of recovery or relief by any other means. Fletcher's hope is, along with maeterlinck, that there will come a day when science will protest its errors and will shorten our sufferings." As one will be able to see after reading this chapter, Fletcher, as always, is in favor of euthanasia--sometimes to the extreme.

657) _____. Stopping Treatment With or Without Consent. 62 min. B&W Videocassette. Rental. Georgia Regional Medical TV Network, Emory University.

Dr. Joseph Fletcher discusses the ethics of euthanasia followed by a thirty minute lecture on medical aspects.

658) Foley, Thomas, and Bernard, Lo. "Is 'Futility' a Prerequisite to a 'Do Not Resuscitate' Decision?" Archives of Internal Medicine 145 (December 1985): 2266, 2268.

Two physicians exchange views on DNR orders and different policies pertaining thereto.

659) Fox, Maurice, and Helen Levens Lipton. "The Decision to Perform Cardiopulmonary Resuscitation." New England Journal of Medicine 309 (September 1983): 607, 608.

A brief discussion of decisions to initiate or forego life-prolonging procedures, such as cardiopulmonary resuscitation. Each decision is a challenge to the physician. An amalgam of conflicting forces and values is not always rationally reached. Physicians are facing decisions with greater frequency. The author refers to an attempt to develop criteria to assist physicians with difficult decisions. He refers to Lo and Jonsen's "Clinical Decisions to Limit Treatment" Annals of Internal Medicine 93 (1980) 764-768.

660) Freund, Paul A. "Organ Transplants: Ethical and Legal Problems." In Ethics in Medicine: Historical Perspectives and Contemporary Concerns, ed. Stanley Joel Reiser, Arthur J. Dyck, and William J. Curran, 173-177. Cambridge, Mass.: MIT, 1977.

Freund discusses problems concerning the allocation of resources--from whom they should come and to whom organs should be transferred. Implications raised by the questions concern moral, legal, and medical considerations. Each differs on removal of organs after death and during life. He briefly discusses the question of whether or not a dying patient should be allowed to consent to surgical intervention for the purpose of saving another's life.

661) Fried, Charles. "Terminating Life Support: Out of the Closet." New England Journal of Medicine 295 (August 12, 1976): 390, 391.

An attorney comments on the publicity given to changing attitudes of hospital administrators who promulgate and discuss, openly, policies about deliberate withdrawal or non-application of life-prolonging measures.

662) Friedman, H. "Serious Gap Between Theory and Practice Seen in Physicians' Management of Terminal Patients." Geriatric Focus (September 1970).

A critique discussing the inability of doctors to face death-and-dying issues with their patients. Friedman suggests that the care of terminal patients be given over to those more proficient in coping with the problems, namely, psychiatrists and social workers.

663) Gillon, Raanan. "Ordinary and Extraordinary Means." British Medical Journal 292 (January 1986): 259-261.

A scholarly discussion on the Roman Catholic view of ordinary and extraordinary means. The importance of the patient's permission is tantamount relative to withholding or discontinuing treatment. Burdensomeness of treatment (risks, cost, and other difficulties) is also taken into consideration, along with burdens on others. Withholding of nutritional support for infants with anencephaly, severe brain damage, and total necrotising enterocolitus would be appropriate because of prolonged treatment for the remainder of the infant's life.

664) Goff, W. "How Can a Physician Prepare His Patient for Death?" Journal of The American Medical Association 201 (July 1967): 280.

Goff believes that children should never be told they are going to die unless they ask. Adults, he believes, should have hope for a cure of their ills and hope of eternal life. This article should be read together with Friedman's "Serious Gap Between Theory and Practice Seen in Physicians' Management of Terminal Patients." For annotation on Friedman,(see Citation 662).

665) Gonda, Thomas Andrew, and John Edward Ruark. Dying Dignified: The Health Professional's Guide to Care. Menlo Park: Addison-Wesley, 1984.

Lucid case histories are presented at the beginning of the book and are referred to throughout the discussion. Emphasis is placed on the fact that decision-making for the most part resides in the hands of the patient. Broad issues are outlined, such as medical, social, and economic aspects of dying. Suicide and working with dying children comprise a part of the book. Each chapter has an annotated bibliography at its end.

666) Green, M. "Care of the Dying Child." Pediatrics 40 (September 1967): 492-497.

Green discusses management of the terminally ill child, and the child's concept of death. He feels that the child's physician should be available at all times, otherwise, a competent substitute should be available.

667) Guideline for Consent: The Uniform Anatomical Gift Act. New York, N.Y.: 15 min. B&W, 3/4" Video-cassette. 15 Columbus Circle (10023).

A National Continuing Medical Education tape dealing with medical and legal aspects of transplantation. For subscribers' use only.

668) Halley, M. and W. Harvey. "Medical vs. Legal Definitions of Death." Journal of The American Medical Association 204 (May 6, 1968): 423-425.

A discussion of both legal and medical definitions of death. Physicians and lawyers are appealed to in order to arrive at a reasonable criteria for death.

669) Harvard, J. D. J. "Legal Regulation of Medical Practice - Decisions of Life and Death: A Discussion Paper." Journal of The Royal Society of Medicine 75 (May 1982): 351-355.

An examination of the reasons why the medical profession has serious doubts about the role of Anglo-Saxon law regulating certain decisions which doctors have to make in the course of medical practice. The paper discusses legal protection of the child between implantation of the fertilized ovum through the completion of the birth process. Life-threatening abnormalities are presented as a problem now that technological advances have been made which increase the ability to keep such infants alive. The author shows throughout the discussion that Anglo-Saxon law has not been impressive in its ability to keep pace with technological developments in medical science.

670) Harwood, Ann L., ed. Cardiopulmonary Resuscitation. Baltimore and London: Williams and Wilkins, 1982.

Topics for discussion include: ventilation during cardiopulmonary resuscitation, perfusion in cardiopulmonary resuscitation, brain resuscitation after cardiac arrest, pharmacology of resuscitation, defibrillation, pre-hospital management of cardiac arrest, pediatric resuscitation, liability aspects of cardiopulmonary resuscitation and emergency cardiac care and traumatic cardiac arrest.

671) Helpern, Milton with Bernard Knight. Autopsy: The Memoirs of Milton Helpern the World's Greatest Medical Detective. New York: St. Martin's, 1977.

Included in this exciting book are fascinating chapters on techniques of forensic pathology, and the art of being a medical witness. Also, there are gruesome accounts of mercy killing (euthanasia), and the camouflaging effects of drugs and disease. Dr. Milton Helpern was Chief Medical Examiner of the City of New York for twenty years. Bernard Knight, another pathologist, is a Reader in Forensic Pathology at the Welsh National School of Medicine. Together, they create a work which reads like a horror story. Unbelievable, but true. For all who are interested in bizarre medical cases. It should be in all libraries.

672) Hilhorst, Henri W. A. "Religion and Euthanasia in The Netherlands: Exploring a Diffuse Relationship." Social Compass 30 (1983): 491-502.

In this work, the author's intention is to discuss euthanasia and its relationship to religion in The Netherlands. He shows that for the most part religion and euthanasia are opposites, and that religion is not in favor of pro-euthanasia attitudes. As to institutions, the non-religious institutions such as, humanist organizations and euthanasia societies are more in favor of euthanasia based on individual right of self-determination. Concerning individuals who are religious, there seems to be favoritism for euthanasia over and above the stand of religious institutions, however, religious individuals are less in favor of euthanasia than are non-religious individuals. Within the medical profession, doctors, nurses, and other health care professionals act within the framework of their religious beliefs, and are for the most part opposed to euthanasia. Only a small percentage think and act in favor of euthanasia. The author's purpose is realized in this article in that he gives revealing insight into the practice of euthanasia throughout The Netherlands.

673) Hofling, C. K. "Life-Death Decisions May Undermine M.D.'s Mental Health." Frontiers In Hospital Psychiatry 5 (March 1968): 3.

Hofling is emphatic in believing that decision - making with regard to euthanasia should be a team effort composed of a group effort. The expertise of the physician, clergyman, family, and friends should be brought to bear on the decision.

674) Holder, Angela Roddey. Legal Issues in Pediatrics and Adolescent Medicine. New York: Wiley, 1977.

A handbook for the physician who is interested in combating those who are opposed to his rights as he operates within the confines of the medical profession. Holder identifies many legal issues confronting pediatricians, neonatologists, and others who treat minors. Among the problems she discusses are genetic counselling, genetic screening, fetal research, and the physician's liability to treat deformed newborns. Discussion of allowing the malformed infant to die is presented with the fact that it cannot be swept under the rug, but must be openly addressed. Moral issues are also treated which pediatricians are faced with as they must come to terms with the question of whether to treat or not to treat severely deformed infants.

675) Horan, Dennis J. Death, Dying and Euthanasia. Washington, D.C.: University Publications of America, Inc., 1977.

An impressive collection of works by authors from various fields: physicians, attorneys, ethicists, clergy, philosophers, and others who write with conviction on euthanasia. The works, most of which are reprints from periodicals, are classified under seven headings: (1) Death: When Does It Occur and How Do We Define It?, (2) Death as a

Treatment of Choice?: Involuntary Euthanasia of the Defective Newborn, (3) Euthanasia: Ethical, Religious, and Moral Aspects, (4) Euthanasia: The Legal Aspects of "Mercy Killing," (5) How Should Medicine and Society Treat the Dying?, (6) Legalized Euthanasia: Social Attitudes and Governmental Policies, and (7) Suicide and the Patient's Right to Reject Medical Treatment. The editors list the contributors in the back of the book. Good for research.

676) Horan and Dela Hoyde, eds. Infanticide and the Handicapped Newborn. Provo, Utah: Brigham Young University Press: 1981.

A scholarly work which evaluates the moral and medical issues raised by infanticide in America.

677) In The Matter of Karen Quinlan. Vol. I, Washington, D.C.: University Publications of America, Inc., 1977.

An integration of all the legal briefs, court proceedings, and decisions in the Superior Court of New Jersey. A helpful volume for those pursuing legal issues in euthanasia.

678) Irreversible Coma. New York, N.Y.: 16 min. B&W Videocassette. 15 Columbus Circle (10023).

The discussion defines death. A National Continuing Medical Education tape. For subscribers only.

679) "It's Over Debbie." Journal of The American Medical Association 259 (January 1988): 272.

An unknown physician shares in detail the steps he took to kill a terminally-ill patient. A good example of active euthanasia.

680) Jackson, E. "Is Euthanasia Christian?" Christian Century 67 (March 8, 1950): 300-301.

This article is divided into three parts: medical, theological, and legal. Each of these aspects are discussed relative to Christianity.

681) Johnson, A. G. "The Right to Live and the Right to Die." Nursing Times 67 (May 1971): 573-574.

Advice is given to physicians that they can help their patients die without actually becoming involved in euthanasia practices. Emphasis is placed on withholding treatment which actually assists the patient in the normal process of dying, rather than positive action on the part of the doctor.

682) Kantoi, George, Maria R. Silver, and Stuart J. Younger. A Closer Look at the Institutional Ethics Committee. 27 min. Videocassette; VHS and Beta; $90, Ohio: University of Akron, 1985.

This tape looks at many problems which beset ethical committees, such as: the committee's effects on the institution, medical staff, decision processes, and legal liabilities. A hypothetical case is presented in which a physician is faced with the problem of whether to withdraw ventilator support from a patient who had been comatose for four days. The patient's family plays a large role in the tape. Anyone may profit from the production in that some insight into the workings of an ethics committee will be gained and, along with it, some understanding of what pressures are brought to bear on thosewho are involved in decision-making on life-and-death issues.

683) Kapusta, Morton Allan, and Solomon Frank. "The Book of Job and the Modern View of Depression." Annals of Internal Medicine 86 (May 1977): 667-672.

A recommended study of the book of Job and depression. The authors present the book as being an instrument to provide professionals of the day with a realistic approach to the problems of life. Its disclosure of depression is the same as the modern view of depression. There are clues throughout the book that distinguish between normal grief and deep depression. Kapusta and Frank are convinced that Job not only gives a good description and meaning of depression, but that it also provides solutions for dealing with modern depression. Chapter 30 of Job provides answers that are vital for results of depression. The authors say, ". . . part of the wisdom of the Book of Job is a timeless medical masterpiece that provides an unexcelled standard of clinical observation and medical intervention." While this study is not specifically on the subject of euthanasia, it provides insight into the depression that occurs as a result of grief on the part of those who deal with the problems of euthanasia. It is highly recommended for all who experience depression, regardless of the cause.

684) Karnofsky, David A. "Why Prolong the Life of a Patient With Advanced Cancer." CA 10 (January/ February 1960): 9-11.

The belief that a doctor should only be concerned with his duty to sustain the life of his patient. The physician should not make judgements, but should concentrate on comfort for the patient.

685) _____. "Treating Incurables." Science Newsletter 80 (November 4, 1961): 300.

Dr. Karnofsky states that the doctor's responsibility is to keep the patient living as long as possible. Not only is the physician responsible medically, but also legally.

686) Katz, Jay, and Alexander Morgan Capron. Catastrostrophic Diseases: Who Decides What? New York: Russell Sage Foundation, 1975.

Two law professors, one of whom is a psychiatrist (Jay Katz), write on catastrophic diseases (a catastrophic disease is a disease for which expensive and unusual equipment must be made available for treatment and which can sustain life for a period of time), and goals and values proposed to treat such diseases. A brief account is given of the state of the art of hemodialysis and organ transplantation. The definition of death, and the right to refuse life-sustaining treatment are examined that surround the issues. The work is scholarly, and merits extensive readership, especially among those who want to know who will be making decisions on the future use of equipment for those less fortunate than most of us.

687) Kleinman, Eli J. "Foregoing Life-Sustaining Treatment." Annals of Internal Medicine 105 (August 1986): 307.

An opposing view to Braithwaite and Thomasma in their proposed anti-cruelty policy. See Braithwaite and Thomasma, Citation number 631.

688) Kohl, Marvin, ed. Infanticide and the Value of Life. Buffalo, New York: Prometheus Books, 1978.

Examined are the religious, medical, legal, and ethical issues surrounding infanticide. Familiar personalities writing are: Joseph Fletcher, Arval A. Morris, Glanville Williams, Joseph Margolis, Richard Brandt, Peter Black, Immanuel Jababovits, and Leonard Weber. Indexed, with bibliography.

689) Koop, C. Everett The Right To Live: The Right To Die. Wheaton, Ill.: Tyndale House, 1976.

A famous pediatric surgeon gives his views on abortion and mercy killing. He examines current attitudes and trends from different perspectives:

medical, personal, social, and theological. He discusses the Supreme Court ruling and the Quinlan case. As the Surgeon General of the U.S., what Dr. Koop has to say in this book is highly significant and important.

690) Lachs, John. "Humane Treatment and Treatment of Humans." New England Journal of Medicine 294 (April 1976): 838-840.

A presentation of a classic case having to do with the treatment and attitude of care toward hydrocephalic-infants. Infants such as these are looked upon by the author as non-persons--not humans, but human shapes.

691) Lamb, David. Death, Brain Death and Ethics. Albany: State University of New York Press, 1985.

"What is considered so essential to human life, such, that when it is lost we consider the individual dead?" This question sets one's thinking for the author's discussion on death, the brain, and ethics. A series of lectures inquiring into what death is relative to the brain. Lamb's thesis is that death of the brain stem is death of the individual organism. He provides a philosophical framework for criteria for determining death. The book is well written, up to date, and more philosophical than practical. Good for anyone looking for a definition of death.

692) Lantos, John, "Baby Doe Five Years Later." New England Journal of Medicine 317 (August 1987): 444-447.

The author reviews the unfortunate case of Baby Doe who was allowed to die of starvation in an Indiana hospital, and the controvery which erupted between the Reagan administration and the Supreme Court decision legalizing abortion. For additional reference see "The Story of Baby Doe." New England Journal of Medicine 309 (1983):644.

693) <u>Learning To Live With The Dying.</u> New York, N.Y.:
39 min. Color. Videocassette. Rental. 15 Columbus
Circle (10023).

A National Continuing Medical Education tape
sharing management of the terminally-ill patients
with patients and family. A discussion involving
medical students, physicians, and a minister. For use
by NCME subscribers only.

694) Lewis, H. P. "Medicine, Machines, and Their Relation
to the Fatally Ill." <u>Journal of The American Medical
Association</u> 206 (October 7, 1968): 387-388.

Moral, ethical, and legal problems have resulted
from advanced medical technology. The meaning
of death and extraordinary means are examined,
along with a summation of modern medical techniques and procedures.

695) Lo, Bernard. "The Death of Clarence Herbert: Withdrawing Care Is Not Murder." <u>Annals of Internal
Medicine</u> 101 (August 1984): 248-251

Discussion of a case where two physicians were
charged with murder of a comatose patient for
discontinuing a ventilating machine and intravenous fluids.

696) _____. "The Case of Claire Conroy: Will Administrative Review Safeguard Incompetent Patients?
<u>Annals of Internal Medicine</u> 104 (June 1986): 869-73.

A review by the New Jersey Supreme Court in
the case of Claire Conroy, who was an 84-year-old
resident of a nursing home, and an incompetent. A
review of ordinary and extraordinary treatment.

697) _____. "Behind Closed Doors." <u>New England
Journal of Medicine</u> 317 (July 1987): 46-49.

Dr. Lo deals with three important questions
relative to ethics committees: (1) are such committees

ethical?, (2) is agreement by ethics committees always desirable?, and (3) are ethics committees effective? He discusses promises and pitfalls in ethics committees, goals and procedures of ethics committees, pitfalls of committee discussions, and evaluating ethics committees.

698) Lockwood, Michael, ed. Moral Dilemmas in Modern Medicine. London: Oxford University Press, 1985.

Three sets of issues comprise the volume. Set one consists of reproductive techniques which include: in vitro fertilization, surrogate mothering, frozen embryos, gene therapy, growing human embryos in the laboratory, and genetic engineering. Medical paternalism and patient autonomy are dealt with in the second set. The nature of moral arguments and reasoning in medicine comprise the third set. These philosophical studies will enhance one's knowledge and respect for those who deal with the issues presented.

699) Lygre, David G. Life Manipulation. New York: Walker and Co., 1970.

All that can be thought of relative to "life manipulation," from test-tube babies to aging, is included in Lygre's well written book. The human implications of cloning, biofeedback, partho-genesis (virgin birth), psychosurgery, delayed aging, redesigned organs, artificial wombs, selective abortions, human gene splicing, artificial insemination, sex preselection of fetuses, life sustenance after brain death, prenatal diagnosis of birth defects, and other interesting subjects relative to biomedical research are treated. After reading this work, one will conclude that these issues cannot and should not be avoided, for everyone's life will be touched somehow as bio-medical research reaches more and more into the lives of all humans.

700) Lynn, Joanne, ed. By No Extraordinary Means: The Choice to Forgo Life-Sustaining Food and Water. Bloomington: Indiana University Press, 1986.

The authors present the medical, moral, ethical, social, and legal perspectives of the nutrition and hydration issue. Situations discussed have to do with the newborn, terminally ill, unconscious persons (permanently), and the chronically ill but not terminal patient who has decided to refuse food and water. This collection of papers was prepared for the Society for Health and Human Values and should be purchased by all who are interested in the subject because it compiles the views of different authors.

701) Mack, Arien, ed. Death in the American Experience. New York: Schocken Books, 1973.

A paperback book reprinted from the Fall issue of Social Research. A compilation of essays including: "Being and Becoming Dead," by Eric Cassell; "The Sacral Power of Death in Contemporary Experience," by William May; "Death in the Judaic and Christian Tradition," by Roy Eckhardt; and Johannes Fabian writes on "How Others Die-Reflections on the Anthropology of Death."

702) McKengney, F. and P. Lange. "The Decision To No Longer Live On Chronic Hemodialysis." American Journal of Psychiatry 128 (September 1971): 267-274.

A discussion of four hemodialysis patients and their attitude toward death. The authors stress that there is a life not worth living.

703) Marty, Martin E. Health and Medicine in the Lutheran Tradition: Being Well. New York: Crossroads, 1983.

An exploration of health and medicine in the Lutheran tradition. It covers such themes as well-being, sexuality, passages, morality, dignity, madness, healing, caring, suffering, and dying.

704) Matheson, J. C. M. "Infanticide." Medico-Legal and Criminological Review 9 (July 1941): 135-152.

A look at medical questions involving infanticide. Also presents several case histories of abortions.

705) Medicine, Morality and The Law: Euthanasia. 30 min. B&W. Rental/Sale. University of Michigan T.V. Center.

A panel discussion of the legal and moral aspects of 3 case studies on the subject of euthanasia.

706) Meyers, David W. "The Legal Aspects of Medical Euthanasia." Bioscience 23 (August 1973): 467-470.

The term "euthanasia" is analyzed and defined. A discussion of withholding treatment and the termination of ordinary medical treatment is presented. Extraordinary means of keeping a patient alive is also part of the discussion.

707) _____. "Legal Aspects of Withdrawing Nourishment From an Incurably Ill Patient." Archives of Internal Medicine 145 (January 1985): 125-128.

A-well-thought-through discussion presenting a list of arguments for and against the practice, with a number of court cases decided to date (the time of the article's publication).

708) Micetich, Kenneth, Patricia H. Steinecker and David C. Thomasma. "Are Intravenous Fluids Morally Required for a Dying Patient?" Archives of Internal Medicine 143 (May 1983): 975-978.

An argument that under certain circumstances, IV fluids are not morally required for dying patients. A hypothetical case is put forth. The authors hold that the use of fluids in certain cases constitutes heroic efforts.

709) Milbauer, Barbra and Bert N. Oberentz. The Law Giveth: Legal Aspects of the Abortion Controversy. Atheneum, N.Y.: McClelland and Stewart, 1983.

The facts on abortion are well summarized in this book. The reader is taken on a journey through case law and pertinent American history. Social, medical, religious, and moral aspects of the abortion debate are discussed. The book assists greatly in helping to understand abortion in our time. The bearing of the book on euthanasia is simply this: if abortion is allowed to be performed on the healthy unborn, the "green light" for aborting the already-born deformed is certainly a permissive sign.

710) Miles, Steven H., and Timothy J. Crimmins. "Orders to Limit Emergency Treatment for an Ambulance Service in a Large Metropolitan Area." Journal of The American Medical Association 254 (July 1985): 525-527.

A description of a policy which allows paramedics and emergency physicians to honor orders from nursing home records not to perform resuscitation or endotracheal intubation on patients.

711) Modell, Walter. "A 'Will' to Live." New England Journal of Medicine 290 (April 1970): 907, 908.

A doctor shares a statement of intent given to him by a friend. It is a personal directive, and a model for anyone who is interested in making out his or her "living will."

712) Mueller, Daniel Mark. "Involuntary Passive Euthanasia of Brain-Stem-Damaged Patients: The Need for Legislation - An Analysis and A Proposal." San Diego Law Review 14 (July 1977): 1277-1297.

Mueller points out the deficiency of physician guides to terminate treatment of brain-stem-damaged patients. Medical practices and maintaining or withdrawing treatment are examined regarding such patients. A proposal is introduced which would legalize withholding treatment from brain-stem-damaged patients.

713) Nash, Irwin. "An ICU Death: A Gordian Knot in Search of Alexander." New England Journal of Medicine 311 (December 1984): 1705.

A physician relates a visit with his seventy-three-year-old uncle who was terminally ill in an intensive care unit of a major medical center, and how he was somewhat neglected by those who could have relieved his suffering by an act of active euthanasia.

714) Noyles, Russell, Jr. "The Art of Dying." Perspectives in Biology and Medicine 35 (Spring 1971): 432-447.

Traces the art of dying through the Classical, Middle Ages, and Renaissance periods to the present. Early medical euthanasia is discussed, together with psychological theory and the physician's role.

715) Parham, Allan M., Donald J. Higby, Jean-Pierre Kaufmann, and Sharon Murphy. "Last Rights." New England Journal of Medicine 295 (November 1976): 1139-1142.

Ten letters written by physicians, both pro and con, on views which have bearing on terminating life-support systems for terminal patients. Patients' families are also discussed.

716) Paris, John J., and Frank E. Reardon. "Court Responses to Withholding or Withdrawing Artificial Nutrition and Fluids." Journal of The American Medical Association 253 (April 1945): 2243-2245.

A presentation and review of different court cases and decisions which effect health-care personnel who withhold artificial nutrition and fluids from terminally-ill and comatose patients.

717) Potts, Malcolm, Peter Diggory, and John Peel. Abortion. New York: Cambridge University Press, 1977.

A scholarly thesis which is well documented. The hypothesis presented is that no society has been able to adjust or advance socio-economically without recourse to abortion. The authors are sympathetic to the illegal abortionists, one of whom was the inventor of the Karman Curette for vacuum aspiration. The authors' presentation supports their thesis that abortion precedes a society's effective use of contraception, and is a necessary adjunct to contraception. Those who are anti-abortionist will not agree that abortion on a large or small scale is the answer to any society's socio-economic problems.

718) President's Commission for the Study of Ethical Problems in Medicine and Biomedical and Behavioral Research. Defining Death: A Report on the Medical, Legal and Ethical Issues in the Determination of Death. Washington, D.C.: U.S. Government Printing Office, 1984.

This is a report to the President on the "definition" of death, and a recommendation of a statute by Congress to provide a clear and socially accepted basis for making determinations of death. Chapter one deals with the question, "Why 'update' death?" Chapter two presents the 'state of the art' in medicine. "Understanding the meaning of death" is the topic of chapter three. "Who ought to define death?" is answered in chapter four, and chapter five inquires, "What 'definition' ought to be adopted?" The book is a must for professionals.

719) Rachels, James. "Active and Passive Euthanasia." New England Journal of Medicine 292 (January 1975): 78-80.

Dr. Rachels takes issue with the conventional view that there is a difference between active euthanasia and passive euthanasia. He challenges the doctrine for several reasons: (1) active euthanasia in many cases is more humane than passive euthanasia, (2) the conventional doctrine leads to decisions concerning life and death on irrelevant grounds, (3) the doctrine rests on a distinction between killing and letting die and that in itself has no moral importance, and (4) the most common arguments favoring the doctrine are invalid. The doctor illustrates his arguments by presenting some hypothetical cases of actively taking part in the deaths of individuals, and passively standing by and allowing someone to die. He concludes: "So, whereas doctors may have to discriminate between active and passive euthanasia to satisfy law, they should not do any more than that. In particular, they should not give the distinction any added authority and weight by writing it into official statements of medical ethics."

720) Ramsey, Paul. Ethics at the Edge of Life: Medical and Legal Interactions. New Haven, Conn.: Yale University Press, 1978.

A serious study of the medical, legal and moral issues which come together in a depressing society. Ramsey, one of the more conservative theologians and ethicists of the present, addresses moral issues at the "first of life." These issues involve the Supreme Court decision regarding a Missouri statute which regulates abortion. The last six chapters which address the "last of life" discuss "dying well enough," the care of infants, and the Quinlan case, followed by a study of treatment withdrawn from a mentally incompetent man. Throughout Ramsey's study, discouragement and distress are obvious due to the fact that he sees very little hope in society's attempt to better the situation, i.e., take a stand against the low respect and regard for life. Those who share Ramsey's views will be encouraged to know that there are still those who stand in the gap for human dignity and right to life.

721) Reiser, Stanley Joel, Arthur J. Dyck, and William J. Curran, eds. Ethics in Medicine: Historical Perspectives and Contemporary Concerns. Cambridge, Mass.: MIT, 1977.

This text was developed while teaching graduate and undergraduate courses at Harvard University. It is practical for practitioners and students in medicine, law, ethics, counselling, and for individual patients and groups who are concerned with medical care. The volume is separated into eight sections: (1) Ethical Dimensions of the Physician-Patient Relationship, (2) Moral Basis of Medical Ethics, (3) Regulation, Compulsion, and Consumer Protection in Clinical Medicine and Public Health, (4) TruthTelling in the Physician-Patient Relationship, (5) Medical Experimentation on Human Subjects, (6) Procreative Decisions, (7) Suffering and Dying, and (8) Rights and Priorities in the Provision of Medical Care. Each section contains articles, essays, and class lectures. An excellent textbook.

722) Ricci, Lawrence R. "A Death in the Family." Journal of The American Medical Association 257 (May 1987): 2485.

A touching account of the death of a doctor's father, and the son's hurt because of the cold and callous care given during the course of his father's hospitalization.

723) "Right to Die - Opinion of Physicians, Church-Men and Press." Literary Digest 120 (November 23 1935): 17.

Can an individual who is racked with pain and incurable choose to die mercifully? The issue is discussed from various viewpoints.

724) Robertson, John A., and Norman Fost. "Passive Euthanasia of Defective Newborn Infants: Legal Considerations." The Journal of Pediatrics 88 (May 1976): 883-889.

The reason for this article is to consider legal ramifications in light of the fact that little mention has been made in reports of passive euthanasia of defective infants. The authors feel that parents, physicians, nurses, and administrators are liable on several grounds; homicide by omission, child neglect, and failure to report child neglect. Increasing publicity of passive euthanasia practices is thought to increase the probability of prosecution. The appeal of this writing is to persuade open discussion and debate to change existing laws, not to try and subvert them through private action. Two alternative policies are described: (1) establishment of criteria for a class of infants who can be allowed to die, and (2) a better process of decision making. Their conclusion is that a commitment to process would be preferable.

725) Rodin, C. M., J. Chmara, J. Ennis, S. Fenton, H. Locking, and K. Steinhouse. "Stopping Life-Sustaining Medical Treatment: Psychiatric Considerations in the Termination of Renal Dialysis." Canadian Journal of Psychiatry 26 (December 1981): 540-544.

A presentation of data regarding the decision by medical staff and patients to discontinue renal dialysis. The patient's mental competence, motivations, and psychiatric state are discussed. Medical factors involved in decision-making are mentioned. The patient's active participation is emphasized.

726) Rosner, Fred. "Withholding or Withdrawing Treatment." Archives of Internal Medicine 147 (January 1947).

A disagreement with the position of The American Medical Association Council on Ethical Affairs that under certain very limited circumstances "it is not unethical to discontinue all means of life-prolonging medical treatment." Rosner's view is that the physician is responsible to heal and should not assist in hastening death.

727) _____. Medicine in the Bible and the Talmud. New York: KTAV Publishing House, Yeshiva University Press, 1977

While this work is not on euthanasia per se, it presents Biblical and Talmudic references to organs, diseases, manifestations of diseases, treatment, and other topics of medical interest. The essays are heavy on interpretation. A broad sketch of health and disease in ancient and medieval Jewish society. One may gather from these essays an understanding of death and dying in the Jewish community.

728) _____. "Judaism and Medical Ethics." Annals of Internal Medicine 101 (November 1984): 721, 722.

A physician writes to discuss Judaism's view that life is of infinite value, and that restoration of health and preservation of life is the physician's responsibility.

729) _____. Modern Medicine and Jewish Ethics. New York: Yeshiva University Press, 1986.

A compilation of essays on Jewish ethics as they pertain to issues such as: artificial insemination, in vitro fertilization, genetic engineering, organ transplantation, and extraordinary life support measures. Jewish thought in other areas are brought forth which touch on contraception, abortion, euthanasia, and autopsy. Specific biomedical issues are dealt

with in each chapter, and contain Biblical passages, interpretations, and codified Jewish laws on
ethical issues. Modern day interpretations by
rabbinical councils are also included. Anyone
wanting to familiarize themselves with Jewish
thought on the vital issues of health-care and
ethics will want to peruse this volume.

730) Sanes, Samuel. A Physician Faces Cancer in Himself.
Albany: State University of New York Press, 1979.

Dr. Samuel Sanes, a pathologist, found that he
had reticulum-cell carcinoma. He lived a little
longer than five years after the diagnosis, during
which time he wrote a series of articles on which
this book is based. His thesis throughout is that
female physicians tend to care for cancer patients
better than male physicians, and he emphasizes that
physicians have had some failures in caring for
cancer patients in that they do not know what the
patients need. His message is clear: patients need to
know what they have, and what can be expected
and predicted. They need support. Sanes advises
how physicians can and should communicate with
their patients. Dr. Sanes is not only one that knows
the body, but he also knows how a cancer patient
feels. This book is written from first-hand
experience.

731) Scott, B. "Physicians' Attitude Survey: Doctors and
Dying: Is Euthanasia Now Becoming Accepted?"
Medical Opinion and Review 3 (May 1974): 31-44.

"This survey outlines the opinions of nine
hundred thirty-three of three thousand doctors sent
a questionnaire on euthanasia. Four out of five
physicians believe that a patient has a right to
choose the way he dies, with only one out of
fourteen disagreeing. This opinion cuts across
clinical specialties, although psychiatrists seemed
more willing to end their own suffering should the
situation arise. More physicians than one might
normally believe, claim to have thought about their

own deaths, with pediatricians and obstetricians having done the least thinking about their own deaths. There is also a breakdown by religion and age." (For source of quotation see Citation 1: Clouser, Danner K., and Arthur Zucker. Abortion and Euthanasia: An Annotated Bibliography. Philadelphia, Pennsylvania: Society for Health and Human Values, 1974.)

732) Selzer, Richard. Mortal Lessons. New York: Simon and Schuster, 1976.

Dr. Selzer writes to find some meaning in the ritual of surgery. The book is in four sections: The Art of Surgery, The Body, Essays, and Down From Troy. Among some metaphors the author shares is that of a man who is slowly dying in an intensive care unit. The "Exact Location of the Soul" is among the essays discussed. One would certainly not want to discard such a book after reading it.

733) _____. Letters to a Young Doctor. New York: Simon and Schuster, 1982.

In his chapter on "Mercy," page 70, Dr. Selzer gives a vivid description of his involvement in actively participating in the attempted death of a patient by injection, all of which was requested by the patient and family members. A good example of active euthanasia.

734) Siegler, Mark, and Alan J. Weisbard. "Against the Emerging Stream: Should Fluids and Nutrition Support Be Discontinued?" Archives of Internal Medicine 145 (January 1985): 129-131.

Two physicians take a strong stand "against the stream" of those colleagues who are caught up in the present trend to go against the traditions of medical care, that of withdrawing treatment (fluids or nutritional supports) from certain classes of patients. They offer several arguments in an effort to stem the tide.

735) Stehbens, William E. "Euthanasia." New Zealand Medical Journal 99 (March 1986): 190-193.

A debate of the inconsistency of society's view of death and euthanasia, especially voluntary euthanasia. Dr. Stehbens sees no difference between active and passive euthanasia. In the light of techniques which enable the patient to be kept alive indefinitely, he believes that doctors should be allowed to decide when it is useless to keep a patient alive, without fear of being charged with unprofessional conduct. Regarding deformed infants, Stehbens believes that interference to prolong the lives of those incapable of ever experiencing a near normal existence is undesirble, in not cruel. He points out that involuntary active euthanasia is unacceptable in a free society and that non-voluntary euthanasia which includes severe irremedial brain damage, grossly malformed infants, and irreversible coma patients, is a form of life that has caused untold misery and cost to family members. He agrees with others that arguments for moral mercy killing outweigh those that oppose it, and concludes that the moralists are beginning to concede that there will be an irreversible trend toward mercy killing.

736) Steinbrook, Robert, Bernard Lo, Jill Tirpack, James W. Dilley, eds. "Ethical Dilemmas in Caring for Patients with the Acquired Immunodeficiency Syndrome." Annals of Internal Medicine 103 (November 1985): 787-790.

This piece discusses ethical dilemmas - - when to provide life-sustaining treatments, such as mechanical ventilation and cardiopulmonary resuscitation for AIDS patients.

737) Steinfels, Peter, and Robert M. Veatch, eds. Death Inside Out. New York: Harper and Row, 1975.

Being the result of a continuing interest in the problems of death and dying, these articles present a clarification of death attitudes during the past eight centuries. They show the change in the relationship of medicine and the dying. The "death with dignity" issue is also discussed. An impressive collection of articles.

738) Takagi, Kentaro. "Medical Problems at Birth and Death." Japanese Journal of Medicine 23 (August 1984): 268-269.

A discussion of "brain death" and the importance of determining criteria for it as quickly as possible, and to strive for national consensus regarding it. Organ transplantation should be used as effectively as possible. Organs should be given to patients who seriously need them in order to prolong their lives. On euthanasia, the author feels that those patients who are in the terminal stage should be given pain medication, and every effort should be made to prolong their lives. He further discusses artificial termination of pregnancy, and external fertilization.

739) Temkin, Owsei, William K. Frankena, and Sanford H. Kadish. Respect for Life in Medicine, Philosophy, and the Law. Baltimore: The Johns Hopkins University Press, 1976.

Respect for life is approached from different perspectives which shed light on the subject in different ways. Temkin discusses the history of medicine, and how early medicine understood respect for life. The philosophical approach by William Frankena interprets respect for life and how moral philosophy should define it. Kadish presents how the law treats different cases of taking human life. Euthanasia, abortion, infanticide, and other means of taking life are interwoven throughout the book.

740) The Mercy Killers. 30 min. B&W. Film/Rental: Visual Aids Department, University of Illinois.

Physicians, clergymen, and four terminally ill patients discuss euthanasia.

741) "The Prognosis for Babies with Meningomyelocele and High Lumbar Paraplegia at Birth." Lancet 8462 (November 1985): 996-997.

A comment by a working group on whether or not there continues to be an ethical justification for selective treatment of spina-bifida babies. The group is convinced that in certain cases, active steps to shorten a baby's life should not be taken.

742) Thomasma, David C., and Joe Brumlik. "Ethical Issues in the Treatment of Patients with a Remitting Vegetative State." The American Journal of Medicine 87 (August 1984): 373-377.

A case of remitting vegetative state is presented, illustrating the need to draw a distinction between persistent and remitting vegetative states in brain-damaged patients. When a patient is unable to permit the withdrawal of treatment, this work emphasizes the importance of preserving life until the course becomes, evidently, downhill.

743) Thomson, A. R. A Dictionary of Medical Ethics and Practice. Bristol: John Wright and Sons, 1977.

Among other things, the author gives accounts of bereavement, moment of death, brain death, suicide, and euthanasia. There is also a piece on "care of the dying". One will find the work moralistic and sincere.

744) Troup, Stanley B., and William A. Greene, ed. The Patient, Death, and The Family. New York: Charles Scribner's Sons, 1974.

A compilation of twelve essays that grew out of a conference sponsored by Rochester General Hospital in New York. Medicine, nursing, philosophy, the chaplaincy, and sociology are represented. They relate effectively because each participant had the opportunity to read and review the others' essays before sharing his or her thoughts on the theme of the conference. The central thought throughout the book is that the dying patient goes through the process of relating to two systems: the hospital or institution which provides the care, and the family, each of which assumes that the other is meeting the patient's needs. Historical, symbolical, and philosophical views of death are treated. The physician is seen as one who has difficulty in grappling with the issues facing the dying patient, and it is pointed out that the chaplain and/or clergy can be of tremendous help and assistance with the terminally ill patient, if trained correctly. This book will be especially helpful for the family, as well as health care personnel.

745) U.S. House of Representatives. Discursive Dictionary of Health Care. Washington, D.C.: Prepared by the staff for the use of the Subcommittee on Health and the Environment of The Committee on Interstate and Foreign Commerce. U.S. Government Printing Office, 1976.

This dictionary was prepared for legislators and the public due to unfamiliar terms which have become part of the National Health Insurance debate. The work defines such terms as "audit," "peer review," "third party," "kitting," "me-to-drug," and "ping-ponging" (the practice of passing a patient from one physician to another for the purpose of spreading out health care business--for unnecessary examinations and tests). Many terms used throughout this dictionary would be beneficial to those who are involved in counselling situations. A great help for $2.40 from the Government Printing Office.

746) Vaux, Kenneth, ed. Powers That Make Us Human: The Foundations of Medical Ethics. Urbana, Ill.: University of Illinois Press, 1985.

These essays are brought together to give the reader insight into the complex problems of health and illness. They deal with reason, hope, virtue, feeling, honor, and mortality. Two essays by Leon Kass and William May are well worth purchasing the book. They are on mortality (to what extent is longer life no good for individuals), and honor (a critique of medical and social attitudes toward care for the aged).

747) Veatch, Robert M. Death, Dying, and the Biological Revolution: Our Last Quest for Responsibility. New Haven: Yale University Press, 1976.

A well-knit view of developments in dying persons. He deals with topics such as the definition of death, life-prolonging care of the moribund, the patient's right to refuse treatment, and the medical use of bodily parts. Dr. Veatch proposes a statutory definition of death, and a bill which would permit the refusal of medical treatment. He believes that legal provision is the best manner in which to handle death-and-dying issues, and has a mistrusting attitude toward physicians in the matter. He is critical of the ways in which physicians handle the matter of informing the patient who has serious progressive illness. Veatch defends his position very well, and contributes a work worth the reader's attention.

748) _____. Case Studies in Medical Ethics. Cambridge, Mass.: Harvard University Press, 1977.

Veatch employs the case method as a pedagogic tool for fastening abstract thought and intellectual theory into an operational unit relative to a particular problem. He incorporates such topics as abortion, contraception, death and dying problems, allocation of resources, human experimentation, and rights which have to do with accepting or refusing treatment. The book is most profitable, and makes one aware of the needs of the patient, family, and physician.

749) _____. "Deciding Against Resuscitation: Encouraging Signs and Potential Dangers." Journal of The American Medical Association 253 (January 1985): 77-78.

A brief discussion on a study which gave evidence that the decision against resuscitation is having an important impact on the care of critically and terminally ill patients.

750) Venes, Joan, Joseph C. Maroon, Thomas Shannon, Barbara Geach, et al. "Severely Deformed Infants." New England Journal of Medicine 295 (July 1976): 115-116.

Six letters by physicians in answer to an article in the New England Journal of Medicine 294: 838, April, 1976, by Dr. Lacks, who characterized hydrocephalic children as being "non persons."

751) Visscher, Maurice B. Humanistic Perspectives in Medical Ethics. Buffalo: Prometheus Books, 1972.

A collection of essays written by leading physicians, psychiatrists, social scientists, and philosophers. This edition comprises the following contents:

1) The Humanistic Tradition in the Health Professions - Chauncey D. Leake
2) Medical Ethics in Philosophical Perspective- Patrick Romanell
3) The Sanctity of Life Principle - Marvin Kohl
4) The Right to Die - Walter C. Alvarez
5) The Evolution of the Right-to-Health Concept in the U.S. - Carleton B. Chapman and John M. Talmadge
6) The Fee-for-Service System - H. Roy Kaplan
7) The Ethics of the Physician in Human Reproduction - Howard C. Taylor
8) Birth Defects - Leroy Augenstein
9) Human Experimentation - Louis Lasagna
10) Medical Ethics and Psychotropic Drugs- Mervin F. Silverman and Deborah B. Silverman
11) Prison Doctors - Tom Murton
12) Medicine and The Military - Gordon Livingston
13) Beyond Atrocity - Robert J. Litton
14) Social Ethics for Medical Educators - John G. Bruhn and Douglas C. Smith

752) Wade, Ellen V., and Rajiv Jain. "Nutritional Support: Enhancing the Quality of Life of the Terminally Ill Patient with Cancer." Journal of The American Dietetic Association 84 (September 1984): 1044-1045.

The emphasis of this article is on providing quality care. The focus is on life, and not death; therefore, nutrition is a means whereby quality care is provided for patients with terminal disease on a palliative-care unit at the Salem Veterans Administration Medical Center, Salem, Va. A description of the palliative-care unit is presented, emphasizing nutrition-related facilities, such as the kitchen, dining room, and equipment, all of which serve to provide the patient with the right surroundings for adequate support. The role of the dietician is discussed, together with an initial nutritional assessment of newly admitted patients, which becomes part of the patient's record.

753) Walker, Earl A., ed. Cerebral Death. Baltimore: Urban and Schwarzenberg, 1985.

The author served on the President's Committee to evaluate guidelines for the determination of death. He is a neurosurgeon, and in this work he attempts to define brain death. Walker reviews the history of brain death (medical views of brain death), and the reaction of medical professions throughout the world to brain death definition, along with religious reaction. Legal problems which present themselves in brain-death situations are also discussed.

754) Wecht, Cyril H., ed. Legal Medicine. Philadelphia: W. B. Saunders, 1982.

While the book covers many areas in legal medicine by different authors, the one entitled "Death: Defining and Determining" by a physician and attorney, Dr. McCarthy DeMere, is excellent. Its fifteen pages chronicle an eight year battle between The American Bar Association, The American Medical Association, and The National Conference of Commissioners on Uniform State Laws, out of which came a compromise on a death definition--the Uniform Determination of Death Act. For those interested in the question, "when is one really dead?," this article is most appropriate.

755) Weiss, Ann E. Bioethics: Dilemmas in Modern Medicine. Hillside, N.J.: Enslow, 1985.

Weiss makes difficult subjects comprehensible, such as right to life, organs for sale, the Baby Doe rule, experimenting on humans, who gets health care, genetic engineering, rights of patients, and the right to die. After reading this book, one will have a good understanding of what bioethics is all about.

756) Whitelaw, Andrew. "Death as Option in Neonatal Intensive Care." Lancet 8502 (August 1986): 328-331.

According to Whitelaw, many physicians believe there are circumstances in which infants should be allowed to die without having their lives prolonged. He mentions that seventy-five infants were so seriously ill that withdrawal of treatment was considered. Criteria for withdrawal of treatment from a particular infant had to be based on certainty of total incapacity and a unanimous decision among the nursing staff caring for the child. Treatment was withdrawn from fifty-one of the seventy-five patients. The parents of forty-seven infants accepted the decision, and all the infants died. Parents of four chose continued intensive care, and two infants survived with disabilities. Treatment of twenty-four cases was continued. Seventeen survived and seven die. Agreement was unanimous amoung staff and parents that treatment should be withdrawn, and that treatment on purely legal grounds is not justifiable.

757) Williams, Samuel D. "Euthanasia." The Popular Science Monthly 3 (July 1872): 90-96.

This is the sixth article of seven published by The Speculative Club in 1870 wherein the author defends the administration of chloroform for the relief of pain. Williams states: "'That in all cases of hopeless and painful illness it should be the recognized duty of the medical attendant, whenever so desired of the patient, to administer chloroform, or such other anaesthetic as may by-and-by supersede chloroform, so as to destroy consciousness at once, and put the sufferer at once to a quick and painless death; all needful precautions being adopted to prevent any possible abuse of such duty; and means being taken to establish, beyond the possibility of doubt or question, that the remedy was applied at the express wish of the patient.'" He also believes that such action demonstrates respect for the sacredness of life. Other articles and publications are mentioned in order to present opposing views to that of Mr. Williams. Since this article was written in 1870, it is important in that it reveals the thinking of society on the subject of euthanasia at that time. Interesting and highly recommended for reading.

758) Wilson, Jerry B. Death By Decision: The Medical, Moral, and Legal Dilemmas of Euthanasia. Philadelphia: Western, 1975.

An attempt to shed light on the euthanasia debate. A well organized study of the subject, which traces ancient practices of euthanasia to the present day. The author examines the medical, moral, and legal aspects of the subject, and presents pros and cons on its different forms. He has a tendency to support limited practices of euthanasia. The book is easy to read, and has an extensive bibliography.

759) Winken Werder, William Jr. "Ethical Dilemmas for House Staff Physicians: The Care of Critically Ill and Dying Patients." Journal of The American Medical Association 254 (December 1985): 3454-3457.

This article addresses the issue of ethical dilemma faced by residents who care for critically-ill patients. A case study is presented.

760) Winter, Arthur. "When Do We Die?" In Is It Moral to Modify Man?, ed. Claude A. Frazier, 248-255. Springfield, Ill.: Charles C. Thomas, 1973.

A medical doctor presents six case histories of patients and how difficult it is to determine death today. In the first two cases (irreparable brain damage and a malignant brain tumor), death was definable and fulfilled the criteria as indicated by the ad hoc committee of Harvard. According to the new criteria, when the brain has died, the patient is dead. This cannot be thought of as euthanasia because the doctor has not interrupted life.

761) _____, ed. Life and Death Decisions. Springfield, Ill.: Charles C. Thomas, 1980.

This edited work is based on a symposium held in 1978 by The Academy of Medicine of New Jersey, and presents the many problems which arise having to do with decision-making during life-and-death situations--decisions made by physicians. Pastors and chaplains who work with or come in contact with physicians should read it in order to get a "feel" of the problems which beset physicians and health-care personnel.

762) Younger, Stuart, Wendy Lewandowski, Donna K. McClish, Barbra W. Jukanialis, Claudia Coulton, and Edward T. Bartlett. "'Do Not Resuscitate' Orders: Incidence and Implications in a Medical Intensive Care Unit." Journal of The American Medical Association 253 (January 1985): 54-57.

A study which focuses on DNR orders of patients who had been selected for intensive care. Patients and methods, the results of demographic and clinical characteristics, resource consumption, documentations, and justifications of DNR orders are presented.

763) Yudkin, John S., Len T. Doyal, and Brian S. Hurwitz. "Interpreting Survival Rates for the Treatment of Decompensated Diabetes: Are We Saving Too Many Lives?" Lancet 2 (November 1987): 1192-1195.

A conflict of attitudes is revealed as the result of a discussion among diabetologists concerning the case of a patient admitted with decompensated diabetes. Two hundred diabetologists were surveyed in the United Kingdom, which revealed that three elderly patients admitted with decompensated diabetes were more likely to be resuscitated than were cardiac arrest patients.

The reasons for different approaches to the two conditions are discussed, along with suggestions for a greater involvement by patients in decision making about future resuscitation.

764) Zachary, R. B. "Life with Spina Bifida." British Medical Journal (December 1977): 1460-1462.

A presentation of the many problems which beset spina bifidas. The doctor's attitude depends on their longevity of life. Criteria for selecting babies for surgery is offered. Regardless of the treatment, some will die. Others require surgery if they are to survive.

765) Zimmerman, Jack, William A. Knaus, Steven M. Sharpe, Andrew S. Anderson, Elizabeth A. Draper, and Douglas P. Wagner. "The Use and Implications of Do-Not-Resuscitate Orders in Intensive Care Units." Journal of The American Medical Association 255 (January 1986): 351-356.

Written to describe current DNR practices and to understand their implications, along with descriptions of the characteristics of ICU patients with DNR orders, variations in order-writing practices in different ICUs, and subsequent treatment decisions, etc.

Moral Reaction

766) Bayles, Michael D., and Dallas M. High, eds. Medical Treatment of the Dying: Moral Issues. Cambridge, Mass.: G. K. Hall-Schenkman, 1978.

Mostly consists of a collection of papers presented at a symposium which was held in October 1974. Moral issues concerning medical treatment of the dying are brought to the fore.

767) Behnke, John, and Sissela Bok, ed. The Dilemmas of Euthanasia. Garden City, N.Y.: Anchor/Doubleday, 1975.

This paperback incorporates seven chapters dealing with the historical, moral, ethical, legal, and diagnostic aspects of euthanasia. A good work for the general reader. There is enough detail on the subject to inform one quite satisfactorily. Legal and other documents are appended.

768) Campbell, A. V. Moral Dilemmas in Medicine: A Coursebook in Ethics for Doctors and Nurses. 2nd Edition. Churchill Livingston, 1975.

A basic ethics coursebook dealing with theoretical and practical issues, among which are: abortion; resuscitation and euthanasia; human experimentation; and transplantation. Included is a limited bibliography.

769) Campbell, M., and R. Duff. "Moral and Ethical Dilemmas in the Special Care Nursery." New England Journal of Medicine 289 (October 1973): 890-894.

Moral and ethical issues surrounding dicisions to allow certain babies to die are presented by Campbell and Duff. They believe it is perfectly alright to allow infants to die who have poor "quality of life" (withhold treatment). A review of records in a special-care nursery found that over a two-and-one-half-year period, fourteen percent of the deaths were the result of withholding treatment from abnormal infants. The family is taken into consideration as being the ultimate decision makers in allowing the infant to die. Special guidelines are suggested in order that the decision to withhold treatment should not be abused.

770) Clouser, K. D. "'The Sanctity of Life': An Analysis of a Concept." Annals of Internal Medicine 78 (1973): 119-125.

Clouser shows that the phrase "sanctity of life" is muddled and inconclusive. He thinks it should be expressed in a moral rule, such as "do not take human life." He explains and analyzes the rule.

771) Etzoioni, Amitai. "Moral and Social Implications of Genetic Manipulation." In Is It Moral to Modify Man?, ed. Claude A. Frazier, 267-269. Springfield, Ill.: Charles C. Thomas, 1973.

A brief discussion of how genetic control and manipulation can be a curse to man rather than a blessing. One danger mentioned is the fact that defective genes may be found in a floating fetus and lead to abortion (infanticide). This short article raises serious questions.

772) Freund, Paul A. "Organ Transplants: Ethical and Legal Problems." In Ethics in Medicine: Historical Perspectives and Contemporary Concerns, ed. Stanley Joel Reiser, Arthur J. Dyck, and William J. Curran, 173-177. Cambridge, Mass.: MIT, 1977.

Freund discusses problems concerning the allocation of resources: from whom they should come and to whom organs should be transferred. Implications raised by the question concern moral, legal, and medical considerations. Each differs on removal of organs after death and during life. He briefly discusses briefly the question of whether or not a dyingpatient should be allowed to consent to surgical intervention for the purpose of saving another's life, which borders on euthanasia practices.

773) Glover, Jonathan. Causing Death and Saving Lives. Harmondsworth: Penguin Books, 1977.

A lucid discussion presenting the arguments used in prohibiting or justifying the killing of others. It deals with: moral theory, autonomy and rights, ends and means; not striving to keep alive; abortion, infanticide, suicide, voluntary and involuntary euthanasia, choices between people in allocating resources, assassination, and war. A skillful work and highly recommended for those interested in euthanasia and problems surrounding it.

774) Gregg, W. W. "Right to Kill." North American Review 237 (March 1934): 239-249.

Active and passive euthanasia are discussed, along with abortion, infanticide, and capital punishment. An analysis of legal and moral implications is offered.

775) Holland R. F. "Suicide." In Moral Problems, ed. J. Rachels. New York: Harper and Row, 1971.

The author tries to find out what one may count as suicide, and the factors that cause it. He differentiates between taking one's life for others, and killing oneself for selfish reasons. He seems to think that religion is rather hard on suicide and blankets it as all wrong.

776) Horan, Dennis J., and David Mall, eds. Death, Dying and Euthanasia. Washington, D.C.: University Publications of America, 1977.

Controversial aspects of euthanasia are discussed, such as: involuntary euthanasia of the defective newborn; ethical, moral, and legal aspects of "mercy killing"; the feasibility of legalized euthanasia; and the right of the individual to reject treatment.

777) Horan and Dela Hoyde, eds. Infanticide and the Handicapped Newborn. Provo, Utah: Brigham Young University Press: 1981.

A scholarly work which evaluates the moral and medical issues raised by infanticide in America.

778) Lockwood, Michael, ed. Moral Dilemmas in Modern Medicine. London: Oxford University Press, 1985.

Three sets of issues comprise the volume. Set one consists of reproductive techniques, which include: in vitro fertilization, surrogate mothering, frozen embryos, gene therapy, growing human embryos in the laboratory, and genetic engineering. Medical paternalism and patient autonomy are dealt with in the second set. The nature of moral arguments and reasoning in medicine studies will enhance one's knowledge and respect for those who deal with the issues presented.

779) Lynn, Joanne, ed. By No Extraordinary Means: The Choice to Forgo Life-Sustaining Food and Water. Bloomington: Indiana University Press, 1986.

The authors present the medical, moral, ethical, social, and legal perspectives of the nutrition-and-hydration issue. Situations discussed have to do with the newborn, terminally ill, unconscious persons (permanently), and the chronically ill but not terminal patient who has decided to refuse food and water. This collection of papers was prepared for the Society for Health and Human Values and should be purchased by all who are interested in the subject because it compiles the views of different authors.

780) Macklin, Ruth. Bioethics in Today's World. New York: Pantheon Books, 1987.

A pioneer in bioethics discusses problems and analyzes many real-life episodes relative to "mortal choices." She writes that these choices are made in the following areas: ethical dilemmas in medicine, applying moral principles, gaining informed consent, aggressive treatment, foregoing life-sustaining therapy, determining incompetency, deciding for others, the best interest of the child, treating the family, allocating scarce resources, conflicting obligations, experimenting on human subjects, harming and wronging patients, and resolving the issues. The book is well indexed, and her notes on each chapter suggest a cross-section of bibliographical material pertinent to each subject discussed.

781) Medicine, Morality and The Law: Euthanasia. 30 min. B&W. Rental/Sale. T.V. Center, University of Michigan.

A panel discussion of the legal and moral aspects of three case studies on the subject of euthanasia.

782) Mercy Killing. Toronto: 30 min. Audio tape. Sale. CBC.

The technical and moral aspects of euthanasia presented by way of a panel discussion. For private and group use only.

783) Milbauer, Barbra and Bert N. Oberentz. The Law Giveth: Legal Aspects of the Abortion Controversy. Atheneum, N.Y.: McClelland and Stewart, 1983.

The facts on abortion are well summarized in this book. The reader is taken on a journey through case law and pertinent American history. Social, medical, religious, and moral aspects of the abortion debate are discussed. The book assists greatly in helping to understand abortion in our time. The bearing of the book on euthanasia is simply this: if abortion is allowed to be performed on the healthy unborn, the "green light" for aborting the already-born deformed is certainly a permissive sign.

784) Ramsey, Paul. The Patient As Person. New Haven, Conn.: Yale University Press, 1970.

A comprehensive moral analysis of euthanasia, the use of ordinary and extraordinary means for preserving life, and moral responsibilities toward the dying.

785) Reiser, Stanley Joel, Arthur J. Dyck, and William J. Curran, eds. Ethics in Medicine: Historical Perspectives and Contemporary Concerns. Cambridge, Massachusetts: MIT, 1977.

This text was developed while teaching graduate and undergraduate courses at Harvard Univerrsity. It is practical for practitioners and students in medicine, law, ethics, counselling, and for individual patients and groups who are concerned with medical care. The volume is separated into eight sections: (1) Ethical Dimensions of the Physician-Patient Relationship, (2) Moral Basis of Medical Ethics, (3) Regulation, Compulsion, and Consumer Protection in Clinical Medicine and Public Health, (4) Truth-Telling in the Physician - Patient Relationship, (5) Medical Experimentation on Human Subjects, (6) Procreative Decisions, (7) Suffering and Dying, and (8) Rights and Priorities in the Provision of Medical Care. Each section contains articles, essays, and class lectures. An excellent textbook.

786) Rosner, Fred and J. David Bleich, ed. "Organ Transplantation". In Jewish Bioethics. New York: Sanhedrin, 1979.

Two chapters dealing with organ transplantation reveals Jewish thinking on the subject: "What is the Halakhah for Organ Transplants?" and "Organ Transplantation in Jewish Law." The first mentioned chapter answers the question " . . .may one administer a treatment which will, if it fails, kill him immediately, but, if it succeeds, prolong his life?" The other chapter deals with theological, moral, ethical, social, legal, and philosophical problems surrounding heart transplantation; the halakhah in eye transplants; the halakhah in kidney transplants; and the halakhah in heart transplants. Each of these chapters has bearing on euthanasia--at least in the Jewish view.

787) Russell, Ruth O. Freedom to Die: Moral and Legal Aspects of Euthanasia. New York: Human Sciences, 1975.

An articulate presentation of a pro-euthanasia view. The author leaves the impression that those in antiquity who held anti-euthanasia views were superstitious and religiously inflexible. On page 283, she writes: "It seems certain that it is only a matter of time until laws will be passed that will permit the administration of painless death when the only alternative is an agonizing or meaningless existence. It is a challenge to every citizen to hasten that day." The author won the Humanist Pioneer Award as a result of this work.

788) The Patient's Right to Die. Washington, D.C.: 60 min. B&W, Videocassette. Videotape Library, Walter Reed Army Medical Center (20307).

Discusses moral and ethical dilemmas on pre-servation of life, and active and passive euth-thanasia. Theological in approach.

789) The Right to Die. Chatsworth, Calif.: Filmstrip and Audiocassette. Sale. Career Aids Inc., 20417 Nordhoss (91311).

A discussion on the moral, legal, and practical implications of life-extending technology.

790) Visscher, Maurice B. Humanistic Perspectives in Medical Ethics. Buffalo: Prometheus Books, 1972.

A collection of essays written by leading physicians, psychiatrists, social scientists, and philosophers. This edition comprises the following contents:

1) The Humanistic Tradition in the Health Professions - Chauncey D. Leake
2) Medical Ethics in Philosophical Perspective - Patrick Romanell
3) The Sanctity of Life Principle - Marvin Kohl
4) The Right to Die - Walter C. Alvarez
5) The Evolution of the Right-to-Health Concept in the U.S. - Carleton B. Chapman and John M. Talmadge
6) The Fee-for-Service System - H. Roy Kaplan
7) The Ethics of the Physician in Human Reproduction - Howard C. Taylor
8) Birth Defects - Leroy Augenstein
9) Human Experimentation - Louis Lasagna
10) Medical Ethics and Psychotropic Drugs Mervin F. Silverman and Deborah B. Silverman
11) Prison Doctors - Tom Murton
12) Medicine and The Military - Gordon Livingston
13) Beyond Atrocity - Robert J. Litton
14) Social Ethics for Medical Educators - John G. Bruhn and Douglas C. Smith

791) Wilson, Jerry B.   Death By Decision: The Medical, Moral, and Legal Dilemmas of Euthanasia. Philadelphia: Western, 1975.

An attempt to shed light on the euthanasia debate. A well organized study of the subject which traces ancient practices of euthanasia to the present day. The author examines the medical, moral, and legal aspects of the subject, and presents pros and cons on its different forms. He has a tendency to support limited practices of euthanasia. The book is easy to read, and has an extensive bibliography.

Philosophical Reaction

792) Bandman , Elsie L., and Bertram Bandman, eds. Bioethics and Human Rights. Boston: Little, Brown, 1978.

The volume comprises fifty-two essays by professionals in philosophy, medicine (doctors and nurses), educators, and attorneys. Listed under four topics are: foundations of human rights in health care, the right to life, the right to live as persons and the responsibilities for changing behavior, and health care rights. Opposing views are presented on a number of subjects.

793) Battin, Pabst M., and David J. Mayo. Suicide: The Philosophical Issues. New York: St. Martin's, 1980.

Contemporary essays by philosophers, psychiatrists, legal theorists, literary, and religious personalities, which bring together a body of material answering to the issues which are relative to suicide. Explored are such questions as: Does a person have a right to end his or her own life? Is suicide always an irrational choice? Is suicide evidence of insanity? Do other persons have a right to intervene into a suicidal attempt or assist someone in taking his or her life? Can suicide be meaningful, legal, or morally right? Debated are the following philosophical issues:

Did Socrates Commit Suicide?
    The Concept of Suicide
    Suicide and Self-Sacrifice
Suicide: Some Theological Reflections
    Suicide and Covenant
    Apologia for Suicide
The Ethics of Not-Being: Individual Options
    for Suicide
The Rationality of Suicide
    Irrational Suicide
    On Choosing Death
    Suicide and False Desires
Suicide as Instrument and Expression

The Art of Suicide
Manipulated Suicide
The Ethics of Suicide
Choosing the Time to Die
Suicide Prevention and the Value of Human Life
The Right to Suicide: A Psychiatrist's View
Suicide and the Inalienable Right to Life
A Constitutional Right to Suicide
Assisting Suicide: A Problem for the Criminal Law
Suicide: A Fundamental Human Right?
Suicide and Virtue

The reader will discover that the discussions in this work involve primarily conceptual and moral issues. Also spoken to are professionals in areas of psychiatry, counselling, nursing, general medicine, religious practice, and law. A book which calls forth respect for the intelligent scholarly gifts of its contributors.

794) Behnke, J. A., and S. Bok, eds. The Dilemmas of Euthanasia. Garden City, N.Y.: Anchor/Doubleday, 1975.

Four anthologies on philosophical, legal, theological, and medical articles, active and passive euthanasia, suicide, and care for the dying.

795) Bell, Nora K., ed. Who Decides? Conflicts of Rights in Health Care. Clifton, N.J.: Humana, 1982.

Included are sixteen essays by outstanding personalities in the field of philosophical and medical ethics: Tristam Engelhardt, Guenter Risse, Daniel Callahan, Ruth Macklin, and Thomas Szasz, along with others. Of interest are four controversial areas: the limits of professional autonomy, refusing and withdrawing treatment, "heroic measures" for the dying patient, and reproductive technology.

796) Choron, J. Death and Western Thought. New York: Collier, 1963.

If one is interested in what the great western philosophers thought about death and dying, this is a classic which should not be avoided. It incorporates pre-Socratic views to the present day. Highly recommended.

797) Clements, Colleen D. Medical Genetics Casebook: A Clinical Introduction to Medical Ethics. Clifton, N.J.: Humana, 1982.

The author maintains that ethicists approach problems in medical ethics with theories that ignore realities of medical practice. They make little allowances for feedback from medical experience. She follows 130 cases which involve problems such as: working with information, trial and reality testing, self-image, experimental research and procedures, selective abortion, and societal and individual interest conflicts. She reviews basic principles of moral and ethical philosophy. Clements also recommends that her book be used as a source for prenatal diagnosis. Her book should be a significant help for all who are concerned for life and the impact of medical technology on that life.

798) Englehardt, H. Tristram, Jr., and Stuart F. Spicker, eds. Philosophy and Medicine. Vol. 18, Medical Ethics in Antiquity: Philosophical Perspectives on Abortion and Euthanasia, by Paul Carrick. Boston: D. Reidel, 1985.

An exploration of the origins and development of medical ethics as practiced by the ancient Greek and Roman physicians, together with their views on abortion and euthanasia. Infanticide and suicide are also examined. The Hippocratic Oath is dissected relative to abortion, infanticide, euthanasia, and suicide. The book is in three parts. Part One explores the social setting of

Greek medicine. Part Two specifically deals with the beginning of Greek medical ethics, and Part Three examines a variety of divergent Greco-Roman ethical views and opinions on abortion and euthanasia. An excellent work and should be in the libraries of those who are interested in the historical aspects of euthanasia and related subjects.

799) Foot, Philippa. "Euthanasia." Philosophy and Public Affairs 6 (Winter 1977): 85-112.

Foot believes that euthanasia should be performed for the dying person. Patients are encouraged to make their wishes known to their physicians, rather than others. This, according to Foot, will alleviate the psychological barrier of "killing."

800) Gruman, Gerald J. "An Historical Introducion to Ideas About Voluntary Euthanasia: With a Bibliographic Survey and Guides for Interdisciplinary Studies" Omega 4 (Summer 1973): 87-138.

A progressive study of the ideas of voluntary euthanasia. For a brief and quick accumulation of information about the subject, this article is highly recommended.

801) Horan, Dennis J. Death, Dying and Euthanasia. Washington, D.C.: University Publications of America, Inc., 1977.

An impressive collection of works by authors from various fields: physicians, attorneys, ethicists, clergy, philosophers, and others who write with conviction on euthanasia. The works, most of which are reprints from periodicals, are classified under seven headings: (1) Death: When Does It Occur and How Do We Define It?, (2) Death as a Treatment of Choice?: Involuntary Euthanasia of the Defective Newborn, (3) Euthanasia: Ethical, Religious, and Moral Aspects, (4) Euthanasia: The Legal Aspects of "Mercy Killing," (5) How Should Medicine and Society Treat the Dying?, (6) Legalized Euthanasia: Social Attitudes and Governmental Policies, and (7) Suicide and the Patient's Right to Reject Medical Treatment. The editors list the contributors in the back of the book. Good for research.

802) Kluge, Eike-Henner. The Practice of Death. New Haven: Yale University Press, 1975.

A philosophical discussion of decision-making on the subjects of euthanasia, suicide, abortion, infanticide, and senicide. Straightforward.

803) Kreeft, Peter J. Love Is Stronger Than Death. New York: Harper and Row, 1979.

Both Christian and philosophical in answering the questions; what is death and why do we die?

804) Ladd, John, ed. Ethical Issues Relating to Life and Death. New York and Oxford: Oxford University Press, 1979.

Nine essays which are concerned with euthanasia from the philosophical and ethical points of view. References to the essays are mostly to non-medical literature.

805) Lamb, David. Death, Brain Death and Ethics. Albany: State University of New York Press, 1985.

"What is considered so essential to human life such that when it is lost we consider the individual dead?" This question sets one's thinking for the author's discussion on death, the brain, and ethics. A series of lectures inquiring into what death is relative to the brain. Lamb's thesis is that death of the brain stem is death of the individual organism. He provides a philosophical framework for criteria for determining death. The book is well written, up to date, and more philosophical than practical. Good for anyone looking for a definition of death.

806) Lockwood, Michael, ed. <u>Moral Dilemmas in Modern Medicine.</u> London: Oxford University Press, 1985.

Three sets of issues comprise the volume. Set one consists of reproductive techniques, which include: in vitro fertilization, surrogate mothering, frozen embryos, gene therapy, growing human embryos in the laboratory, and genetic engineering. Medical paternalism and patient autonomy are dealt with in the second set. The nature of moral arguments and reasoning in medicine comprise the third set. These philosophical studies will enhance one's knowledge and respect for those who deal with the issues presented.

807) Macklin, Ruth. <u>Bioethics in Today's World</u>. New York: Pantheon Books, 1987.

A pioneer in bioethics discusses problems and analyzes many real-life episodes relative to "mortal choices." She writes that these choices are made in the following areas: ethical dilemmas in medicine, applying moral principles, gaining informed consent, aggressive treatment, foregoing life-sustaining therapy, determining incompetency, deciding for others, the best interest of the child, treating the family, allocating scarce resources, conflicting obligations, experimenting on human subjects, harming and wronging patients, and resolving the issues. The book is well indexed, and her notes on each chapter suggest a cross-section of bibliographical material pertinent to each subject discussed.

808) Meier, Levi, ed. <u>Jewish Values in Bioethics.</u> New York: Human Sciences, 1986.

A collection of addresses on biomedical issues echoing the voices of many Jewish authorities: Orthodox and Conservative, legal and philosophical, medical and literary, and wrestles with modern dilemmas in the health care field.

809) Meyer, J. E. Death and Neurosis. Vol. 12, New York: International Universities Press, 1975.

A theory that man's fear of death is the beginning of neuroses. A presentation of theological and philosophical concepts about dying.

810) Murray, Thomas, and Arthur L. Caplan, eds. Which Babies Shall Live?: Humanistic Dimensions of the Care of Imperiled Newborns. Clifton, New Jersey: Humana, 1985.

A collection of essays discussing seriously-ill newborns. This work draws on the insights of philosophers, a historian, theologian, an anthropologist and others. The essays are in four groups: "The Child: Medicine and Science"; "Caretakers: Images and Attitudes"; "Religion, Suffering and Mortality"; and "Images of the Abandoned." Truly, this book offers a new perspective in the cause of catastrophically-ill newborns.

811) Raanan, G. "Suicide and Voluntary Euthanasia: Historical Perspective." In Euthanasia and the Right to Die, ed. A. B. Downing, New York: Humanities, 1970.

A brief historical sketch of ideas surrounding suicide and voluntary euthanasia, along with various reasons for and against suicide are stated. Personalities, movements, and philosophies are discussed.

812) Robison, Wade L., and Michael S. Pritchard, eds, Medical Responsivility: Paternalism, Informed Consent, and Euthanasia. Clifton, N.J.: Humana, 1979.

A collection of essays by philosophers. The first two discuss the general nature of paternalism and its medical implications. The third essay sets forth the subject of genetic screening. A series of six chapters follow on problems of paternalism in obtaining informed consent for therapy and medical experimentation. A study on fetal research done for the National Commission for the Protection of

Human Subjects is presented by Toulmin, and is followed by four chapters on euthanasia and death and dying. This is a masterful compilation of essays which carry a philosophical theme.

813) Rosner, Fred and J. David Bleich, ed. "Organ Transplantation." In Jewish Bioethics. New York: Sanhedrin, 1979.

Two chapters dealing with organ transplantation reveal Jewish thinking on the subject: "What is the Halakhah for Organ Transplants?" and "Organ Transplantation in Jewish Law." The first mentioned chapter answers the question ". . . may one administer a treatment which will, if it fails, kill him immediately, but, if it succeeds, prolong his life?" The other chapter deals with theological, moral, ethical, social, legal, and philosophical problems surrounding heart transplantation; the halakhah in eye transplants; the halakhah in kidney transplants; and the halakhah in heart transplants. Each of these chapters has bearing on euthanasia--at least in the Jewish view.

814) Temkin, Owsei, William K. Frankena, and Sanford H. Kadfsh. Respect for Life in Medicine, Philosophy, and the Law. Baltimore: The Johns Hopkins University Press, 1976.

Respect for life is approached from different perspectives which shed light on the subject in different ways. Temkin discusses the history of medicine, and how early medicine understood respect for life. The philosophical approach by William Frankena interprets respect for life and how moral philosophy should define it. Kadish presents how the law treats different cases of taking human life. Euthanasia, abortion, infanticide, and other means of taking life are interwoven throughout the book.

815) Visscher, Maurice B., ed. Humanistic Perspectives in Medical Ethics. Buffalo, N.Y.: Prometheus Books, 1972.

Essays examining issues on medical ethics. Physicians, psychiatrists, social scientists, and philosophers develop guidelines for the future. Discussed are such issues as population control, drug abuse, the National Health Program, human experimentation, euthanasia, and birth defects. Anyone concerned with these moral issues will benefit from this excellent work.

816) Wasserman, H. P. "Problematical Aspects of the Phenomenon of Death." World Medical Journal 14 (September - October 1967): 146-149.

A philosophical study of death and dying. After defining death, Wasserman believes that it should be looked upon as inevitable. He believes that medical science should provide a means of euthanasia without suffering.

817) Williams, Samuel D. "Euthanasia." The Popular Science Monthly 3 (July 1872): 90-96.

This is the sixth article of seven published by The Speculative Club in 1870 wherein the author defends the administration of chloroform for the relief of pain. Williams states: "'That in all cases of hopeless and painful illness it should be the recognized duty of the medical attendant, whenever so desired of the patient, to administer chloroform, or such other anaesthetic as may by-and-by supersede chloroform, so as to destroy consciousness at once, and put the sufferer at once to a quick and painless death; all needful precautions being adopted to prevent any possible abuse of such duty; and means being taken to establish, beyond the possibility of doubt or question, that the remedy was applied at the express wish of the patient.'" He also believes that such action demonstrates respect for the sacredness of life.

Other articles and publications are mentioned in order to present opposing views to that of Mr. Williams. Since this article was written in 1870, it is important in that it reveals the thinking of society on the subject of euthanasia at that time. Interesting and highly recommended for reading.

Psychological Reaction

818) Battin, Pabst M., and David J. Mayo. Suicide: The Philosophical Issues. New York: St. Martin's, 1980.

Contemporary essays by philosophers, psychiatrists, legal theorists, literary and religious personalities, which bring together a body of material answering to the issues which are relative to suicide. Explored are such questions as: Does a person have a right to end his or her own life? Is suicide always an irrational choice? Is suicide evidence of insanity? Do other persons have a right to intervene into a suicidal attempt or assist someone in taking his or her life? Can suicide be meaningful, legal, or morally right? Debated are the following philosophical issues:

Did Socrates Commit Suicide?
   The Concept of Suicide
   Suicide and Self-Sacrifice
Suicide: Some Theological Reflections
   Suicide and Covenant
   Apologia for Suicide
The Ethics of Not-Being: Individual Options
for Suicide
   The Rationality of Suicide
   Irrational Suicide
   On Choosing Death
   Suicide and False Desires
Suicide as Instrument and Expression
   The Art of Suicide
   Manipulated Suicide
   The Ethics of Suicide
Choosing the Time to Die

Suicide Prevention and the Value of Human Life
The Right to Suicide: A Psychiatrist's View
Suicide and the Inalienable Right to Life
A Constitutional Right to Suicide
Assisting Suicide: A Problem for the Criminal Law
Suicide: A Fundamental Human Right?
Suicide and Virtue

The reader will discover that the discussions in this work involve primarily conceptual and moral issues. Also spoken to are professionals in areas of psychiatry, counselling, nursing, general medicine, religious practice, and law. A book which calls forth respect for the intelligent scholarly gifts of its contributors.

819) Beswick, David E. "Attitudes to Taking Human Life." The Australian and New Zealand Journal of Sociology 6 (1970): 120-130.

An exceptional survey which was taken by third-year psychology students. The interviews conducted in April and May, 1969 resulted in responses from various sections of the Canberra population. The study centers on attitudes to taking of human life.

820) Clark, David B., Jr. "Voluntary Euthanasia and the Hemlock Society." American Journal of Psychiatry 143 (November 1986): 1503, 1504.

A defense of the Hemlock Society in response to an article "Is It Normal for The Terminally Ill Patients to Desire Death?" The article states that the Hemlock Society condones and assists in suicide by terminally-ill patients.

821) Deutsch, Felix. "Euthanasia: A Clinical Study." Psychoanalytic Study 5 (1936): 347-368.

Deutsch contributes what he has learned at the bedside of the dying patient - - a psychological understanding of peaceful dying. He presents case histories of dying patients, and their experiences during the process of death. He discusses under what conditions euthanasia occurs, when the fear of death has been dispelled, when there is no further question of the fear of guilt, and what makes happiness possible during the process of dying. One will find new "food for thought" in this article.

822) Foot, Philippa. "Euthanasia." Philosophy and Public Affairs 6 (Winter 1977): 85-112.

Foot believes that euthanasia should be performed for the dying person. Patients are encouraged to make their wishes known to their physicians, rather than others. This, according to Foot, will alleviate the psychological barrier of "killing."

823) Friedman, H. "Serious Gap Between Theory and Practice Seen in Physicians' Management of Terminal Patients." Geriatric Focus (September 1970).

A critique discussing the inability of doctors to face death-and-dying issues with their patients. Friedman suggests that the care of terminal patients be given over to those more proficient in coping with the problems, namely, psychiatrists and social workers.

824) Garfield, Charles A., ed. Psychosocial Care of the Dying Patient. New York: McGraw-Hill, 1978.

A comprehensive account of the many problems faced by the dying person and those who are engaged in caring for the terminally ill. It offers detailed help for the physician and the nurse. The patient's family can also find much that is helpful in the book. This work can be considered to be--up until the 80's when more was written on the subject--among the best.

825) Hofling, C. K. "Life-Death Decisions May Undermine M.D.'s Mental Health." Frontiers In Hospital Psychiatry 5 (March 1968): 3.

Hofling is emphatic in believing that decision-making with regard to euthanasia should be a team effort composed of a group effort. The expertise of the physician, clergyman, family, and friends should be brought to bear on the decision.

826) Katz, Jay and Alexander Morgan Capron. Catastrophic Diseases: Who Decides What? A Psychosocial and Legal Analysis of the Problems Posed by Hemodialysis and Organ Transplantation. New York.: Russell Sage Foundation, 1975.

The nature and effects of catastrophic illness are explored. Especially interesting is the section on the reduction of suffering.

827) Keleman, Stanley. Living Your Dying. New York: Random House, 1976.

A psychological viewpoint on man's traditional images of death. Keleman's belief is that man should be free to die his own death.

828) Kubler-Ross, Elizabeth. On Death and Dying. New York: MacMillan, 1969.

Kubler-Ross gives a classic statement of the five stages of dying: denial, anger, bargaining, depression, and acceptance. Dr. Kubler-Ross wrote this book as a result of two hundred interviews with terminally-ill patients. The book is certainly an eye opener to the reactions of terminal patients during the dying process.

829) Lygre, David G. Life Manipulation. New York: Walker, 1970.

All that can be thought of relative to "life manipulation," from test-tube babies to aging, is included in Lygre's well written book. The human implications of cloning, biofeedback, parthogenesis (virgin birth), psychosurgery, delayed aging, redesigned organs, artificial wombs, selective abortions, human gene splicing, artificial insemination, sex preselection of fetuses, life sustenance after brain death, prenatal diagnosis of birth defects, and other interesting subjects relative to biomedical research are treated. After reading this work, one will conclude that these issues cannot and should not be avoided, for everyone's life will be touched somehow as biomedical research reaches more and more into the lives of all humans.

830) May, A. E. "An Assessment of Homicidal Attitudes." The British Journal of Psychiatry 114 (April 1968): 479, 480.

An assessment of homicidal attitudes was made using three groups: normals, psychiatric patients, and homicidal patients. Inquiry into each of these groups was based on the attitude of a psychiatric patient who believed that anyone with physical or mental imperfections should be exterminated. The Respiratory Grid technique was used on all three groups to see if the psychiatric patient's attitude was abnormal. In summary, "a high correlation between 'feeling love for the family' and 'being in favor of mercy killing' was predicted for a patient with psychotic and sadistic idealtion. This prediction was confirmed."

831) Meyer, J. E. Death and Neurosis. Vol. 12, New York: International Universities Press, 1975.

A theory that man's fear of death is the beginning of neuroses. A presentation of theological and philosophical concepts about dying.

832) Noyles, Russell, Jr. "The Art of Dying." Perspectives in Biology and Medicine 35 (Spring 1971): 432-447.

Traces the art of dying through the Classical, Middle Ages, and Renaissance periods to the present. Early medical euthanasia is discussed, together with psychological theory, and the physician's role.

833) Please Let Me Die. 30 min. Color Videocassette. Rental/ Sale. Library of Clinical Psychiatric Syndromes; Dr. Robert B. White, Department of Psychiatry, University of Texas Medical Branch, Galveston, Tex. 77550.

A twenty-seven-year-old man is interviewed, who wants to be allowed to die as a result of being severely burned and handicapped. His argument for being allowed to die is compelling.

834) Restak, Richard M. Pre-Meditated Man: Bioethics and the Control of Future Human Life. New York: Viking, 1973.

A three-part book discussing the issues raised in psychosurgery. The most dramatic form of behavior modification in use is discussed in part one. Part two explores the implications of genetic engineering of different kinds. The third part analyzes experiences and the frightful lesson of the past and present having to do with human experimentation.

835) Rodin, C. M., J. Chmara, J. Ennis, S. Fenton, H. Locking, and K. Steinhouse. "Stopping Life-Sustaining Medical Treatment: Psychiatric Considerations in the Termination of Renal Dialysis." Canadian Journal of Psychiatry 26 (December 1981): 540-544.

A presentation of data regarding the decision by medical staff and patients to discontinue renal dialysis. The patient's mental competence, motivations, and psychiatric state are discussed. Medical factors involved in decision making are mentioned. The patient's active participation is emphasized.

836) Schulz, Richard. The Psychology of Death and Dying. Reading, Mass.: Addison-Wesley, 1978.

The text presents the following topics: research strategies, thinking about death, demography of death, the terminal phase of life, extending life, grief and bereavement, and death education.

837) Strauss, Anselm L. Chronic Illness and The Quality of Life. St. Louis: C. V. Mosby, 1975.

A study on how chronic illness effects the quality of life. The psychosocial aspects of living with chronic illness focuses on the patient and the family. Renal failure and dying in the hospital are discussed, along with how to gather information from such patients in order to better understand their needs. An informative piece of literature.

838) The Right to Die: Decision and Decision Makers. New York: Group for the Advancement of Psychiatry. Symposium No. 12, 1973.

A collection of essays dealing with a sensitive subject. Interesting ideas and discussions which may or may not be of interest.

839) Turpin, Joe P. "Some Psychiatric Issues of Euthanasia." In Beneficient Euthanasia, ed. Marvin Kohl, 193-203. Buffalo, N.Y.: Prometheus Books, 1975.

Turpin begins with the assumption that a person has a right to consent to his or her demise. He proceeds to discuss important practicalities relative to the exercise of that right. Informed consent, competence, and pain are factors which determine the freedom of a patient to exercise freedom to die.

840) van den Berg, Jan H. Medical Power and Medical Ethics. New York: W. W. Norton, 1978.

The brief work comprises 91 pages and was originally published in The Netherlands. The author is a psychiatrist, and brings into question the Hippocratic Oath that all human lives must be saved or prolonged by whatever means available. The author believes that a new and fundamental code of ethics should be required because of the technological advances in the science of medicine. Although the work is short, the case histories presented are well worth the reading time.

841) Veatch, Robert M. "Saying 'No' To Hemodialysis: Should A Minor's Decision Be Respected?" Hastings Center Report (September 1974): 8-10.

A case study in bioethics reflecting the attitudes of a 16 year-old girl who underwent transplant surgery. After receiving her father's kidney, it eventually failed to function, resulting in deep depression for both Karen and her parents. A shunt was placed in Karen's arm for dialysis, and soon became infected. It was judged that other transplantations would also fail, and the decision was made by Karen and her parents to discontinue hemodialysis. Two professionals study her case and give some interesting comments. I would encourage those who may be undergoing serious decisions concerning life - and - death - situations confronting teenage children to read Karen's case.

842) Vincent, Merville O. "Suicide - A Christian Perspective: Suicide Prevention - Where There's Hope There is Life." In Is It Moral to Modify Man?, ed. Claude A. Frazier, 129-147. Springfield, Ill.: Charles C. Thomas, 1973.

A Christian psychiatrist looks at the question "'. . .what role, if any, does Christianity have in alleviating the kind of suffering that results in self-destructive behavior? Does Christianity have anything to offer except. . .thou shalt not?'" Dr. Vincent appeals to Scripture and finds that while the Bible does not moralize on certain suicidal acts, it does not condone the practice. He lists and discusses the myths about suicide and faith as being the factor of preventing suicide. He emphasizes that Christians should change society and provide hope for the hopeless. Anyone reading this article will find neither justification nor encouragement in committing suicide by euthanasia.

843) Visscher, Maurice B., ed. Humanistic Perspectives in Medical Ethics. Buffalo, New York: Prometheus Books, 1972.

Essays examining issues on medical ethics. Physicians, psychiatrists, social scientists, and philosophers develop guidelines for the future. Discussed are such issues as population control, drug human experimentation, euthanasia, and birth defects. Anyone concerned with these moral issues will benefit from this excellent work.

Social Reaction

844) Breo, Dennis. Extraordinary Care: The Medical Treatment of Adolph Hitler, Howard Hughes, Elvis Presley, President Ronald Reagan, Barney Clark,... Chicago: Review, 1986.

A not-so-serious examination of the issues facing society today. A collection of interviews which shed light on outstanding personalities and their patient-physician relationship. The interview format touches on perplexing issues, such as surrogate motherhood, the right to choose forms of cancer therapy, and the subject which has real bearing on all our lives--euthanasia. The discussions involving the author and VIPs will interest all who care to read the assemblage.

845) Clements, Colleen D. Medical Genetics Casebook: A Clinical Introduction to Medical Ethics. Clifton, N.J.: Humana, 1982.

The author maintains that ethicists approach problems in medical ethics with theories that ignore realities of medical practice. They make little allowances for feedback from medical experience. She follows one hundred thirty cases which involve problems such as: working with information, trial and reality testing, self-image, experimental research and procedures, selective abortion, and societal and individual interest conflicts. She reviews basic principles of moral and ethical philosophy. Clements also recommends that her book be used as a source for prenatal diagnosis. Her book should be a significant help for all who are concerned for life and the impact of medical technology on that life.

846) Cohen, Bernice H., Abraham M. Lilenfeld, and P. C. Huang, eds. Genetic Issues in Public Health and Medicine. Springfield, Ill.: Charles C. Thomas, 1978.

Brings into focus genetic knowledge and concomitant problems in the social, political, legal, and moral-ethical areas. Space is given to the discussion of genetic material and the environment, prenatal diagnosis of genetic disorders, population and programs in special population segments, genetic counselling and intervention, and present capabilities and future possibilities. Anyone interested in genetics and where society is headed in this area would find the book of interest. Includes bibliographical references and index.

847) Crane, Diane. The Sanctity of Social Life: Physician's Treatment of Critically Ill Patients. New Brunswick, N.J.: Transactions Books, 1977.

Crane addresses social and ethical problems of the dying in America. A search for ethical guidelines is continued by a seven-year research among physicians who are faced with decision-making when confronted with terminally ill and severely handicapped infants. Criteria are investigated by which physicians treat critically ill patients. Circumstances are investigated under which physicians take part in active euthanasia. A social policy is sought in this work, i.e., a different criteria for establishing a person's worth to society other than that of meeting physical criteria of life.

848) Etzoioni, Amitai. "Moral and Social Implications of Genetic Manipulation." In Is It Moral to Modify Man?, ed. Claude A. Frazier, 267-269. Springfield, Ill.: Charles C. Thomas, 1973.

A brief discussion of how genetic control and manipulation can be a curse to man rather than a blessing. One danger mentioned is the fact that defective genes may be found in a floating fetus and lead to abortion (infanticide). This short article raises serious questions.

849) Fox, Renee C., and Judith P. Swazey. The Courage to Fail: A Social View of Organ Transplants and Dialysis. Chicago and London: The University of Chicago Press, 1978.

A paperback revised edition. An analysis of the emotional, social, and economic problems of heart and kidney transplantation besetting both patient and doctor.

850) Fulton, Robert. "Death and Dying: Some Sociologic Aspects of Terminal Care." Modern Medicine (May 1972): 74-77.

Fulton presents sociologic and demographic facts, along with dying in an institution, and the importance of recognizing the dignity of a person during the process of dying.

851) Garfield, Charles A., ed. Psychosocial Care of the Dying Patient. New York: McGraw-Hill, 1978.

A comprehensive account of the many problems faced by the dying person and those who are engaged in caring for the terminally ill. It offers detailed help for the physician and the nurse. The patient's family can also find much that is helpful in the book. This work can be considered to be--up until the 80's when more was written on the subject--among the best.

852) Gonda, Thomas Andrew, and John Edward Ruark. Dying Dignified: The Health Professional's Guide to Care. Menlo Park: Addison-Wesley, 1984.

Lucid case histories are presented at the beginning of the book, and are referred to throughout the discussion. Emphasis is placed on the fact that decision making for the most part resides in the hands of the patient. Broad issues are outlined, such as medical, social, and economic aspects of dying. Suicide and working with dying children comprise a part of the book. Each chapter has an annotated bibliography at its end.

853) Horan, Dennis J. Death, Dying and Euthanasia. Washington, D.C.: University Publications of America, Inc., 1977.

An impressive collection of works by authors from various fields: physicians, attorneys, ethicists, clergy, philosophers, and others who write with conviction on euthanasia. The works, most of which are reprints from periodicals, are classified under seven headings: (1) Death: When Does It Occur and How Do We Define It?, (2) Death as a Treatment of Choice?: Involuntary Euthanasia of the Defective Newborn, (3) Euthanasia: Ethical, Religious, and Moral Aspects, (4) Euthanasia: The Legal Aspects of "Mercy Killing," (5) How Should Medicine and Society Treat the Dying?, (6) Legalized Euthanasia: Social Attitudes and Governmental Policies, and (7) Suicide and the Patient's Right to Reject Medical Treatment. The editors list the contributors in the back of the book. Good for research.

854) Humber, James and Robert F. Almeder, eds. <u>Biomedical Ethics and The Law</u>. New York: Plenum, 1976.

This work covers social problems brought about by the revolution of medical technology, such as: abortion, mental illness, human experimentation, NIH guidelines on research with human subjects, human genetics, and dying. Capron and Katz have a thoughtful discussion on definitions of death, (see Citation 282).

855) Kantrowitz, Adrian, et al. <u>Who Shall Live and Who Shall Die?</u> New York: Union of American Hebrew Congregations (Pamphlet), 1968.

Discusses the ethical implications of the new medical technology, and its effect on society.

856) Lynn, Joanne, ed. <u>By No Extraordinary Means: The Choice to Forgo Life-Sustaining Food and Water</u>. Bloomington: Indiana University Press, 1986.

The authors present the medical, moral, ethical, social, and legal perspectives of the nutrition and hydration issue. Situations discussed have to do with the newborn, terminally ill, unconscious persons (permanently), and the chronically ill but not terminal patient who has decided to refuse food and water. This collection of papers was prepared for the Society for Health and Human Values and should be purchased by all who are interested in the subject because it compiles the views of different authors.

857) Mack, Arien, ed. <u>Death in the American Experience</u>. New York: Schocken Books, 1973.

A paperback book reprinted from the Fall issue of Social Research. A compilation of essays including: "Being and Becoming Dead," by Eric Cassell; "The Sacral Power of Death in Contemporary Experience," by William May; "Death in the Judaic and Christian Tradition," by Roy Eckhardt;

and Johannes Fabian writes on "How Others Die-Reflections on the Anthropology of Death."

858) Milbauer, Barbra and Bert N. Oberentz. The Law Giveth: Legal Aspects of the Abortion Controversy. Atheneum, N.Y.: McClelland and Stewart, 1983.

The facts on abortion are well summarized in this book. The reader is taken on a journey through case law and pertinent American history. Social, medical, religious, and moral aspects of the abortion debate are discussed. The book assists greatly in helping to understand abortion in our time. The bearing of the book on euthanasia is simply this: if abortion is allowed to be performed on the healthy unborn, the "green light" for aborting the already-born deformed is certainly a permissive sign.

859) Milunsky, Aubrey and George J. Annas, eds. Genetics and The Law. New York: Plenum, 1976.

In this book a distinguished faculty of scientists, physicians, lawyers, and ethicists explore the major issues in modern genetics which confront the law. Topics discussed are: the legal rights of the fetus; the xyy controversy, law and pre-natal diagnosis of hereditary disorders; informed consent requirements in genetic counselling, legal implications of genetic screening; legal aspects of artificial insemination; sterilization of the mentally handicapped; malpractice risks in genetic counselling, and governmental and social restriction of experiments involving gene manipulation, cloning, and in vitro fertilization. A thorough discussion of the medical and legal aspects of the non treatment of defective newborns is set forth. This book is a must for all professionals, and anyone concerned about the effects of genetics on society.

860) Moberg, David C., ed. Spiritual Well-Being: Sociological Perspectives. Lanham, Md.: University Press of America, 1979.

A Judeo-Christian orientation on the religious beliefs of the aged. Death, preparation for death, and the right to die are presented with hope for immortality. Today, while many writers leave the dying without any hope, Moberg presents a positive outlook for those who must enter death's door. An excellent work.

861) Reilly, Philip. Genetics, Law, and Social Policy. Cambridge, Mass.: Harvard University Press, 1977.

Reilly succeeds in pulling together material in the broad and diverse areas of genetics, law, and policy making. Section one of the book deals with human genetics and technology, with commentary on legal ramifications. Genetic legislation is discussed in section two, and provides comprehensive treatment of genetic screening legislation and its future. Reilly favors that genetic screening be modelled after the law passed by the State of Maryland, in which a Commission on Hereditary Diseases was created. Important issues on applied human genetics, and advances in reproductive technology are raised in section three. For those interested in how laws on human genetics in the present and future are being effected, the book is recommended.

862) Rosner, Fred and J. David Bleich, ed. "Organ Transplantation." In Jewish Bioethics. New York: Sanhedrin, 1979.

Two chapters dealing with organ transplantation reveal Jewish thinking on the subject: "What is the Halakhah for Organ Transplants?" and "Organ Transplantation in Jewish Law." The first mentioned chapter answers the question ". . .may one administer a treatment which will, if it fails, kill him immediately, but, if it succeeds, prolong his life?" The other social, legal, and philosophical problems surrounding heart transplantation; the halakhah in eye transplants; the halakhah in kidney transplants; and the halakhah in heart transplants. Each of these chapters has bearing on euthanasia--at least in the Jewish view.

863) Science and Society: Biomedical Engineering. Terrytown, N.Y.: 2 Filmstrips and Long-Play Recording or Audiocassette. Sale. Schloat Productions, 150 White Plaines (10591).

Life-support machines, transplants, genetic surgery, results of social interference, defining death, and making choices are discussed.

864) Sempos, Christopher, and Richard Cooper. "Passive Euthanasia." Archives of Internal Medicine 143 (July 1983): 1492.

A letter written to oppose the thought that parents may be justified in allowing their children with profound mental retardation to be killed, which is incompatible with social experiences.

865) Simpson, Michael A. "Brought in Dead." Omega 7 (No. 3, 1976): 243-248.

The author presents social factors which are influential as determinants deciding on whether or not to resuscitate in emergency rooms.

866) Strauss, Anselm L. Chronic Illness and The Quality of Life. St. Louis: C. V. Mosby, 1975.

A study on how chronic illness effects the quality of life. The psychosocial aspects of living with chronic illness focuses on the patient and the family. Renal failure and dying in the hospital are discussed, along with how to gather information from such patients in order to better understand their needs. An informative piece of literature.

867) Vaux, Kenneth, ed. Powers That Make Us Human: The Foundations of Medical Ethics. Urbana, Ill.: University of Illinois Press, 1985.

These essays are brought together to give the reader insight into the complex problems of health and illness. They deal with reason, hope, virtue, feeling, honor, and mortality. Two essays by Leon Kass and William May are well worth purchasing the book. They are on mortality (to what extent is longer life no good for individuals) and honor (a critique of medical and social attitudes toward care for the aged).

868) Visscher, Maurice B. Humanistic Perspectives in Medical Ethics. Buffalo: Prometheus Books, 1972.

A collection of essays written by leading physicians, psychiatrists, social scientists, and philosophers. This edition comprises the following contents:

1) The Humanistic Tradition in the Health Professions - Chauncey D. Leake
2) Medical Ethics in Philosophical Perspective - Patrick Romanell
3) The Sanctity of Life Principle - Marvin Kohl
4) The Right to Die - Walter C. Alvarez
5) The Evolution of the Right-to-Health Concept in the U.S. - Carleton B. Chapman and John M. Talmadge
6) The Fee-for-Service System - H. Roy Kaplan
7) The Ethics of the Physician in Human Reproduction - Howard C. Taylor
8) Birth Defects - Leroy Augenstein
9) Human Experimentation - Louis Lasagna
10) Medical Ethics and Psychotropic Drugs - Mervin F. Silverman and Deborah B. Silverman
11) Prison Doctors - Tom Murton
12) Medicine and The Military - Gordon Livingston
13) Beyond Atrocity - Robert J. Litton
14) Social Ethics for Medical Educators - John G. Bruhn and Douglas C. Smith

869) Wallace, Samuel E., and Albin Eser, eds. Suicide and Euthanasia. Knoxville: The University of Tennessee Press, 1981.

An edited work by a professor of sociology at the University of Tennessee, and a professor of criminal and comparative law at the University of Tubingen in West Germany. The essays address a wide variety of issues related to suicide and euthanasia: social suicide, suicide among cancer patients, defending suicide, the right to live and the right to die, voluntary euthanasia, "sanctity" and "quality" of life in a historical-comparative view, and legal structure of the "living will." Collectively, the essays apply a variety of perspectives on unexplored areas relating to the study of death. The book provides a very helpful bibliography, citing works which directly relate suicide and euthanasia, and is highly recommended.

870) Whiter, Walter. Dissertation on the Disorder of Death: Or, That State of The Frame Under The Signs of Death Called Suspended Animation. New York: Arno, 1976.

A description of resuscitation experiences. Whiter believes that society fails to revive individuals because death, according to popular belief, is inevitable. A good work on the importance of life-prolongation.

871) Yondorf, Barbara. "The Declining and Wretched." Public Policy 23 (Fall 1975): 465-482.

An emphasis on problems confronted by the dying, aged and incurably ill. Every effort should be put forth to direct policies not only toward the dying, but also toward all who are declining and wretched.

CHAPTER 8

EUTHANASIA:
THE TECHNOLOGICAL CHALLENGE

Drugs

872) Alsop, Stewart. "The Right to Die with Dignity." Good Housekeeping 179 (August 1974): 130-132.

Alsop, a distinguished journalist, shares his viewpoints on euthanasia, and believes that a terminal patient has the right to decide his or her fate and be allowed to receive pain-killing medication, including heroin.

873) Ayd, F. Jr. "Voluntary Euthanasia: The Right To Be Killed." Medical Counterpoint (June 1970): 12.

Arguments against legalization of euthanasia are presented effectively throughout by Ayd. He is positive that under certain circumstances it is good medicine to withdraw treatment and allow nature to take its course. He also contends that euthanasia is not necessary in light of pain-killing drugs given in large doses.

874) Dignity of Death. New York: ABC News, 30 min. Color. Rental/Sale. St. Christopher's Hospice and Pain Control.

A visual study of pain control in terminal patients. Maybe should be titled "An Easy Death with Dignity."

875) "Drug That Left a Trail of Heartbreak: Thalidomide." Life 53 (August 10, 1962): 24-36.

A descriptive account of the tragic results of the drug thalidomide - - deformed infants, heartaches, and grief.

876) Fordyce, Wilbert. Behavioral Methods for Chronic Pain and Illness. St. Louis: C. V. Mosby, 1976.

A valuable work for those who are involved in terminal care. Reviews of pain as a clinical problem, psychogenic pain, orientation, pain cocktails, and maintenance of performance are very well covered.

877) Goldberg, Malitz and Kutscher, ed. Psychopharmacological Agents for the Terminally Ill and Bereaved. New York: Columbia University Press, 1973.

A study of the use of drugs in the care of the dying and bereaved. Reviews of the use of chlorpromazine, heroin, and LSD are presented, along with a discussion of the nature of grief and pain.

878) Hoyle, J. C. "The Care of the Dying." In Medical Ethics, ed. M. Davidson. London: Lloyd-Luke Medical Books, 1957.

Emphasis is placed on drug medication for pain in the care of the dying. Hoyle believes that nothing is more important than comfort for the patient. He holds that if the doctor of a patient decides to kill by drugs, he should do so in secret. No third party should be involved. The family should be told that the patient is dying and the end is near.

879) Manney, James, and John C. Blattner. "Infanticide: Murder or Mercy?" Journal of Christian Nursing (Summer 1985): 10-14.

Manney and Blattner mention in brief how unwanted infants have been disposed of in the past which, if compared to present-day practices, show very little difference. The authors are opposed to infanticide in any form, and present a strong defense against it by pointing out the dark side of human thinking in its attitude toward helpless infants who are malformed, but still human beings. According to the writers, it is imperative that a true definition of infanticide be understood, that the new ethic of "quality of life" be rejected, which opposes the old ethic of Judeo-Christian moral tradition (there is intrinsic worth and equal value of every human life regardless of its stage of development or condition).

880) Munk, William. Euthanasia, Or, Medical Treatment in Aid of an Easy Death. New York: Arno, 1976.

Holds for good terminal care rather than the up-to-date use of euthanasia. Deals with the phenomena, symptoms, and different ways of dying. Includes near-death experiences, and the use of opium for symptom control. A good advisory on management of pain.

881) Persaud, T., ed. Problems of Birth Defects. Baltimore: University Park Press, 1977.

From Hippocrates to Thalidomide and beyond. A compilation of fifty-seven papers on historical aspects, epidemiology, mechanisms, genetics, causes, prenatal diagnosis, management, and social aspects of birth defects. Good for basic reference and physical problems of unborn and newborn infants.

882) Selzer, Richard. Letters to a Young Doctor. New York: Simon and Schuster, 1982.

In his chapter on "Mercy," page 70, Dr. Selzer gives a vivid description of his involvement in actively participating in the attempted death of a patient by injection, all of which was requested by the patient and family members. A good example of active euthanasia.

883) Shanbrom, E. "Malthus, Morality and Miracle Drugs." Journal of The American Medical Association 182 (November 24, 1962): 856-857.

A statement that with increased use of antibiotics, nature has not been allowed to take its course, and the result is that the number of aged and infirmed has increased. This leaves the question: not "whom should we kill?", but "whom should we let live?"

884) Takagi, Kentaro. "Medical Problems at Birth and Death." Japanese Journal of Medicine 23 (August 1984): 268-269.

A discussion of "brain death" and the importance of determining criteria for it as quickly as possible, and to strive for national consensus regarding it. Organ transplantation should be used as effectively as possible. Organs should be given to patients who seriously need them in order to prolong their lives. On euthanasia, the author feels that those patients who are in the terminal stage should be given pain medication, and every effort should be made to prolong their lives. He further discusses artificial termination of pregnancy and external fertilization.

885) West, Jessamyn. The Woman Said Yes: Encounters With Life and Death. New York: Fawcett Book Group, 1977.

West gives an account of her own fight for life, and supports her sister's desire for death rather than a drug-dominated existence. She also gives an account of assist suicide, whereby she helped her sister commit suicide rather than face a prolonged dying process resulting from cancer of the bowel.

886) Williams, Samuel D. "Euthanasia." The Popular Science Monthly 3 (July 1872): 90-96.

This is the sixth article of seven published by The Speculative Club in 1870 wherein the author defends the administration of chloroform for the relief of pain. Williams states: "'That in all cases of hopeless and painful illness it should be the recognized duty of the medical attendant, whenever so desired of the patient, to administer chloroform, or such other anaesthetic as may by-and-by supersede chloroform, so as to destroy consciousness at once, and put the sufferer at once to a quick and painless death; all needful precautions being adopted to prevent any possible abuse of such duty; and means being taken to establish, beyond the possibility of question, that the remedy was applied at the express wish of the patient.'" He also believes that such action demonstrates respect for the sacredness of life. Other articles and publications are mentioned in order to present opposing views to that of Mr. Williams. Since this article was written in 1870, it is important in that it reveals the thinking of society on the subject of euthanasia at that time. Interesting and highly recommended for reading.

Genetics

887) Barnes, E. W. "Science, Religion and Moral Judgement." Nature 166 (September 16, 1950): 455-457.

A bishop discusses euthanasia's role in solving many of the world's problems; its role in capital offenses, the eradication of abnormal genes, and over-population.

888) Clements, Colleen D. Medical Genetics Casebook: A Clinical Introduction to Medical Ethics. Clifton, N.J.: Humana, 1982.

The author maintains that ethicists approach problems in medical ethics with theories that ignore realities of medical practice. They make little allowances for feedback from medical experience. She follows one hundred thirty cases which involve problems such as: working with information, trial and reality testing, self-image, experimental research and procedures, selective abortion, and societal and individual interest conflicts. She reviews basic principles of moral and ethical philosophy. Clements also recommends that her book be used as a source for prenatal diagnosis. Her book should be a significant help for all who are concerned for life and the impact of medical technology on that life.

889) Cohen, Bernice H., Abraham M. Lilenfeld, and P. C. Huang, eds. Genetic Issues in Public Health and Medicine. Springfield, Ill.: Charles C. Thomas, 1978.

Brings into focus genetic knowledge and its concomitant problems in the social, political, legal, and moral-ethical areas. Space is given to the discussion of genetic material and the environment, prenatal diagnosis of genetic disorders, population screening and surveillance, investigations and pro- grams in special population segments, genetic coun- selling and intervention, and present capabilities and future possibilities. Anyone interested in genetics and where society is headed in this area would find the book of interest. Includes bibliographical references and index.

890) Davis, John W., Barry Hoffmaster, and Sarah Shorten, eds. Contemporary Issues in Biomedical Ethics. Clifton, N.J.: Humana, 1978.

A compilation of comments and papers presented at a colloquium on biomedical ethics at the University of Western Ontario. Contained in the volume are issues such as rights and moral decisions, legalism, and the rights of the terminally ill. Among other issues brought to the reader's attention are issues in genetics, the role of the physician, informed consent and paternalism, and professional responsibility.

891) Etzoioni, Amitai. "Moral and Social Implications of Genetic Manipulation." In Is It Moral to Modify Man?, ed. Claude A. Frazier, 267-269. Springfield, Ill.: Charles C. Thomas, 1973.

A brief discussion of how genetic control and manipulation can be a curse to man rather than a blessing. One danger mentioned is the fact that defective genes may be found in a floating fetus and lead to abortion (infanticide). This short article raises serious questions.

892) Fletcher, Joseph. Humanhood: Essays in Biomedical Ethics. Buffalo, N.Y.: Prometheus Books, 1979.

Perplexities confronting modern man, such as genetic engineering, transplantation, fetal research, recombinant DNA, abortion, suicide, and euthanasia are discussed by this well known ethicist. In the early chapters he establishes standards of individuals. These essays are well written.

893) Haring, Bernard. <u>Ethics of Manipulation: Issues in Medicine, Behavior Control and Genetics.</u> New York: Seabury, 1975.

The core of the book deals with manipulation of man through behavior management and genetics-- behavior modification through surgical, chemical, and electrical means, and genetic therapy and engineering. Father Haring gives a vigorous and thorough discussion of the issues surrounding the subject. A superb book.

894) Humber, James and Robert F. Almeder, eds. <u>Biomedical Ethics and The Law.</u> New York: Plenum, 1976.

This work covers social problems brought about by the revolution of medical technology, such as: abortion, mental illness, human experimentation, NIH guidelines on research with human subjects, human genetics, and dying. Capron and Katz have a thoughtful discussion on definitions of death, (see Citation 282).

895) Lockwood, Michael, ed. <u>Moral Dilemmas in Modern Medicine.</u> London: Oxford University Press, 1985.

Three sets of issues comprise the volume. Set one consists of reproductive techniques, which include in-vitro fertilization, surrogate mothering, frozen embryos, gene therapy, growing human embryos in the laboratory, and genetic engineering. Medical paternalism and patient autonomy are dealt with in the second set. The nature of moral arguments and reasoning in medicine comprise the third set. These philosophical studies will enhance one's knowledge and respect for those who deal with the issues presented.

896) Lygre, David G. <u>Life Manipulation.</u> New York: Walker, 1970.

All that can be thought of relative to "life manipulation," from test-tube babies to aging, is

included in Lygre's well written book. The human
implications of cloning, biofeedback, parthogenesis
(virgin birth), psychosurgery, delayed aging, redesigned organs, artificial wombs, selective abortions,
human gene splicing, artificial insemination, sex
preselection of fetuses, life sustenance after brain
death, prenatal diagnosis of birth defects, and
other interesting subjects relative to biomedical
research are treated. After reading this work, one
will conclude that these issues cannot and should
not be avoided, for everyone's life will be touched
somehow as biomedical research reaches more and
more into the lives of all humans.

897) McCormick, Richard A. How Brave A New World?:
Dilemmas in Bioethics. Garden City, N.Y.: Doubleday, 1951.

The issues which continually make headlines
are brought forth in McCormick's How Brave A New
World. Birth control, abortion, fetal and genetic
research, test-tube reproduction, human experimentation, and euthanasia are thoroughly discussed.
Much, if not all of the book, is a compilation of
articles which have appeared in different
periodicals and other publications.

898) Milunsky, Aubrey and George J. Annas, eds. Genetics
and The Law. New York: Plenum, 1976.

In this book a distinguished faculty of scientists, physicians, lawyers, and ethicists explore
the major issues in modern genetics which confront
the law. Topics discussed are: the legal rights of
the fetus; the xyy controversy; law and pre-natal
diagnosis of hereditary disorders; informed-consent
requirements in genetic counselling; legal implications of genetic screening; legal aspects of artificial
insemination; sterilization of the mentally handicapped; malpractice risks in genetic counselling; and
governmental and social restriction of experiments
involving gene manipulation, cloning, and in-vitro
fertilization. A thorough discussion of the medical

and legal aspects of the non treatment of defective newborns is set forth. This book is a must for all professionals and anyone concerned about the effects of genetics on society.

899) Nelson, Leonard J., ed. The Death Decision. Ann Arbor, Mich.: Servant Books, 1984.

A collection of essays from the Fourth Annual Christianity and Law Seminar presented November 11-13, 1982 at the City of Faith Continuing Education Center in Tulsa, Oklahoma, sponsored by the O. W. Coburn School of Law of Oral Roberts University. The contributors are composed of such men as Harold O. J. Brown, John Eidsmore, Leonard J. Nelson III, John T. Noonan, Walter Probert, Charles E. Rice, Peter J. Riga, and George Huntston Williams. The above experts address the legal and ethical issues emerging on the frontier of today's new biology, including: abortion, euthanasia, treatment of newborns, genetic screening, bioengineering, and reproductive techniques. "Who decides when it's time for someone to die?" is what the book is all about. A book which presents the Christian stand on important issues.

900) Ostheimer, Nancy C. and John M., ed. Life or Death--Who Controls? New York: Springer, 1976.

Composed of twenty-two chapters which deal with important issues, such as eugenics, abortion on demand, compulsory sterilization, and euthanasia. Written by authors from various fields. Informative.

901) Reilly, Philip. Genetics, Law, and Social Policy. Cambridge, Mass.: Harvard University Press, 1977.

Reilly succeeds in pulling together material in the broad and diverse areas of genetics, law, and policy making. Section one of the book deals with human genetics and technology, with commentary on legal ramifications. Genetic legislation is discusssed in section two, and provides comprehensive treatment of genetic screening legislation and its future. Reilly favors that genetic screening be modelled after the law passed by the State of Maryland, in which a Commission on Hereditary Diseases was created. Important issues on applied human genetics, and advances in reproductive technology are raised in section three. For those interested in how laws on human genetics in the present and future are being effected, the book is recommended.

902) Restak, Richard M. <u>Pre-Meditated Man: Bioethics and the Control of Future Human Life</u>. New York: Viking, 1973.

A three-part book discussing the issues raised in psychosurgery. The most dramatic form of behavior modification in use is discussed in part one. Part two explores the implications of genetic engineering of different kinds. The third part analyzes experiences, and the frightful lesson of the past and present having to do with human experimentation.

903) Rosner, Fred. <u>Modern Medicine and Jewish Ethics</u>. New York: Yeshiva University Press, 1986.

A compilation of essays on Jewish ethics as they pertain to issues such as: artificial insemination, in vitro fertilization, genetic engineering, organ transplantation, and extraordinary life support measures. Jewish thought in other areas are brought forth which touch on contraception, abortion, euthanasia, and autopsy. Specific biomedical issues are dealt with in each chapter, and contain Biblical passages, interpretations, and codified Jewish laws on ethical issues. Modern day interpretations by rabbinical councils are also included. Anyone wanting to familiarize themselves with Jewish thought on the vital issues of health care and ethics will want to peruse this volume.

904) "The Spirit: Who Will Make the Choice of Life and Death?" Time 97 (April 19, 1971): 48.

The sanctity of life and the family are seriously threatened by the new genetics. Already experiments in the field are developing and multiplying at a speed faster than humans can cope with them. Human freedom, as a result, can either be promoted or restrained. It is not always easy to tell them apart, according to the author.

905) Vaux, Kenneth. Biomedical Ethics: Morality for the New Medicine. New York: Harper and Row, 1974.

Dr. Vaux is a Presbyterian minister and professor of ethics, and brings a wealth of material out of his experience. He shares many insights on ethical problems. The book is a help for physicians and others who need assistance in making decisions in the sensitive area of health care. Dr. Vaux points out that disciplines which were at one time helpful are now outdated because they are pre-technological and, therefore, new disciplines need to be formulated. The first part of the book is a summary of historical roots of medical ethics. It discusses Judaism, Islam, Catholicism, Protestantism, and Marxism, and ends with some insight into the Nuremburg trials. The second half of the book centers on ethical concerns in biomedicine: genetic manipulation, organ transplantation, controlling man, and immortalizing man, which deals with death. Theological terms are used which should be appealing to the clergy, as well as to theologians.

906) Veatch, Robert M. Case Studies in Medical Ethics. Cambridge: Harvard university Press, 1977.

A collection of case studies in the field of bioethics. One hundred and twelve problems in the area of medical ethics are discussed, and case histories are presented for each. There are also commentaries on the cases by other parties. The topics covered are: values in health and illness, problems in health care delivery, confidentiality, truth telling, abortions, sterilizations, contraceptives, genetics, transplantations, the allocation of scarce resources, psychiatry and control of human behavior, experimentation on human beings, consent and the right to refuse treatment, and death-and-dying problems. The book is easy to read, and is a good case book for anyone concerned with ethical problems in the health care field. Veatch is rated as one of the best, if not the best, in the field of ethics.

907) Weiss, Ann E. Bioethics: Dilemmas in Modern Medicine. Hillside, N.J.: Enslow, 1985.

Weiss makes difficult subjects comprehensible, such as: right to life, organs for sale, the baby Doe rule, experimenting on humans, who gets health-care, genetic engineering, rights of patients, and the right to die. After reading this book, one will have a good understanding of what bioethics is all about.

908) Williams, P., ed. To Live and Die: When, Why and How. New York: Springer-Verlag, 1973.

Covers a wide range of topics dealing with current important and vital issues, such as genetic engineering, contraception, abortion, euthanasia, transplant ethics, marriage, and other issues.

Machines

909) Caroline, N. L. "Dying in Academe." The New Physician 21 (November 1972): 655-657.

A prize-winning essay about a man who chose to die rather than linger in "life" on a respirator. The author has little to support her claim that it is wrong to sustain patients on life-support systems, but is to be congratulated on her stand.

910) Furlow, Thomas W. "Euthanasia and the Tyranny of Technology." In Beneficent Euthanasia, ed. Marvin Kohl, 169-179. Buffalo, N.Y.: Prometheus Books, 1975.

> Furlow contends that the physician has been given, through technology, the means whereby he is able to exasperate the great enemy, Death, and therefore has lost sight of allowing the patient a normal, natural, and easy passage out of life. Major by-products of medical progress have become tyrannical in that they have prevented a realistic approach to death. The author discusses different forms of euthanasia toward the end of the article.

911) Hiscoe, S. "Awesome Decision to Stop Heroic Measures." American Journal of Nursing 73 (February 1973): 291-293.

> The family of a patient whose vegetative existence would continue is helped by a nurse who answers their questions honestly with to-the-point frankness. She helped them arrive at a decision to discontinue life-supporting machinery.

912) Kelly, G. "The Duty of Using Artificial Means of Preserving Life." Theological Studies 11 (1950): 203.

> A review of Catholic literature on the difference between ordinary and extraordinary means. The distinction between preserving life when there is no hope and preserving life when there is hope of recovery is also made by Kelly. According to Catholic teaching, treatment may be withheld from the hopeless as long as sacraments have been given.

913) Lewis, H. P. "Machine Medicine and Its Relation to the Fatally Ill." Journal of The American Medical Association 206 (October 1968): 387-388.

> Lewis feels that if a patient must be maintained on a machine while registering a flat EEG, he should be taken off and allowed to die (indeed, he is

already dead if a flat EEG is the criteria for death). It seems that Lewis' purpose is to find a distinct difference between ceasing life-support systems (euthanasia) and killing.

914) "M.D.'s, Clergy Discuss Prolonging Life." American Medical Association News 9 (May 9 1966): 1.

Bishop Fulton J. Sheen, Paul S. Rhoads, Reverend Granger E. Westberg, and Gotthard Booth engage in a discussion of prolonging a patient's life by extraordinary means. Artificial devices such as the artificial kidney and artificial heart are discussed.

915) Mercy Killing. CBC, 30 min. Audio tape. Sale. Toronto.

The technical and moral aspects of euthanasia presented by way of a panel discussion. For private and group use only.

916) Ogg, Elizabeth. Facing Death and Loss. Lancaster, Pa., 1985.

A sensitive book which considers the subject of death and the individual's needs and concerns during the process of dying. The patient's right to choose death in a hospice rather than a hospital and its torturous machine-like technological life-sustaining practices is discussed, along with financing terminal care.

917) Powills, Suzanne. "Coalition Asks 'Life At Any Price?'" Hospital (May 1985): 110, 114.

A discussion on a report by The Minnesota Coalition on Health Care Costs. The report was prompted by the high cost of technological advances. "The report suggests that promoting the patient's right of self-determination and reducing the emphasis on life-prolonging technology may by terminally ill patients."

918) Science and Society: Biomedical Engineering. Terrytown, N.Y.: 2 Filmstrips and Long-Play Recording or Audiocassette. Sale. Schloat Productions, 150 White Plaines (10591).

Life-support machines, transplants, genetic surgery, results of social interference, defining death, and making choices are discussed.

919) Steinbrook, Robert, Bernard Lo, Jill Tirpack, James W. Dilley, eds. "Ethical Dilemmas in Caring for Patients with the Acquired Immunodeficiency Syndrome." Annals of Internal Medicine 103 (November 1985): 787-790.

This piece discusses ethical dilemmas--when to provide life-sustaining treatments, such as mechanical ventilation and cardiopulmonary resuscitation for AIDS patients.

920) The Right to Die. 56 Min. Color. Rental/Sale. EMC No. 9193. University of Michigan: MacMillan Films, 1974.

An ABC documentary presenting a well-done production on actual cases of life prolongation by machines, and suffering patients who want to die. Euthanasia is explored effectively and efficiently.

921) The Right to Die. Chatsworth, Calif.: Filmstrip and Audiocassette. Sale. Career Aids Inc., 20417 Nordhoss (91311).

A discussion on the moral, legal, and practical implications of life-extending technology.

Transplants

922) Bacon, Francis. The Historie of Life and Death with Observations Naturall and Experimentall for the Prolonging of Life. New York: Arno, 1976.

Bacon's treatise on death, prolongation of life, euthanasia, transfusion, and transplantation. The first edition of the work: London, 1638.

923) Beecher, H. K. "Ethical Problems Created by the Hopelessly Unconscious Patient." New England Journal of Medicine 278 (June 27, 1964): 1425-1430.

This article stresses the importance of the inappropriateness of keeping patients alive by extraordinary means, and that society cannot afford to discard the organs of these patients when there is a dire need by other patients whose lives can be saved. Death definitions are discussed relative to organ transplantations.

924) Caplan, Arthur L. "Ethical and Policy Issues in the Procurement of Cadaver Organs for Transplantation." New England Journal of Medicine 311 (October 1984): 981-983.

Questions are posed concerning availability, cost, and donors of organ transplantations. A policy of "required request" is discussed, which concerns patients whose situations are hopeless, and that no one on a respirator who might serve as a donor should be declared legally dead until a request for organ donation has been made of any available next of kin or legal proxy.

925) Curran, Charles and Michael de Bakey. Decisions: Life or Death. 30 min. B&W. Rental/Sale. Association Films and MacMillan Films, n.d.

The ethics of heart transplants and medical technology are discussed by a leading heart surgeon.

A religious professional also takes part in the discussion.

926) Deaton, John G. New Parts for Old: The Age of Organ Transplants. Palisade, N.J.: Franklin, 1974.

A brief account written for the general public on the biology of transplantation and the many accomplishments that have transpired in the area of kidney, heart, lung, liver, and other transplantations. While there is no direct link of transplants to the subject of euthanasia, it is always good to keep in mind that indirectly one has bearing on the other in that questions often arise relating the two.

927) Dempsey, David. The Way We Die: An Investigation of Death and Dying in America Today. New York: MacMillan, 1975.

A competent work on death, transplants, longevity, the right to die, the experience of dying, mourning, and burial. Another book pointing out the process of dying in the U.S.

928) Fletcher, Joseph. Humanhood: Essays in Biomedical Ethics. Buffalo, N.Y.: Prometheus Books, 1979.

Perplexities confronting modern man, such as genetic engineering, transplantation, fetal research, recombinant DNA, abortion, suicide, and euthanasia are discussed by this well known ethicist. In the early chapters he establishes standards of humanhood, and chooses progress and rationalism over the rights and loving concern of individuals. These essays are well written.

929) Fox, Renee C., and Judith P. Swazey. The Courage to Fail: A Social View of Organ Transplants and Dialysis. Chicago and London: The University of Chicago Press, 1978.

A paperback revised edition. An analysis of the emotional, social, and economic problems of heart and kidney transplantation besetting patient and doctor.

930) Freund, Paul A. "Organ Transplants: Ethical and Legal Problems." In Ethics in Medicine: Historical Perspectives and Contemporary Concerns, ed. Stanley Joel Reiser, Arthur J. Dyck, and William J. Curran, 173-177. Cambridge, Mass.: MIT, 1977.

Freund discusses problems concerning the allocation of resources -- from whom they should come and to whom organs should be transferred. Implications raised by the questions concern moral, legal, and medical considerations. Each differs on removal of organs after death and during life. He briefly discusses the question of whether or not a dying patient should be allowed to consent to surgical intervention for the purpose of saving another's life.

931) Gift of Life/Right to Die. Champaign, Ill.: 15 min. B&W. Rental, EMC No. 7320. Indiana University Audio-Visual Center and Visual Aids Service, Division of University Extension, University of Illinois (61822), 1968.

A short film discussing one person's death , and another becomes an organ recipient of the former. Other ethical issues are mentioned, such as euthanasia for infants who are malformed, and individuals who suffer from catastrophic disease.

932) Goldberg, J. H. "The Dying Patient: Tackling the New Ethical and Legal Questions." Hospital Physician 36 (June 1968): 41-45.

Because of new medical techniques, Goldberg stresses the importance of new death definitions. The age of transplants requires such. Doctors should be given more freedom in forming opinions, and allowed to implement them, depending on each case.

933) Guideline for Consent: The Uniform Anatomical Gift Act. New York, N.Y.: 15 min. B&W, 3/4" Video-cassette. 15 Columbus Circle (10023).

　　A National Continuing Medical Education tape dealing with medical and legal aspects of transplantation. For subscribers' use only.

934) Jonasson, Olga. "Organ Transplantation: Interview With Olga Jonasson." An interview by Illinois Medical Journal 171 (May 1987): 301-310.

　　An outstanding dialogue on organ transplantation; costs, availability of donors, donor choice, and types of patients sought for donorship. While euthanasia is not discussed, the subject should be considered relative to imminent-death-patients who may be candidates as donors.

935) Katz, Jay and Alexander Morgan Capron. Catastrophic Diseases: Who Decides What? A Psychosocial and Legal Analysis of the Problems Posed by Hemodialysis and Organ Transplantation. New York: Russell Sage Foundation, 1975.

　　The nature and effects of catastrophic illness are explored. Especially interesting is the section on the reduction of suffering.

936) Kolff, W. J. Artificial Organs. New York: Halsted, 1976.

　　This work is tops in its field because it was done by the "father" of artificial organs. With his vast experience behind him, he discusses three major areas having to do with artificial organs. Much of the book describes artificial organ research, especially that having to do with the artificial heart, artificial hearts driven by atomic energy, and significant research surrounding the artificial heart. Dr. Kolff developed and demonstrated clinical effectiveness of hemodialysis for the treatment of patients with chronic renal failure early in his career, and in the present volume describes the future of the artificial kidney; transplantation versus dialysis, and the cost of dialysis. This book would benefit pastors, psychologists, and those who are interested in specifics which have to do with transplants and artificial organs, especially in light of the fact that counsellors are called upon more often to advise in the area of death and dying.

937) Lygre, David G. Life Manipulation. New York: Walker, 1970.

All that can be thought of relative to "life manipulation," from test-tube babies to aging, is included in Lygre's well-written book. The human implications of cloning, biofeedback, parthogenesis (virgin birth), psychosurgery, delayed aging, redesigned organs, artificial wombs, selective abortions, human gene splicing, artificial insemination, sex preselection of fetuses, life sustenance after brain death, prenatal diagnosis of birth defects, and other interesting subjects relative to biomedical research are treated. After reading this work, one will conclude that these issues cannot and should not be avoided, for everyone's life will be touched somehow as biomedical research reaches more and more into the lives of all humans.

938) MacNeil-Lehrer Newshour (PBS) April 8, 1988. Discussion on bone marrow transplants and the cost involved.

In a very real sense, this report was a good example of active euthanasia in that two young children in dire need of bone marrow transplants were denied help by the State of Oregon. The state had money available, but due to policy refused to pay one hundred thousand dollars for each of the children. The result was tragic--both children died a very short time after the refusal.

939) Oden, Thomas C. <u>Should Treatment Be Terminated?</u>
<u>Moral Guidelines for Christian Families and Pastors</u>.
New York: Harper and Row, 1976.

Arguments which favor and oppose ending
treatment of the terminally ill are addressed, along
with problems having to do with truth telling, organ
donation, home care, and legal limits. Disagreements between families and physicians are discussed,
with other issues, such as "living wills" and refusal
of medical treatment.

940) Pattison, Mansell E., ed. <u>The Experience of Dying</u>. New
York: Spectrum/Prentice-Hall, 1976.

A clinically relevant work dealing with the
malformed and burned child, childhood leukemia,
middle childhood and hemophilia, trauma, and
cancer; adolescence and cardiac pacemakers, renal
transplants, and cancer; young adults and M.S.,
trauma, and leukemia; middle age and the I.C.U.,
cancer, leukemia, and hemodialysis; the elderly and
euthanasia; and two chapters which review different styles of dying.

941) Revkin, Andrew C. "Organ Hunter." <u>Discover</u> 9
(February 1988): 65-69.

Revkin's account is of a former detective, Bill
Contirina (an organ recipient), who became known
as "organ hunter." Contirina seeks out families
e memberswhose recently died as a result of
accidents, natural causes, etc., for the purpose of
procuring organs for transplantation. As one reads
this article, there will immediately come to mind
the subject of euthanasia and the danger of organ
procurement through immoral means (actually
allowing someone to die for the purpose of passing
on his or her body parts to others). The article is
well written and is not suggestive of any wrong
doing on the part of those involved, however, the
subject raises many questions to the imaginative
reader.

942) Rosner, Fred and J. David Bleich, ed. "Organ Transplantation." In Jewish Bioethics. New York:
Sanhedrin, 1979.

Two chapters dealing with organ transplantation reveal Jewish thinking on the subject: "What is
the Halakhah for Organ Transplants?" and "Organ
Transplantation in Jewish Law." The first mentioned chapter answers the question ". . . may one
administer a treatment which will, if it fails, kill
him immediately, but, if it succeeds, prolong his
life?" The other chapter deals with theological,
moral, ethical, social, legal, and philosophical problems surrounding heart transplantation; the halakhah
in eye transplants; the halakhah in kidney transplants; and the halakhah in heart transplants. Each
of these chapters has bearing on euthanasia--at
least in the Jewish view.

943) Rosner, Fred. Modern Medicine and Jewish Ethics.
New York: Yeshiva University Press, 1986.

A compilation of essays on Jewish ethics as they
pertain to issues such as: artificial insemination, in-
vitro fertilization, genetic engineering, organ transplantation, and extraordinary life support measures.
Jewish thought in other areas are brought forth
which touch on contraception, abortion, euthanasia,
and autopsy. Specific biomedical issues are dealt
with in each chapter, and contain Biblical passages,
interpretations, and codified Jewish laws on ethical
issues. Modern day interpretations by rabbinical
councils are also included. Anyone wanting to familiarize themselves with Jewish thought on the vital issues of health-care and ethics will want to
peruse this volume.

944) Science and Society: Biomedical Engineering. Terrytown, N.Y.: 2 Filmstrips and a Long-Play Recording
or Audiocassette. Sale. Schloat Productions, 150
White Plaines (10591).

Life-support machines, transplants, genetic
surgery, results of social interference, defining
death, and making choices are discussed.

945) Simmons, Roberta G. and Julie Fulton. "Ethical Issues in
Kidney Transplantation." In Is It Moral to Modify
Man?, ed. Claude A. Frazier, 171-188. Springfield,
Ill.: Charles C. Thomas, 1973.

Simons addresses serious ethical issues and
treats such vital questions as: What are the criteria
by which potential recipients should be selected for
transplantation and others refused life-saving treatment?; How can a donor be protected against
premature termination of his life (a practice of
euthanasia is implied here)?; What is an acceptable
definition of death?; Should living donors be used?
Other vital issues are treated. Excellent!

946) Takagi, Kentaro. "Medical Problems at Birth and
Death." Japanese Journal of Medicine 23 (August
1984): 268-269.

A discussion of "brain death" and the importance of determining criteria for it as quickly
as possible, and to strive for national consensus
regarding it. Organ transplantation should be used
as effectively as possible. Organs should be given
to patients who seriously need them in order to
prolong their lives. On euthanasia, the author
feels that those patients who are in the terminal
stage should be given pain medication, and every
effort should be made to prolong their lives. He
further discusses artificial termination of pregnancy, and external fertilization.

947) Vaux, Kenneth. Biomedical Ethics: Morality for the New Medicine. New York: Harper and Row, 1974.

Dr. Vaux is a Presbyterian minister and professor of ethics, and brings a wealth of material out of his experience. He shares many insights on ethical problems. The book is a help for physicians and others who need assistance in making decisions in the sensitive area of health care. Dr. Vaux points out that disciplines which were at one time helpful are now outdated because they are pre-technological and, therefore, new disciplines need to be formulated. The first part of the book is a summary of historical roots of medical ethics. It discusses Judaism, Islam, Catholicism, Protestantism, and Marxism, and ends with some insight into the Nuremburg trials. The second half of the book centers on ethical concerns in biomedicine; genetic manipulation, organ transplantation, controlling man, and immortalizing man, which deals with death. Theological terms are used which should be appealing to the clergy, as well as to theologians.

948) Veatch, Robert M. Case Studies in Medical Ethics. Cambridge: Harvard University Press, 1977.

A collection of case studies in the field of bioethics. One hundred and twelve problems in the area of medical ethics are discussed. A case history is presented for each. There are also commentaries on the cases by other parties. The topics covered are: values in health and illness, problems in health care delivery, confidentiality, truth telling, abortions, sterilizations, contraceptives, genetics, transplantations, the allocation of scarce resources, psychiatry and control of human behavior, experimentation on human beings, consent and the right to re- fuse treatment, and death and dying problems. The book is easy to read, and is a good case book for anyone concerned with ethical problems in the health care field. Veatch is rated as one of the best, if not the best, in the field of ethics.

949) Williams, P., ed. <u>To Live and Die: When, Why and How.</u> New York: Springer-Verlag, 1973.

Covers a wide range of topics dealing with current, important, and vital issues such as genetic engineering, contraception, abortion, euthanasia, transplant ethics, marriage, and other issues.

ADDENDUM

After the manuscript for this book was completed, an incident occurred which engaged the interests and emotions of the public throughout the U.S. and other countries around the world. Consequently, it has become a classic case study for those interested in the subject of euthanasia. Therefore, because of the significance and nature of the following case it should be added to this work.

On April 26, 1989, Rodolfo Linares, a Cicero, Illinois father, held security guards and medical personnel at bay as he disconnected his young son from life-support systems. Among the many publications reporting the incident were the Chicago Tribune and the American Medical News.

The Chicago Tribune did an excellent job covering the story through a series of articles written over a period of two months. Following is a chronology of the case with the date, section, column, and page number of each article as listed in the Chicago Tribune Index, April-May, 1989.

Linares charged with murder (April 27-1,1:2)

Linares case causes controversy over life-support use and legality of pulling the plug (April 28-1,1:14)

Developments in trial of Linares are noted (April 29-A,5:6)

Editorial advocates judicial and medical leadership involving terminally comatose patients (April 30-4,2:1)

Medical and other state welfare monies discussed
relative to care of comatose Linares boy (May 5-
2C,1:2)

Discussion by States Attorney Cecil Partee on grand
jury investigation underway for trial of Linares
(May 13-1, 5:2)

Father John J. Paris, a medical ethics teacher at
Holy Cross College comments on Linares case
(May 15-15:2)

Linares to appear before grand jury to face possible
murder charges (May 18-2C, 4:4)

Linares not indicted. Grand jury drops murder charges
(May 19-1,1:2)

Linares appeared before grand jury who refused to
return indictment on murder charges (May 21-2C,1:2)

In light of surrounding Linares case, Joan Beck discusses
issues surrounding artificial life support (May 22-1,
15:1)

Linares describes events leading up to his disconnecting
the life-support system from his child (May 24-25,6:5)

A Cook County Illinois Commission formed to study the
ethical, social and medical aspects of euthanasia - -
spurred by Linares case (May 31-2C, 3:3)

The American Medical News (AMN) carried two pieces;
annotations are as follows:

Somerville, Janice. "Hospital blamed for failing to aid parents." American Medical News (May 12, 1989): 1,12.

An excellent discussion on the fears that hospitals have without any clear-cut legal guidelines relative to removing life-support systems. Rush Presby-
terian-St. Luke's Medical Center is taken to task by

medical ethicists who strongly feel that the hospital was negligent in its responsibilities toward the Linareses.

Lantour, Paul A., Lovis J. Dolinar, and Donald M. Clough. "Fear of unknown determines behaviour," "Why was charge ever considered?", and "Treatment of dad 'Unconscionable'." <u>American Medical News</u> (June 23/30, 1989): 27.

Letters by three physicians who express their opinions relative to the context of the above article: "Hospital blamed for failing to aid parents." Two are in sympathy with the hospital and one is embarrassed because Rodolfo Linares was put in a predicament which caused him to remove his son from the ventilator.

Hopefully, the actions of Linares and the death of his young son will not have been in vain. The above articles provide much "food for thought" and, no doubt, will be helpful to those who must decide on future courses of action; whether they be parents, physicians, hospital administrators, attorneys, ethicists or clergy.

REFERENCE LIST

Chafer, Lewis S. 1947. Systematic Theology. Vol. 2, Soteri-
ology. Dallas: Dallas Seminary Press.

Fletcher, John. 1975. Abortion, Euthanasia and Care of Defective Newborns. New England Journal of Medicine 292
(January): 75-77.

Hensley, Jess L. 1983. The Zero People. ed., Ann Arbor, Michigan: Servant Books.

It's Over Debbie. 1988. Journal of The American Medical
Association 259 (January 8): 272.

Jensen, Albert R., and Garland, Michael A., eds. 1976. Ethics of
Newborn Intensive Care. Berkley: Institute of Governmental Studies.

Johnson, Eric W. 1986. Older and Wiser. New York: Walker and
Co.

Keil, C. F., and F. Delitzch. 1975. Commentary on The Old
Testament. Vol. 1, Genesis. Grand Rapids: William B.
Eerdmans Publishing Co.

Lammers, Stephen and Verhey, Allen. 1987. On Moral Medicine: Theological Perspectives In Medical Ethics. Grand
Rapids: William B. Eerdmans Publishing Co.

Lawerman, Connie. 1987. Life After Transplant. Sunday
Magazine: The Chicago Tribune, 24 May, 10: 10, 11.

Lo, Bernard. 1984. The Death of Clarence Herbert: Withdrawing Care is Not Murder. Annals of Internal Medicine 101 (August): 248.

Manchester, William. 1978. American Caesar. Boston: Little, Brown and Co.

Meyers, David W. 1985. Legal Aspects of Withdrawing Nourishment from an Incurably Ill Patient. Archives of Internal Medicine. 145 (January): 127.

Muggeridge, Malcolm. 1977. Abortion to Euthanasia: A Slippery Slope. The Human Life Review 3 #4 (Fall 1977): 5-10

Muller, Richard A. 1985. Dictionary of Latin and Greek Theological Terms. Grand Rapids: Baker Book House.

Quinlan, Joseph and Quinlan, Julia. 1977. Karen Ann. New York: Doubleday and Company.

Rollin, Betty. 1985. Last Wish. New York: Linden Press /Simon and Shuster.

Scott, Ralph. 1979. A New Look at Biblical Crime. New York: Dorsey Press.

Webster's New Collegiate Dictionary. 1981. Springfield: G&C. Merriman Co.

Will, George F. 1987. The Killing Will Not Stop. Washington Post, 22 April.

AUTHOR INDEX

(Indexed according to citation number)

Author

TITLE INDEX

(Indexed according to citation number)

ABOUT THE AUTHOR

Don Bailey, an ordained minister, and the son of a coal-mining minister, was born and raised in the southeastern coalfields of the Appalachian Mountains of Kentucky and West Virginia. At the age of seventeen, he was awarded the Distinguished Service Cross, while serving in the Korean War with the U. S. Army's 24th Division Medical Battalion. He is a graduate of Moody Bible Institute, Chicago, Illinois, and holds a B.A. Degree from Arizona Bible College, Phoenix, Arizona, an M.A. Degree from Calvary Bible College, Kansas City, Missouri, and the Doctor of Ministry degree from Trinity Evangelical Divinity School, Deerfield, Illinois. He has served in the health-care field for a period of thirty-eight years. He recently completed twenty-five years service as chaplain of Bethesda Hospital, Chicago, Illinois. He enjoys running, biking, and treks the Grand Canyon periodically.